Contents at a Glance

T0006457

Italian Workbook

for dummies®
A Wiley Brand

Italian Workbook

by Teresa Picarazzi, PhD

Italian Workbook For Dummies®

Published by: **John Wiley & Sons, Inc.**, 111 River Street, Hoboken, NJ 07030-5774, www.wiley.com

Copyright © 2023 by John Wiley & Sons, Inc., Hoboken, New Jersey

Published simultaneously in Canada

For general information on our other products and services, please contact our Customer Care Department within the U.S. at 877-762-2974, outside the U.S. at 317-572-3993, or fax 317-572-4002. For technical support, please visit https://hub.wiley.com/community/support/dummies.

Wiley publishes in a variety of print and electronic formats and by print-on-demand. Some material included with standard print versions of this book may not be included in e-books or in print-on-demand. If this book refers to media such as a CD or DVD that is not included in the version you purchased, you may download this material at http://booksupport.wiley.com. For more information about Wiley products, visit www.wiley.com.

Library of Congress Control Number is available from the publisher.

ISBN: 978-1-119-98670-6 (pbk); ISBN: 978-1-119-98671-3 (ebk); ISBN: 978-1-119-98672-0 (ebk)

SKY10067998_022224

Table of Contents

CHAPTER 9: Prepositions, and Then Some 113

CHAPTER 10: La Mia Famiglia: Possessive Adjectives and Pronouns 127

CHAPTER 11: Asking with Interrogatives; Pointing Out with Demonstratives 139

PART 4: MORE VERB TENSES 149

CHAPTER 12: Glancing Back at the Past: The Passato Prossimo 151

Introduction

Italian speaks the language of fantastic food, art, design, fashion, cinema, music, and of course, great literature. And it's also the language of great scientists, entrepreneurs, political activists, explorers, and migrants. Italian is spoken by the 60 million inhabitants of Italy and by many people of Italian descent in other countries (about 18 million in the United States alone) around the world.

Derived from Latin, Italian was initially established as the language of literary culture in the 13th century, thanks to the works of many poets and storytellers (the most important one being Dante and his "*Divine Comedy*") who began to shift from writing in Latin to writing in the vernacular. Since the period of Unification (the **Risorgimento**, 1848–1871), one shared language — Italian — has dominated culture.

Perhaps you want to speak to an Italian relative, or you plan to visit Italy and want to be able to converse with the locals while you're there. Or maybe you're taking an Italian class and want some extra help. Whatever has brought you to these pages, this book is here to be your guide through the beautiful Italian language.

About This Book

The language I present in *Italian Workbook For Dummies* is the language of everyday life in today's Italy. You can find it used in newspapers, on TV, in modern novels, in instruction booklets, on the Internet, and so forth. At any given point in time, you can find good ways and bad ways to express yourself, so I give you the correct version of the language and usage. But don't be surprised if you go to Italy and hear or read something different from what you find in this book. Over time, you'll develop your own sensibility for expressions that are interesting variations on the language, rather than merely mistakes.

Italian Workbook For Dummies is a hands-on reference book for beginners of the language. As such, I start with the basic building blocks, and then build on those. Keep in mind that the book does proceed logically from simpler matters to more complex ones, so unless you have the essentials down first, I suggest progressing chronologically. At the same time, the more you expose yourself to authentic Italian during the process, the greater your results. When children are immersed in language and receive constant input, they pick it up naturally, holistically, and communicatively.

Establish your own communicative goals while you go through this book: The discrete points about the Italian language that I offer in this book can provide you with the tools and contexts to navigate a variety of situations, from basic introductions to seeking help at the pharmacy. Try starting with the ten practice dialogues in Chapter 18, and then back up to the very beginning, giving yourself a road map for arriving at the end.

But first, do a positioning exercise that I always ask my new students to do on the first day of class. Take pen and paper, and a timer (and cover the rest of this page). Set the timer for five minutes. Then, write down as many Italian words that you already know, and whose pronunciation you can already begin to sound out. (Think food! Think music!). Challenge your study buddy if you're working through this book with someone else.

After your timer goes off, how did you do? What words do you know already? Bruschetta, spaghetti, biscotti, pizza — whatever you wrote down is a good start to putting words into conversations and building your proficiency.

The first part of the book is devoted to articles, nouns, and the concept of gender. In Part 1, I also introduce you immediately to numbers, dates and times, and interrogatives (or question words). I devote Part 2 to getting you started with Italian verbs. Part 3 adds onto these basics with adjectives and prepositions. Part 4 goes a bit more deeply into verbs, both to their conjugations and to the way you use them in context. The appendixes provide you with some quick-reference tools to check translations.

Because this is a book for beginners, I don't talk about some tenses that are generally reserved for more intermediate and advanced study, such as the subjunctive mood, the passive voice, and the **passato remoto** (*distant past*) tense.

In each chapter, you have the opportunity to practice what you've just read. You may be asked to come up with one word, craft an entire sentence, or select the best word or phrase to complete a sentence. Test your skills so that you can find that information stored in your mind. The Answer Key at the end of each chapter allows you to check your progress.

Conventions Used in This Book

To make this book as easy to use as possible, I used certain conventions throughout:

>> I **bold** all the Italian words so that they stand out in the text; English translations are in *italics*.

>> When a practice exercise has more than one correct answer, I provide both the more and the less common answers.

>> I use some technical grammar terms, in context. Every subject matter has its jargon, and you can more easily learn by example than by engaging in wordy explanations. The more you actively engage and practice with the content, the more familiar it becomes — trust me.

Foolish Assumptions

I made the following assumptions about you (my reader) and your Italian when writing this book:

>> You're a novice writer or speaker. You're already aware that even the simplest sentence in Italian requires an understanding of gender and number options, and the ability to make endings agree.

>> You're committed to learning Italian, and you know that it's okay to make mistakes in order to progress. You also know that sometimes, you just have to commit the material to memory.

>> You understand basic concepts of English grammar. I define them, but I expect you to have encountered the terms before and be able to apply them to any language. From a grammatical point of view, Italian and English are often substantively different, but with a few exceptions, the grammarians who systematized the two languages used the same concepts: A verb is a verb in both languages, as is a pronoun, an adjective, and so on.

>> You want to become more precise when using verbs, pronouns, and other parts of speech. Sure, Italians can understand you if you say **volere caffè** (*to want coffee*) instead of **Vorrei un caffè** (*I'd like a coffee*), but the pleasure of speaking a foreign language comes with effective communication and proficiency in it.

>> You might be planning a trip to Italy.

>> You want to know everyday Italian, rather than the language of a special field, such as economics or medicine.

I do hope that you're the reader I had in mind when I was writing this book. It should be challenging, but approachable and rewarding.

Icons Used in This Book

As in all *For Dummies* books, icons tag information that's unique in some way. I used the following icons throughout this book (you can spot them in the left-hand margin):

TIP

This icon highlights advice that can help you use or remember the information at hand; it can also emphasize minor variations in the topic.

REMEMBER

This icon alerts you to grammar rules, special cases, or points about meaning that you should pay particular attention to.

This icon highlights points where Italian and English differ in important ways.

DIFFERENCES

You see this icon at the start of each practice exercise.

PRACTICE

Beyond this Book

In addition to the abundance of information and guidance related to embracing Italian that I provide in this book, you can get access to even more help and information online at Dummies. com. Check out this book's online Cheat Sheet by going to www.dummies.com and searching for *Italian Workbook For Dummies Cheat Sheet.*

Where to Go from Here

In *Italian Workbook For Dummies,* I think of my readers as highly motivated people who are self-starters and have the patience to work through training exercises as if they were at the gym. Learning a language isn't easy, but you can make it more enjoyable by varying your approach. Because Italian is a living language, grow your listening and speaking proficiency during the process of working through this book. Expose yourself to as much authentic language as is possible, and practice speaking and listening whenever you can!

Work your way through the chapters and test yourself with the practices. Try to immerse yourself in the situations that the different tenses represent. Then, check out some Italian websites or listen to some Italian podcasts. Sing along to Italian songs and get Italian subtitles to your favorite programs to help increase your proficiency. And let this book be a guide that you can come back to whenever you have a question or forget a conjugation. Time to get started!

Buon lavoro! (*Enjoy!* Literally: *Have a good experience with this work!*)

1

Getting Your Bearings with the Basics

IN THIS PART . . .

Get started with the basics of Italian. Learn greetings and salutations, plus pronunciation and more. It's time to start communicating!

Find out about pronouns and articles. Figure out how to use gender in Italian, and when (and when not) to use definite and indefinite articles.

See how to use numbers in Italian, including cardinals, ordinals, dates, and times.

Chapter **1**

Greetings! Getting to Know You

You've picked up this book because you're interested in learning Italian — **molto bene!** (*great!*) Whatever your reasons — heritage, travel, work, food, Italophilia, love of languages — you're in the right place: **Benvenute/Benvenuti!** (*Welcome!*)

What are some essential first steps in getting your feet wet in another language? Communication, making yourself understood, and understanding throughout a variety of social situations, as well as creating a solid foundation on which to build.

This chapter provides you with some Italian basics on using formal and informal conventions. I illustrate the formal and informal with communicative exercises that can help you confidently express — whether you're speaking or writing in Italian — greetings and salutations, and forms of courtesy. This chapter also provides a preliminary consideration of pronunciation and gender, two elements you can't do without.

Deciding between Formal and Informal

The Italian language clearly recognizes and requires two different conventions of address, formal and informal, depending on whom you're addressing and also the situation. When you understand what convention to use, you're better equipped to communicate meaningfully, to convey respect for the person, and to also show regard for cultural differences.

The informal is usually designated with the pronouns **tu/voi** (*you*) and the formal **Lei** (*you*): These pronouns connect concretely to verb forms (see Chapter 4) and possessive adjectives (see Chapter 10). In Italian, you generally use the formal address to write or speak to a stranger, teacher, business acquaintance, customer, waitstaff, salesperson, or boss. You usually use the informal address with family members, friends, people your same age or younger, or children.

REMEMBER

Italian is a living language. I can't emphasize enough how important it is for you to practice saying and hearing Italian while you go through this book. Although you need to approach the language holistically and in context, you also need a grasp on the individual parts of the whole, which is where this book comes in.

TIP

When meeting someone for the first time, Italians customarily shake hands. When you see someone whom you haven't seen in a while, or when you stop by your aunt's house, Italians customarily kiss each other on both cheeks, first on one side, then the other.

To put formal and informal conventions to use, the following sections walk you through Italian greetings and phrases.

Formal greetings

Use the following formal phrases when you want to meet and greet a stranger, someone whom you don't know very well, and/or someone to whom you should show respect. Use titles when you know what titles apply, such as **Dottore/Dottoressa** (*Doctor*), or either **Signore** (*Mr.*) or **Signora** (*Mrs.*).

Table 1-1 provides you with some terms generally associated with greetings and salutations. While you go through this table, make a mental note (or even underline and highlight) some of the differences and similarities between Table 1-1 and Table 1-2 (in the next section), which provides the informal phrases.

REMEMBER

You use **buona notte** when you know it's actually bedtime; consider it another way of saying, *"Have a good sleep."* Start to use **buona sera** in the late afternoon until you go to bed. For example, say it's 10 p.m. and you walk into your hotel. You first greet the concierge by saying, "Buona sera." After you get your key and are on your way to your room, you can say, "**Buona notte.**"

REMEMBER

Cut off the final **e** when using a last name with masculine titles:

» **Signore** becomes **Signor Tarroni**.

» **Dottore** becomes **Dottor Costa**.

» **Professore** becomes **Professor Gambi**.

The title *Ms.* doesn't exist in Italian, so you use either **Signora** (*Miss*) or **Signorina** (*Mrs./Ma'am*).

For female professional titles of doctor and professor, you use **Dottoressa** and **Professoressa**.

Table 1-1   Formal Greetings and Salutations

English	Italian
Hello/Good morning	**Buon giorno/Buongiorno**
Hello	**Salve**
Good afternoon	**Buon pomeriggio**
Good evening	**Buona sera/Buonasera**
Good night	**Buona notte/Buonanotte**
Miss (young woman)	**Signorina**
Mrs./Ma'am (older married or unmarried woman)	**Signora**
Mr./Sir	**Signore**
My name is . . .	**Mi chiamo . . .**
What's your name?	**Come si chiama?**
How are you?	**Come sta?**
Where are you from?	**Di dov'è?**
Sono di . . .	**I'm from . . .**
Well.	**Bene.**
Very well.	**Molto bene.**
So-so.	**Così così.**
Fair/pretty well.	**Abbastanza bene.**
(I'm) not well.	**(Sto) male.**
Not bad.	**Non c'è male.**
Thank you, and you?	**Grazie, e lei?**
Nice to meet you.	**Piacere (di conoscerla).**
It's a pleasure.	**È un piacere.**
It's a great pleasure.	**Molto piacere.**
The pleasure is mine.	**Il piacere è mio.**
Goodbye.	**Arrivederci.**
See you later.	**A dopo.**
See you soon.	**A presto.**
See you tomorrow.	**A domani.**
Have a good day.	**Buona giornata.**
Have a good evening.	**Buona serata.**

Here are a few more titles in both their masculine and feminine forms:

>> **Avvocato/Avvocata** (*Attorney*)

>> **Giudice** (*Judge*)

>> **Sindaco/Sindaca** (*Mayor*)

DIFFERENCES

The title **Dottore/Dottoressa** can have two meanings in Italian: You can use it for someone who has a university degree (meaning a B.A. or a B.S.), as well as for a medical doctor and a person who has a Ph.D. In the United States, the word *doctor* is reserved for medical doctors and people who have Ph.D.s

Informal greetings

Use informal phrases when you want to meet and greet a friend, relative, child, people who are younger than you, and (of course) your beloved pet. Notice that you find some overlap between some of the terms in the formal list (see Table 1-1) and the informal list in Table 1-2.

TIP

A good rule of thumb is that you use the informal when on a first name basis with someone.

Table 1-2   Informal Greetings and Salutations

English	Italian
Hi.	Ciao.
My name is . . .	Mi chiamo . . .
I'm (meaning My name is . . .)	Sono. . .
What's your name?	Come ti chiami?
How are you?	Come stai?
Thank you, and you?	Grazie, e tu?
Well.	Bene.
Very well.	Molto bene.
So-so.	Così così.
Fair./Pretty well.	Abbastanza bene.
Not well.	Male.
Not bad.	Non c'è male.
Where are you from?	Di dove sei?
I'm from . . .	Sono di . . .
It's a pleasure (to meet you).	Piacere (di conoscerti).
How nice it is to see you.	Che piacere vederti.
How's it going?	Come va?
What's new?	Che c'è di nuovo?
What's up?/What's wrong?	Che c'è?
Nothing much.	Niente.
See you later.	Ci vediamo.
See you (very) soon.	A presto.
Until next time.	Alla prossima
See you tomorrow.	A domani.
Have a good day.	Buona giornata.
Have a good evening.	Buona serata.
Bye.	Ciao.

REMEMBER

Prego not only means *You're welcome.* It also means, *Please, come this way*; *Please, by all means, you first*; or *Here you go!*

You're not always spontaneously introducing yourself to someone else. Sometimes, you're introduced. Compare the informal and the formal introductions in the following examples.

> **Ti presento Camilla** (informal). (*This is Camilla./Let me introduce you to Camilla.*)

> **Le presento mia madre, Mary** (formal). (*This is my mother, Mary./Let me introduce you to my mother, Mary.*)

Formal and informal usage distinctions inform your use of everything from possessive adjectives to verbs in all tenses. You can't get away from this convention — but of course, it's okay to make mistakes! You just need to make yourself understood.

PRACTICE

Translate the following.

Q. *What's new?*

A. **Che c'è di nuovo?**

1. My name is. . .

2. Good morning!

3. Hi! (informal)

4. Where are you from? (informal)

5. Good evening, Mr. Marotti.

6. Nothing's new.

7. Have a good day!

8. How are you? (formal)

9. How nice to see you! (informal)

10. See you soon!

11. Thank you. . . You're welcome.

12. Pleasure to meet you.

TIP

Don't panic if the distinctions and terms related to formal and informal address don't seem so straightforward. You can gain a lot of practice by using formal and informal with all of the verb tenses covered in this book, as well as with possessive adjectives (Chapter 10).

PRACTICE

Now fill in the missing term and practice the following mini-dialogue based on the cues provided. Practice reading them aloud.

Q. You see your neighbor, Mrs. Coia.

Buon _____ (day), _____ (Mrs.) **Coia**

_____(how) **sta?**

A. Buon giorno, signora Coia.

Come sta?

13 You see your friend Giorgio.

"(Hi)_____ Giorgio! Come _____ (are you)?"

"Bene, _____ (thanks), e _____ (you)?"

"Non _____ (not bad)."

Forms of courtesy

It's always good to know how to be courteous when communicating with others. Saying *please* and *thank you* in any language goes a long way. Table 1-3 lists common forms of courtesy.

Table 1-3   Being Polite

English	Italian
please	**per favore**
please	**per piacere**
please	**per cortesia**
Thank you.	**Grazie.**
Thanks so much.	**Grazie mille.**
Thank you very much.	**Molte grazie.**
Thank you, that's very kind (of you).	**Grazie, molto gentile.**
You're welcome.	**Prego**
Don't mention it.	**Non c'è di che.**
It was nothing.	**Niente**
Excuse me.	**(Mi) scusi. (formal)**
Excuse me, I need some information, please.	**Mi scusi, un'informazione, per favore.**
Excuse me./I'm sorry.	**Scusa/scusami (informal)**
I'm sorry.	**Mi dispiace.**

Provide the most appropriate response to the following statements/situations by using the forms of courtesy in Table 1-3. (Check the answer key if in doubt!)

Q. You need to ask someone for information.

A. **Mi scusi, un'informazione, per favore.**

14. Someone gives up their seat for you on a crowded bus. Thank them profusely. _____

15. They tell you not to worry about their kind gesture. _____

16. You're late for your aperitivo date with your friend. _____

17. You ask for a glass of water at the bar (caffè): Un bicchiere d'acqua, _____.

18. Your friend has just told you they just lost their job: _____

Working with Pronunciation

Italian provides many opportunities to have fun because the language offers you some new sounds. In this section, I give you some basic pronunciation hints that can help you both surf through this book and have good articulation when you speak Italian.

Next to the Italian words in this chapter, you can find the pronunciation in parentheses. Then I give you some helpful hints about how to read these pronunciations — that is, how to pronounce the Italian words. Follow the code that I give you outlining which letters refer to which sounds all through this book.

TIP

The best way to understand Italian pronunciation though, is to listen to it. I highly recommend finding some reliable sites on the Internet, from the alphabet to podcasts to cartoons to music, to help you get this pronunciation down. Listen, read, and repeat as much as you need to!

In the pronunciations, I separate the syllables with a hyphen, like this: **casa** (<u>kah</u>-sah) (*house*). Furthermore, I underline the stressed syllable, which means that you emphasize your tone on the underlined syllable. If you can figure out the correct pronunciation in this chapter, starting with the alphabet (see Table 1-4), you'll read Italian like, well, a real Italian.

Table 1-4 Alfabeto (ahl-fah-beh-toh)

Letter	Pronunciation	Letter	Pronunciation	Letter	Pronunciation
a	ah	l	el-le	U	ooh
b	bee	m	<u>em</u>-me	V	vooh
c	chee	n	en-ne	Z	<u>dzeh</u>-tah
d	dee	o	oh		
e	eh	p	pee		
f	<u>ef</u>-fe	q	kooh		
g	jee	r	ehr-reh		
h	<u>ahk</u>-kah	s	<u>ehs</u>-she		
i	ee	t	Tee		

Stressing Words Properly

In Romance languages, accents can make a big difference. In Italian, you write the accent only on vowels.

Stress is the audible accent that you put on a syllable when you speak it. One syllable always gets more stress than all the others.

Some words give you a hint as to where to stress them: They have an accent — (`) or (´) — above one of their letters. The accent falls on the vowel at the end of the last syllable, as in **città** (*city*) and **virtù** (*virtue*). You should memorize the spelling of these common words with an accented final vowel.

Here are some examples:

>> **caffè** (kahf-<u>feh</u>) (*coffee*)

>> **città** (cheet-<u>tah</u>) (*city*)

>> **lunedì** (loo-neh-<u>dee</u>) (*Monday*)

>> **perché** (pehr-<u>keh</u>) (*why*)

>> **però** (peh-<u>roh</u>) (*but*)

>> **università** (ooh-nee-vehr-see-<u>tah</u>) (*university*)

>> **virtù** (veer-<u>tooh</u>) (*virtue*)

If the word doesn't have an accent, you're unfortunately left on your own. Italian tends to have the stress on the *penultimate* (next-to-last) syllable. Although there are too many rules and exceptions to list them all here, keep the following points in mind:

>> The accent tells you where to stress the word.

>> The most important function of an accent is to change a word's meaning.

Fortunately, only a few words have the same spelling and only an accent to distinguish them. But it can be a very important distinction, as in the following examples:

- **la** (*the/her*) and **là** (*there*)

- **da** (*from/by*) and **dà** (*she/he gives*)

- **e** (eh) (*and*) and **è** (eh) (*he/she/it is*) are distinguished only by the accent on the vowel, which means *is*.

REMEMBER

Using Gender in Italian

You can't get around the use of gender in Italian. Nouns are either masculine or feminine: There's no neutral. (Chapter 2 goes into detail about the gender and number of nouns and articles.) Most of the elements that make up a sentence — definite articles (*the*), indefinite articles (*a/an*), contracted prepositions, adjectives, personal pronouns, direct and indirect object pronouns, past participles — must reckon with gender and number, and follow some basic rules. Keep the following in mind:

» Nouns and articles: As in **il gatto** (*the male cat*) or **la gatta** (*the female cat*).

» Adjectives: As in **bello**, **bella**, **belli**, **belle**, **bei**, **bel**, **begli**, or **bell'**, which all mean *beautiful*, have to agree in gender and number with the noun.

» Past participles: Used frequently in compound tenses, as in **andato** and **andati** (*went/gone*, referring to a singular and a plural masculine noun) or **andata** and **andate** (*went/gone*, referring to a singular feminine and plural noun).

» Masculine singular: It is the default gender. In an Italian dictionary, adjectives and other qualifiers that can vary in gender and/or number are listed in the masculine singular (unless they exist only in the feminine, such as **la spia** [*spy*]).

For example, no one is listed under **nessuno** (*nobody*). Only the examples in the entry indicate (if you don't know it already) that you can use **nessuna** (feminine singular). Similarly, the color red is an adjective listed as **rosso** (*red*), even though it can become **rossa**, **rossi**, and **rosse**, depending on the gender and number of the noun it's modifying.

Even though Italian grammar dictates that the gender defaults to masculine, even when referring to a room that has, for example, 14 women and 2 men, things are changing slowly in Italy to become more inclusive.

In the spirit of inclusivity, many of my friends who are high school teachers and college professors use an asterisk (*) or a schwa (ə) when writing (and speaking) to groups of mixed gender, and also where some participants may identify as non-binary or whose gender isn't known, so that they can avoid privileging one gender over the other. They might start an e-mail with, for example: **Car* tutt*** instead of **Cari tutti** (Dear All), which defaults to the masculine.

Other colleagues choose to make the feminine the default gender in the classroom, just to mix things up. Many maintain that women fought so hard and for so long to be recognized that they're not quite willing to subsume themselves in an asterisk or schwa.

Still others refer to both genders: **le mie studentesse e i miei studenti** (*my female students and my male students*) instead of the conventional **i miei studenti** for *my students* (which is masculine by default).

In Italian, you only use **loro/il-la-i-le loro** (*they/theirs*) when you are referring to a plural subject. But what to do with pronouns in the inclusive classroom where *they/theirs* isn't an option because of the very gendered nature of Italian? Some people ask non-binary students to choose which gender they want to use in the classroom, for the purpose of agreement, and with the understanding that they can always change it. Recent progressive initiatives in some Italian schools are also sensitive to naming, asking students and teachers to choose their preferred pronouns. In Italy, like in the United States, some are resistant to inclusive language, while others are actively adopting it.

Answers to "Greetings! Getting to Know You" Practice Questions

1. **Mi chiamo. . .** (*My name is. . .*)

2. **Buon giorno!/Buongiorno!** (*Good morning!*)

3. **Ciao!** (*Hi!* informal)

4. **Di dove sei?** (*Where are you from?* informal)

5. **Buona sera, signor Marotti.** (*Good evening, Mr. Marotti.*)

6. **Niente di nuovo.** (*Nothing's new.*)

7. **Buona giornata!** (*Have a good day!*)

8. **Come sta?** (*How are you?* formal)

9. **Che piacere vederti!** (*How nice to see you!* informal)

10. **A presto!** (*See you soon!*)

11. **Grazie. . . Prego.** (**Thank you. . .You're welcome.**)

12. **Piacere!** (*Pleasure to meet you!*)

13. **"(Hi) Ciao Giorgio! Come stai** (*are you*)**?"**

    "Bene, grazie (*thanks*), **e tu** (*you*)**?"**

    "Non non c'è male (*not bad*)**."**

14. **Grazie mille!** (*Thank you so much!*)**/Molto gentile!** (*That's very kind!*)

15. **Non c'è di che.** (*Don't mention it.*)**/Niente.** (*It was nothing.*)

16. **Scusami!** (*Excuse me!*)

17. **per favore/per piacere/per cortesia** (*please*)

18. **Mi dispiace!** (*I'm sorry!*)

Chapter **2**

Embedded Gender and Number: Nouns and Articles

Nouns are those exciting and diverse basic building blocks that cover every topic under the sun. Nouns serve similar purposes in Italian and English, but there's an important difference that you can't get around. Italian nouns have a gender: They're masculine or feminine (see Chapter 1 for a discussion on gender in the Italian language). When Italian nouns refer to certain things, their grammatical gender is merely a product of convention and usage: **il sole** (*sun*) and **il giorno** (*day*) are masculine, but **la luna** (*moon*) and **la notte** (*night*) are feminine.

Definite articles, which translate as the word *the*, frequently accompany nouns much more than in English usage, and agree with nouns in number and gender.

In this chapter, I show you how to distinguish between feminine and masculine nouns, how to form plural nouns, and which definite and indefinite articles to use.

Distinguishing between Masculine and Feminine Nouns

In most Indo-European languages (the family to which both Italian and English belong), nouns have a gender. In Italian, you deal with two genders: masculine and feminine. Other parts of speech — such as demonstrative pronouns, combined prepositions, articles and adjectives — reflect noun gender, as well, and these other parts of speech have to agree with the gender of the noun.

This section focuses on nouns, discussing what word endings tell you about gender and providing a map for transforming singular nouns into plural nouns.

Grammatically, the noun endings in the singular usually help you figure out to which gender they belong. Like always, you have to watch out for exceptions to the norm, but first things first: the regular guys.

Table 2-1 illustrates the noun endings for masculine and feminine singular and plural nouns. In general, nouns ending in -**a** are feminine and nouns ending in -**o** are masculine.

Table 2-1: Regular Singular and Plural Noun Endings

Gender	Singular	Plural
Masculine	o	i
Feminine	a	e
Masculine or Feminine	e	i

 I give you some clues in the following sections about knowing the gender of nouns that end in –**e** in the singular and –**i** in the plural, but you generally need to determine their gender upon first encounter, and then just memorize that gender.

Some nouns end in –**ore** in the masculine and –**ice** in the feminine, such as the ones in this table.

Masculine	Feminine
attore (*actor*)	**attrice** (*actress*)
pittore (*male painter*)	**pittrice** (*female painter*)

You add an **h** to the plurals of nouns ending in –**ca**, –**co**, –**go**, and –**ga**, to keep the hard sound of *k* or *g*, such as with the word **amica** (*female friend*) to create **amiche** (*female friends*), **barca** (*boat*) to create **barche** (*boats*), and **lago** (*lake*) to create **laghi** (*lakes*). One word that doesn't follow this spelling and pronunciation exception is the plural form of **amico** (*male friend*), which is **amici** (*male friends*). I have no clue why it does that!

Masculine nouns

Masculine nouns often end in **–o** in the singular and **–i** in the plural, like those in the following table.

Singular	Plural
biscotto (*cookie*)	**biscotti** (*cookies*)
libro (*book*)	**libri** (*books*)
amico (*friend*)	**amici** (*friends*)
giorno (*day*)	**giorni** (*days*)
ragazzo (*boy*)	**ragazzi** (*boys*)

REMEMBER

Masculine nouns may also end in a consonant in the singular. These words are often borrowed from another language, and they're *invariable*, which means they have the exact same form in the singular as they have in the plural. With these words, articles come in very handy, as I discuss in the section "Sorting out Definite and Indefinite Articles," later in this chapter. In the following table, I illustrate these unchanging nouns that end in a consonant.

Singular	Plural
un autobus (*a/one bus*)	**due autobus** (*two buses*)
uno sport (*a/one sport*)	**tre sport** (*three sports*)
un bar (*a/one bar/cafe*)	**quattro bar** (*four bars/cafes*)
uno chef (*a/one chef*)	**cinque chef** (*five chefs*)

TIP

When you see the indefinite article **uno** (meaning *a, an,* or *one*) preceding a noun, how do you know whether it means *one* or *a/an*? Let context and common sense be your guide when in doubt. I explain how these articles work in the section "Keeping things general with indefinite articles," later in this chapter. Any word in Italian that has an accented final vowel is invariable. Many feminine nouns follow this rule. But this table shows two important Italian masculine nouns that have an accented final vowel.

Singular	Plural
un caffè (*a coffee*)	**otto caffè** (*eight coffees*)
un lunedì (*a Monday*)	**nove lunedì** (*nine Mondays*)

Some masculine nouns end in **–e** in the singular and in **–i** in the plural, such as with the very common nouns in the following table.

Singular	Plural
ristorante (*restaurant*)	**ristoranti** (*restaurants*)
esame (*exam*)	**esami** (*exams*)
padre (*father*)	**padri** (*fathers*)
latte (*milk*)	

Singular	Plural
bicchiere (*glass*, as in glass of water)	**bicchieri** (*glasses*)
studente (*student*)	**studenti** (*students*)
pesce (*fish*)	**pesci** (*fishes*)
mare (*sea*)	**mari** (*seas*)

Note the very common exceptions of masculine plural nouns in the following table.

Singular	Plural
un uomo (*a/one man*)	**cinque uomini** (*five men*)
un uovo (*a/one egg*)	**sei uova** (*six eggs*) (This noun goes from masculine to feminine.)
un cinema (*a/one cinema*)	**due cinema** (*two cinemas*) (This noun is invariable.)
un frigo (*a/one fridge*)	**tre frigo** (*three fridges*) (This noun is invariable.)

The nouns **cinema** (**cinematografo**) and **frigo** (**frigorifero**) are abbreviations and thus invariable.

REMEMBER Some nouns ending in **–a** are masculine because they derive from classical Greek: **un problema** (*problem*), **un tema** (*theme*), and **un programma** (*program*).

Feminine nouns

Feminine nouns often end in **–a** in the singular and **–e** in the plural. Note the examples in the following table.

Singular	Plural
ora (*hour*)	**ore** (*hours*)
pasta (*pastry*)	**paste** (*pastries*)
pizza (*pizza*)	**pizze** (*pizzas*)
ragazza (*girl*)	**ragazze** (*girls*)
birra (*beer*)	**birre** (*beers*)
macchina (*car*)	**macchine** (*cars*)
studentessa (*female student*)	**studentesse** (*female students*)
amica (*female friend*)	**amiche** (*female friends*)
donna (*woman*)	**donne** (*women*)
penna (*pen*)	**penne** (*pens*)

The noun **pasta** has different meanings depending on the context. It can mean *pasta* (such as a dish of spaghetti), as well as *pastry* (a baked good) and the *dough* you use to make the pastry. Don't confuse the word **pasta** with **pasto**, which means *meal*.

REMEMBER

Some feminine nouns, like masculine nouns, end in **–e** in the singular and in **–i** in the plural. Here's a good hint for remembering that these words are feminine: They all end in **–ione** in the singular. Note the three examples in the following table.

Singular	Plural
una lezione (*one lesson*)	**due lezioni** (*two lessons*)
una regione (*one region*)	**tre regioni** (*three regions*)
una stazione (*one station*)	**quattro stazioni** (*four stations*)

The following table shows a few exceptions to the general rules governing number and gender with feminine nouns. Most are abbreviations. Look to the definite article for a dead giveaway concerning gender.

Singular	Plural
un'auto (*a/one car*; from **automobile**)	**due auto** (*two cars*)
una bici (*a/one bike*; from **bicicletta**)	**tre bici** (*three bikes*)
una mano (*a/one hand*)	**due mani** (*two hands*)
una moto (*a/one motorcycle*; from **motociclette**)	**due moto** (*two motorcycles*)

REMEMBER

Many words for body parts have irregular plurals, such as **mano/mani** in the preceding table. You encounter more body parts in Chapter 17.

Feminine nouns, just like masculine nouns, have some invariable exceptions. When a noun is *invariable*, the word's singular is the exact same as the plural:

» **–i**: **analisi** (*analysis*), **crisi** (*crisis*), **tesi** (*thesis*), **diagnosi** (*diagnosis*)

» **–tà** or **–tù**: **città** (*city*), **virtù** (*virtue*), **verità** (*truth*), **università** (*university*)

Some nouns that end in **–ista** have one identical singular form for both masculine and feminine, and then both a masculine and a feminine plural. The following table shows you some examples.

Singular	Masculine Plural	Feminine Plural
l'artista (*artist*, m/f)	**gli artisti** (*male artists*)	**le artiste** (*female artists*)
il/la pianista (*pianist*, m/f)	**i pianisti** (*male pianists*)	**le pianiste** (*female pianists*)
il/la barista (*barista*, m/f)	**i baristi** (*male baristas*)	**le bariste** (*female baristas*)

In the following section, I explain how the definite articles in the preceding table agree with nouns.

PRACTICE

Decide whether the following singular nouns are masculine or feminine and mark an M or F on the corresponding blank lines.

Q. analisi

A. F

1. algebra: _____

2. gelato: _____

3. amica: _____

4. toast: _____

5. medicina: _____

6. cappuccino: _____

7. pera: _____

8. pino: _____

9. arancia: _____

10. ristorante: _____

PRACTICE

Transform the following singular masculine and feminine nouns to the plural.

Q. uno stato

A. stati (*states*)

11. un pianista

12. una cameriera

13. uno studente

14. un lago

15. una crisi

16. una montagna

17. un fiume

18. un uomo

19. una regione

20. un parco

Sorting out Definite and Indefinite Articles

The section "Distinguishing between Masculine and Feminine Nouns," earlier in this chapter, gives you the basics about gender and number with nouns. In the following sections, you can dive into the articles that frequently accompany them and which must agree with (or match) them.

Because a clear and reliable indicator of a noun's gender is the definite article, I devote the following section and the section "Knowing when (and when not) to use a definite article," later in this chapter, to definite articles.

Italian, like English, has both definite and indefinite articles —*the* and *a/an*, respectively. With the definite article, you point to a specific item.

Il bambino è caduto dall'altalena. (*The child fell off the swing.*)

With the indefinite article, you point to one thing among many like things.

Leggi un libro? (*Are you reading a book?*)

You can find out all about indefinite articles in the section "Keeping things general with indefinite articles," later in this chapter.

TIP

Memorizing new nouns with their articles can help you remember the nouns' genders, as well.

Dealing with definite articles

In Italian, articles vary in gender, number, and spelling.

English and Italian use the definite article to point to a specific thing or person.

Il libro è sul tavolo. (*The book is on the table.*)

I bambini stanno giocando in giardino. (*The children are playing in the garden.*)

Table 2-2 provides the three forms of the singular masculine definite article: **il**, **lo**, and **l'**. You use these forms with singular masculine nouns. It also presents the two forms of the masculine plural definite article, **i** and **gli**, which you use with plural masculine nouns. Commit them to memory if you can.

In Table 2-2, I show you which articles to use with the specific types of masculine nouns.

Table 2-3 lists the two forms of the definite article used with singular feminine nouns, **la and l'**, as well as the plural feminine article, which has only one form: **le**.

Table 2-2   Masculine Definite Articles

Placement	Singular	Singular Example	Plural	Plural Example
Before most single consonants and groups of consonants	il	**il ragazzo** (*the boy*)	i	**i ragazzi** (*boys*)
		il bar (*the bar*)		**i bar** (*the bars*)
		il treno (*the train*)		**i treni** (*the trains*)
Before **gn–**, **pn–**, **ps–**, **s +** another consonant, **x–**, **y–**, and **z–**	lo	**lo gnocco** (*the dumpling*)	gli	**gli gnocchi** (*the dumplings*)
		lo psicologo (*the male psychologist*)		**gli psicologi** (*the male psychologists*)
		lo studente (*the male student*)		**gli studenti** (*the male students*)
		lo zaino (*the backpack*)		**gli zaini** (*the backpacks*)
Before any vowel	l'	**l'uomo** (*the man*)	gli	**gli uomini** (*the men*)
		l'amico (*the male friend*)		**gli amici** (*the male friends*)

Table 2-3   Feminine Definite Articles

Placement	Singular	Singular Examples	Plural	Plural Examples
Before any consonant or group of consonants	la	**la casa** (*the house*)	le	**le case** (*the houses*)
		la mela (*the apple*)		**le mele** (*the apples*)
Before any vowel	l'	**l'amica** (*the female friend*)	le	**le amiche** (*the female friends*)
		l'ora (*the hour*)		**le ore** (*the hours*)

Provide the correct definite article for the noun provided. Look up the word if you're in doubt!

Q. _____ pane

A. Il pane (*bread*)

21   gelato al limone

22   insalata mista

23   lasagne alla bolognese

24   contorno

25   spinaci

26   mozzarella

27   vino bianco

(28) bistecca alla fiorentina

(29) conto

(30) uva

Make the following nouns plural and apply the appropriate definite article.

PRACTICE

Q: la figlia

A: le figlie (*the daughters*)

(31) il raviolo

(32) l'aperitivo

(33) il pomodoro

(34) la cozza

(35) la melanzana

(36) lo scontrino

Knowing when (and when not) to use a definite article

REMEMBER

Deciding when and when not to use the definite article is a tricky topic in Italian. Italian uses the definite article much more than English. And it doesn't always translate as the word *the*! For example, Italian uses articles before

>> Foods: **Amo il pane** (*I love bread*); **Mangio le mele** (*I eat apples*)

>> Dates: **il 25 aprile** (*April 25*)

>> Titles: **il professor Baldini** (*Professor Baldini*)

>> Abstract nouns: such as **la forza** (*strength*) and **l'amore** (*love*)

>> Concrete nouns: **Il cibo è necessario.** (*Food is necessary.*)

>> Possessive adjectives: **la mia borsa** (*my handbag*)

>> Family members (when referred to in the plural): **le mie sorelle** (*my sisters*)

People

In Italian, you use articles when talking about a professional (**il dottor Cecconi**) or before a female name to express affection and familiarity (**La Elena**), but you don't use them in direct address. For example, you use the article when you say

Ho visto il dottor Cecconi martedì sera. (*I saw Dr. Cecconi on Tuesday evening.*)

But you don't use it when you say

Buon giorno, dottor Cecconi. (*Good morning, Dr. Cecconi.*)

Places

You use the Italian definite article with the following geographical features:

>> Mountains, rivers, and lakes: **le Alpi** (*the Alps*), **il Monte Bianco** (*Mont Blanc*), **il Po** (*the Po River*), **il [lago di] Garda** (*Lake Garda*), **il lago Michigan** (*Lake Michigan*)

>> Many large islands and archipelagos: **la Sicilia** (*Sicily*), **l'Inghilterra** (*England*), **le Hawaii** (*Hawaii*)

>> Regions and states: **il Lazio** (*the Lazio region*), **la Puglia** (*Apulia*), **la California** (*California*)

>> Nations (singular or plural) and continents: **l'Italia** (*Italy*), **gli Stati Uniti** (*the United States*), **l'Asia** (*Asia*)

Italian doesn't use the definite article before names of cities and small islands: **Bologna, Roma** (*Rome*), **New York, Capri, Malta.**

The rules for articles change when you use prepositions and idiomatic expressions. See Chapter 9 for more on prepositions.

Things

You use the definite article with the following things:

>> Countable plural nouns: **I gatti i cani sono i nostri amici.** (*Cats and dogs are our friends.*)

>> Uncountable nouns: **il sale** (*salt*), **lo zucchero** (*sugar*), **l'acqua** (*water*), **l'amore** (*love*), **la pazienza** (*patience*)

Keeping things general with indefinite articles

Besides the definite article (which you can read about in the section "Dealing with definite articles," earlier in this chapter), Italian uses the indefinite articles **un, un', una,** and **uno,** which correspond to the English *a* or *an*. Because **un/una** mean *one,* you can use them only with singular nouns, as in **una villa** (*a villa/one villa*) or **un paese** (*a country/one country*). Table 2-4 lays out the forms of the indefinite article used with singular masculine nouns, and Table 2-5 does the same for the feminine article.

The words **un/uno/un'/una** also means *one.*

REMEMBER You use the indefinite article **uno** with the exact same set of words with which you use the singular definite article **lo.** (See the section "Dealing with definite articles," earlier in this chapter, for more on **lo.**)

REMEMBER

Table 2-4   Masculine Indefinite Articles

Article	Placement	Examples
un	Before any vowel or consonant and most groups of consonants	un ufficio (an office)
		un uomo (a man)
		un treno (a train)
uno	Before gn–, pn–, ps–, s + another consonant, x–, y–, and z–	uno psicologo (a male psychologist)
		uno studente (a male student)
		uno gnomo (a gnome)
		uno zio (an uncle)

Table 2-5   Feminine Indefinite Articles

Article	Placement	Examples
una	Before any consonant or group of consonants	una casa (a house)
		una porta (a door)
		una strega (a witch)
		una lezione (a lesson)
un'	Before any vowel	un'arancia (an orange)
		un'ora (an hour)
		un'università (a university)

PRACTICE

Provide the correct indefinite article for the noun provided.

Q. cappuccino

A. un cappuccino (a/one cappuccino)

37 tesi

38 tema

39 radio

40 automobile

41 cameriere

42 ristorante

Answers to "Embedded Gender and Number: Nouns and Articles" Practice Questions

1. F

2. M

3. F

4. M

5. F

6. M

7. F

8. M

9. F

10. M

11. **pianisti** (*male or male and female pianists*)

12. **cameriere** (*waitresses*)

13. **studenti** (*students*)

14. **laghi** (*lakes*)

15. **crisi** (*crises*)

16. **montagne** (*mountains*)

17. **fiumi** (*rivers*)

18. **uomini** (*men*)

19. **regioni** (*regions*)

20. **parchi** (*parks*)

21. **il gelato al limone** (*lemon ice-cream*)

22. **l'insalata mista** (*mixed salad*)

23. **le lasagne alla bolognese** (*lasagna with bolognese sauce*)

24. **il contorno** (*side dish*)

25. **gli spinaci** (*spinach*)

26. **la mozzarella** (*mozzarella*)

(27) **il vino bianco** (*white wine*)

(28) **la bistecca alla fiorentina** (*Florentine steak*)

(29) **il conto** (*check/bill*)

(30) **l'uva** (*grapes*; always singular in Italian)

(31) **i ravioli** (*ravioli*)

(32) **gli aperitivi** (*before dinner drink*)

(33) **i pomodori** (*tomatoes*)

(34) **le cozze** (*mussels*)

(35) **le melanzane** (*eggplants*)

(36) **gli scontrini** (*receipts*)

(37) **una tesi** (*a thesis*)

(38) **un tema** (*a theme*)

(39) **una radio** (*a radio*)

(40) **un'automobile** (*an automobile*)

(41) **un cameriere** (*a waiter*)

(42) **un ristorante** (*a restaurant*)

Chapter **3**

Putting Two and Two Together: Numbers, Dates, and Time

You count the steps you take and the miles you drive to work. You check appointments ten times a day and celebrate birthdays and anniversaries. Numbers are a central part of your life and are used all over the world. But each language has its own words and conventions to convey numbers, to talk about centuries, and to tell the time.

In this chapter, I help you express quantities from one to 1 million in Italian. You can also find out how to set things in numerical order — first, second, third, and so on — and how to manage time and dates.

Counting Items with Cardinal Numbers

If you say that you've seen ten movies, you're using a cardinal number. When written in full, numbers are invariable in Italian (except for the number *one*, which can also be an indefinite article; see Chapter 2). The first ten numbers each have their own words. Those between 11 and 19 add the suffix **–dici** or the prefix **dicia–**, which both mean *ten*. Starting with 21, you encounter a neat pattern that you then repeat from 30 to 99.

Following are the numbers from 0 through 29:

- **zero** (0)
- **uno** (1)
- **due** (2)
- **tre** (3)
- **quattro** (4)
- **cinque** (5)
- **sei** (6)
- **sette** (7)
- **otto** (8)
- **nove** (9)
- **dieci** (10)
- **undici** (11)
- **dodici** (12)
- **tredici** (13)
- **quattordici** (14)

- **quindici** (15)
- **sedici** (16)
- **diciassette** (17)
- **diciotto** (18)
- **diciannove** (19)
- **venti** (20)
- **ventuno** (21)
- **ventidue** (22)
- **ventitré** (23)*
- **ventiquattro** (24)
- **venticinque** (25)
- **ventisei** (26)
- **ventisette** (27)
- **ventotto** (28)
- **ventinove** (29)

From 30 on, you follow the same pattern of 21 through 29. When you add an **uno** (*one*) or an **otto** (*eight*), drop the final **a**; otherwise, you keep the vowel and simply add the number:

- **trenta** + **uno** = **trentuno** (31)
- **trenta** + **due** = **trentadue** (32)
- **quaranta** + **sette** = **quarantasette** (47)
- **quaranta** + **otto** = **quarantotto** (48)
- **cinquanta** + **uno** = **cinquantuno** (51)
- **cinquanta** + **quattro** = **cinquantaquattro** (54)
- **sessanta** + **otto** = **sessantotto** (68)
- **sessanta** + **nove** = **sessantanove** (69)

REMEMBER

Except for the word **tre** (3), all numbers ending in 3 carry an accent, such as **trentatré** (33) and **settantatré** (73).

Table 3-1 lists multiples of 10 and 100, as well as examples of numbers from 101 to 909. Directly after the word **cento** (100), add **–uno** and **–otto** without dropping any vowel, even if another vowel follows, as in **centouno** (101) and **centootto** (108). Add all the other numbers without modifying them: 117 is **centodiciassette**, and 148 is **centoquarantotto**.

You build numbers from 200 to 900 like you do in English, by adding **–cento** to any of the first ten numbers, as in **duecento** (200). For numbers between 200 and 999, add any other number to the number you've just formed, as in **trecentoquarantatré** (343). You write them as one word.

Table 3-1   Cardinal Numbers with Double and Triple Digits

Multiples of 10	Multiples of 100	Numbers 101–909
dieci (10)	**cento** (100)	**centouno** (101)
venti (20)	**duecento** (200)	**duecentodue** (202)
trenta (30)	**trecento** (300)	**trecentotré** (303)
quaranta (40)	**quattrocento** (400)	**quattrocentoquattro** (404)
cinquanta (50)	**cinquecento** (500)	**cinquecentocinque** (505)
sessanta (60)	**seicento** (600)	**seicentosei** (606)
settanta (70)	**settecento** (700)	**settecentosette** (707)
ottanta (80)	**ottocento** (800)	**ottocentootto** (808)
novanta (90)	**novecento** (900)	**novecentonove** (909)

In Italian, 1,000 is **mille**. For numbers between 1,000 and 1,999, you add hundreds to **mille–**. For example, to write 1,100, you add 100 to **mille–** and get **millecento**. To write 1,999, you add 999 to 1,000 and get **millenovecentonovantanove**.

REMEMBER

A common error is to say **un mille** for *a thousand/one thousand* — you just say **mille**. For example, **Vengono mille persone al concerto** (*A thousand people are coming to the concert*). Another common error is to use the English convention of doubling up on the first two numbers: In English to read 1929 you group the numbers when talking about years and say *nineteen twenty-nine*, but in Italian, you must use the following structure: **millenovecentoventinove** (not **diciannoveventinove**, which does not mean anything).

TIP

The plural of **mille** is **mila**.

To form higher numbers, you use **–mila** as follows:

» **duemila** (2,000), **cinquemila** (5,000)

» **undicimila** (11,000), **trentamila** (30,000), **sessantamila** (60,000)

» **duecentomila** (200,000), **settecentomila** (700,000)

When you write numbers as numerals, you use a period to separate thousands and a comma to separate integers from decimals — basically, the opposite of the punctuation in English. For example, 1.000,00 in Italian corresponds to 1,000.00 in English.

When you get to **un milione** (1,000,000), you write it as two separate words, but you link all the lower numbers together and then to the word **milione**, as in 1.300.000 euro: **un milionetrecentomila euro** (1,300,000.00 euro).

Here's an example of how you talk about money. Let's say you've just purchased a book at the bookstore. The salesperson will say **dodici euro e cinquanta**, but it will be written as **12,50 euro**.

> **Quanto costa una Ferrari?** (*How much does Ferrari cost?*)

> **Costa duecentosessantanovemila euro.** (*It costs 269,000 euros.*)

 The plural of **euro** in Italian is **euro**: it's invariable.

TIP

Write out the cardinal numbers in the following exercise.

 Q. 140

PRACTICE **A.** **centoquaranta**

1. 144
2. 813
3. 87
4. 1944 (the year)
5. 200.000
6. 1321 (the year)
7. 15
8. 37
9. 93
10. 7300 euro

Putting Items in Order with Ordinal Numbers

With ordinal numbers, you set things in order, using them to establish ranking. The first ten have special forms:

» **primo** (1st)

» **secondo** (2nd)

» **terzo** (3rd)

» **quarto** (4th)

» **quinto** (5th)

» **sesto** (6th)

- » **settimo** (7th)
- » **ottavo** (8th)
- » **nono** (9th)
- » **decimo** (10th)

REMEMBER In Italian, ordinal numbers behave like adjectives in that they need to agree in gender and number with the nouns or pronouns they refer to. You form ordinal numbers beyond **decimo** by dropping the **–o**, and then adding the ending **–esimo** (masculine singular), **–esima** (feminine singular), **–esimi** (masculine plural), or **–esime** (feminine plural) to the corresponding cardinal number (see the preceding section).

The following are some ordinal numbers from 11th to 100th, in the feminine and masculine singular and plural forms: I transform the first three for you, and then provide just the singular forms for the subsequent ones.

- » **undicesima, undicesimo, undicesime, undicesimi** (11th)
- » **dodicesima, dodicesimo, dodicesime, dodicesimi** (12th)
- » **tredicesima, tredicesimo, tredicesime, tredicesimi** (13th)
- » **quattordicesima** (14th)
- » **quindicesimo** (15th)
- » **sedicesima** (16th)
- » **diciassettesimo** (17th)
- » **diciottesima** (18th)
- » **diciannovesimo** (19th)
- » **ventesima** (20th)
- » **trentesimo** (30th)
- » **quarantesima** (40th)
- » **cinquantesimo** (50th)
- » **sessantesima** (60th)
- » **settantesimo** (70th)
- » **ottantesima** (80th)
- » **novantesimo** (90th)
- » **centesima** (100th)

When you use an ordinal number in the context of a sentence, you usually place it before the word it refers to, accompanied by the article.

Lei è la sua terza moglie. (*She's his third wife*).

Abito all'ottavo piano. (*I live on the eighth floor.*)

TIP

You can write an ordinal number using numerals followed by a superscript letter related to the ordinal number's ending. That is, you use **–o** for **primo** and **–a** for **prima** (both meaning *first*). For example, you write **il 1° maggio** (*May 1st*) or **la 3ª pagina** (*the third page*).

Managing Your Calendar and Your Time

You live in the age of digital planners, e-mail appointment reminders, cellular phones that contain calendars and flight schedules, and clocks on every possible gadget. That's why it's pretty important to know how to handle information about time, starting with centuries and proceeding to years, seasons, months, days of the week, hours, minutes, and seconds.

Il calendario: The calendar

Italy shares the same calendar with the rest of the world. The following sections give you the vocabulary that you can use to talk about centuries, years, seasons, months, dates, and days of the week.

Secoli, anni e stagioni: Centuries, years, and seasons

In Italian, as in English, you refer to a century with Roman numerals, as opposed to ordinal numbers. The Italian word for *century* is **secolo**, so when speaking about a century, you say the Roman numeral as an ordinal number, followed by **secolo**.

> **Artemisia Gentileschi è un'artista importante del XVII (diciassettesimo) secolo.**
> (*Artemisia Gentileschi is an important artist of the seventeenth century.*)

See the section "Putting Items in Order with Ordinal Numbers," earlier in this chapter, for details on writing ordinal numbers.

If you're referring to a particular year, you add the definite article to the cardinal number indicating the year, as in **Il 2000** (**il duemila**) (*the year 2000*).

When you need a preposition, you use the form combined with the article (see Chapter 9), as in **nel 1945** (**millenovecentoquarantacinque**) (*in 1945*).

You can say either **il 1968/il millenovecentosessantotto** (*nineteen sixty-eight*) or **il '68/il Sessantotto** (*sixty-eight*), or either **il 1977/il millenovecentosettantasette** (*nineteen seventy-seven*) or **il '77/il Settantasette**, to refer to certain years that are historically important in Italy.

TIP

The four seasons are **la primavera** (*spring*), **l'estate** (f; *summer*), **l'autunno** (*autumn*), and **l'inverno** (*winter*).

Mesi e date: Months and dates

You don't capitalize the names of the months. Here are the months:

- **gennaio** (*January*)
- **febbraio** (*February*)
- **marzo** (*March*)
- **aprile** (*April*)
- **maggio** (*May*)
- **giugno** (*June*)
- **luglio** (*July*)
- **agosto** (*August*)
- **settembre** (*September*)
- **ottobre** (*October*)
- **novembre** (*November*)
- **dicembre** (*December*)

TIP

If you want to have some fun while trying to figure out proper pronunciation, turn to the Internet. You can look for certain words on YouTube. Or try Googling *I mesi italiani per bambini* (which translates as *"the Italian months for children"*) to hear the months spoken out loud.

REMEMBER

When mentioning a particular date, you use cardinal numbers, except for the first of the month, in which case, you use the ordinal number **primo**. You write dates in the day-month-year format, without commas. (Unlike the common usage in the United States, which is month-day-year).

> **Oggi è il primo maggio.** (*Today is May 1st.*)
>
> **Partiamo il quindici aprile.** (*We will leave on April 15th.*)

If you want to know the specific day of the week that something occurred or occurs on, you say

> **In che giorno . . .?** (*On what day . . .?*)

If you ask for today's date, you usually say one of these two options:

> **Che giorno è?** (*What's the date?*)
>
> **Qual è la data di oggi?** (*What's today?*)

To answer, use this structure:

> **Oggi è il ventinove febbraio** (*Today is February 29th*).

TIP

You can use **Che giorno è (oggi)?** to mean *What day of the week is (today)?* You answer with something like **Oggi è venerdì** (*Today is Friday*).

I giorni della settimana: Days of the week

Just like with months, you don't capitalize the days of the week in Italian. They're all masculine and take **il**, except for **la domenica** (*Sunday*). In Italian calendars, the week starts on Monday and include the following:

» **i giorni feriali** (*weekdays*)

- **lunedì** (*Monday*)
- **martedì** (*Tuesday*)
- **mercoledì** (*Wednesday*)
- **giovedì** (*Thursday*)
- **venerdì** (*Friday*)

» **il fine settimana/il week-end** (*the weekend*)

- **sabato** (*Saturday*)
- **domenica** (*Sunday*)

In Italian, **la domenica** and other holidays are known as **i giorni festivi** (*festivities/holidays*).

Other important words to add to your toolbox include:

» **giorno** (*day*)

» **oggi** (*today*)

» **domani** (*tomorrow*).

REMEMBER

You generally use the definite article with days of the week only when you're talking about a repeated action.

For example, compare the following two sentences:

> **Il venerdì sera faccio sempre Zumba** (*On Friday evenings, I always go to Zumba.*)
>
> **Venerdì sera faccio Zumba.** (*I'm going to Zumba this Friday evening.*)

PRACTICE

Answer the following questions. Use the December calendar for some of them. Don't worry about making full sentences. Answer with the date (Italian style) when specified or complete the response I've started for you.

Dicembre 2023						
Lunedì	Martedì	Mercoledì	Giovedì	Venerdì	Sabato	Domenica
				1	2	3
4	5	6	7	8	9	10
11	12	13	14	15	16	17
18	19	20	21	22	23	24
25	26	27	28	29	30	31

Q. **Quando iniziano le lezioni?** (sounds better in Italian) **or Quando inizia la scuola?** (*What day does school start?*)

A. **Il sette settembre.** (*September seventh*)

11 Che giorno è il trentuno dicembre? (day)

12 Che giorno è la Giornata della donna? (date)

13 Quando è il tuo compleanno? (date)

14 Qual è il tuo mese preferito? Il mio mese preferito è _____

15 Qual è la tua stagione preferita? La mia stagione preferita è _____

16 Che giorno è Natale? _____

17 Write out the days of the week, Italian style, on this mock calendar:

L'ora: Telling time

If you want to catch a train or a plane, make sure the store is open, or check the movie theater's schedule, you need to know the right time. To ask the time, you say:

Che ora è?/Che ore sono? (*What time is it?*)

These questions are interchangeable.

The answer, however, is not. To respond, you must use the third person singular of the verb **essere** (*to be*) — **è** — or with singular time indicators. You must use the third person plural of the verb **essere** — **sono** — if you're answering with plural time indicators.

To use the singular to tell time, follow this structure to talk about times that start at 1:00, noon, and midnight:

È + l' + una (+ **e** or **meno** + a portion of the hour or a number of minutes)

You use **e** (*and*) when giving the minutes within the hour (hour *and* minutes). After you pass the half hour, you generally jump to the next hour and use the word **meno** (*minus*) (hour *minus* minutes).

 >> **È l'una.** (*It's 1:00.*)

 >> **È mezzogiorno.** (*It's noon.* — 12:00 p.m.)

 >> **È mezzanotte.** (*It's midnight.* — 12:00 a.m.)

 >> **È l'una e un quarto.** (*It's a quarter past 1:00.* — 1:15)

 >> **È l'una meno dodici.** (*It's 12 to 1:00.* — 12:48)

 >> **È l'una meno dieci.** (*It's 10 to 1:00.* — 12:50)

 >> **È l'una e mezzo/a.** (*It's half past 1:00.* — 1:30)

To write a time in plural, follow this structure:

Sono + le + hour (any time other than 1:00) + **e** or **meno** + a portion of the hour or a number of minutes

Here are some examples:

 >> **Sono le due e dieci.** (*It's 10 past 2:00.* — 2:10)

 >> **Sono le otto meno un quarto.** (*It's a quarter to 8:00.* — 7:45)

 >> **Sono le dieci e un quarto.** (*It's a quarter past 10:00.* — 10:15)

 >> **Sono le tre meno cinque.** (*It's five to 3:00.* — 2:55)

 >> **Sono le quattro e mezza/o.** (*It's half past 4:00.* — 4:30)

When using the 12-hour system, you can add **di mattina** (*a.m./in the morning*), **di pomeriggio** (*p.m./in the afternoon*), or **di sera** (*p.m./in the evening*) to avoid misunderstandings, as in

"Partono alle 4:00 (alle quattro)." (*"They're leaving at 4:00."*)

Vado a lavorare alle otto di mattina. (*I go to work at 8:00 in the morning*.)

Mio fratello torna a casa alle quattro del pomeriggio. (*My brother gets home at 4:00 in the afternoon.*)

Of course, you can always use the 24-hour system (which in the U.S. is usually associated with the military). This system is much more common in Italy than it is in the United States.

You find the 24-hour system printed on Italian train schedules, event programs, class times and so forth.

Il treno parte alle [ore] 15,45/15:45. (*The train leaves at 15:45 hours [3:45 p.m.].*)

When you tell the time this way, you add minutes to the hour, as in 15:45, which you read as **le quindici e quarantacinque.** Use this system in everyday life when you want to avoid misunderstandings or when you're making appointments.

PRACTICE

Che ora è? or **Che ore sono?** Say what time it is by writing out the time displayed as digits. Make certain to determine first whether the time is singular or plural (whether you need to start your time with **È** or **Sono**).

Q. 3:10

A. Sono le tre e dieci

18 12:22

19 4:15

20 8:50

21 6:30 a.m.

22 22:54

23 5:30 p.m.

A che ora: Saying "at"

To ask *at what time* something begins or ends, you simply say **A che ora** (*at what time?*). To answer, you use a form of the preposition *at* — **a**, **all'**, or **alle** — in your response.

A che ora vai a dormire? (*At what time do you go to sleep?*)

A mezzanotte. (*At midnight.*)

» **a** with no article: It's **mezzogiorno** (*noon*) or **mezzanotte** (*midnight*).

A mezzanotte. (*At midnight.*)

» **all'**: It's 1:00.

All'una. (*At 1:00.*)

» **alle**: The hour is plural, meaning it's later than 1:00.

Alle due. (*At 2:00.*)

Answers to "Putting Two and Two Together: Numbers, Dates, and Times" Practice Questions

1. centoquarantaquattro
2. ottocentotredici
3. ottantasette
4. millenovecentoquarantaquattro
5. duecentomila
6. milletrecentoventuno
7. quindici
8. trentasette
9. novantatrè
10. settemilatrecento euro
11. domenica
12. l'otto marzo
13. (sample response) **il sette novembre**
14. **Il mio mese preferito è giugno.** (*My favorite month is June.*)
15. **La mia stagione preferita è l'autunno.** (*My favorite season is Autumn.*)
16. **Quando è Natale? Lunedì venticinque dicembre.** (*When is Christmas? Monday, December 25th.*)
17.

lunedì	martedì	mercoledì	giovedì	venerdì	sabato	domenica

18. **È mezzogiorno e ventidue.** (*It's 22 past noon.*)/**È mezzanotte e ventidue.** (*It's 22 past midnight.*)/**Sono le dodici e ventidue.** (*It's 22 past 12:00.*)
19. **Sono le quattro e un quarto.** (*It's a quarter past 4:00.*)/**Sono le quattro e quindici.** (*It's 15 past 4:00.*)
20. **Sono le nove meno dieci.** (*It's 10 to 9:00.*)/**Sono le otto e cinquanta.** (*It's 8:50.*)
21. **Sono le sei e mezzo di mattina** (*It's half past 6:00 in the morning*).
22. **Sono le ventidue e cinquantaquattro.** (*It's 22:54.*)/**Sono le undici meno sei di sera.** (*It's 6 to 23:00.*)
23. **Sono le cinque e mezzo di sera.** (*It's half past 5:00 in the evening.*)

Verbs as Building Blocks

2

Meet **essere** and **avere**: two very important verbs in Italian. Along with them, you get to know subject pronouns.

Find out how to speak in the present. Get versed in how to describe what's happening at certain moments and in current situations and get acquainted with regular verbs.

Staying in the present, learn about irregular verbs and how to conjugate them, as well as get the lowdown on modal auxiliaries and stressed pronouns.

IN THIS CHAPTER

» Knowing whom you're talking to
with personal pronouns

» Being happy to be here with
essere

» Having it all with avere

Chapter **4**

Noting to Be or to Have with Essere and Avere

The verbs **essere** (*to be*) and **avere** (*to have*) are the cornerstones of the Italian language when it comes to verbs. Both are irregular, and both are essential to successfully navigating the language. In addition to the standard, easily translatable into English, uses such as **Io sono felice** (*I am happy*) and **Io ho un cane stupendo** (*I have a stupendous dog*), these two verbs are also the auxiliary verbs you need to construct compound tenses, such as the present perfect tense (see Chapter 12). The verb **avere** also has a host of other idiomatic meanings (other than *to have*), such as in the expression **Ho fame** (*I am hungry*),

First in this chapter, you get your feet wet with the subject pronouns, also known as personal pronouns, because they're essential to verb conjugation and sentence building.

I also show you how to conjugate the verbs **essere** (*to be*) and **avere** (*to have*). I walk you through combining **essere** with other expressions, including **dov'è?** (*where is*) and **dove sono?** (*where are?*). You can also practice with the myriad idiomatic uses of **avere**, such as when **avere** means *to be* in certain contexts.

Meeting the Subject Pronouns

Grammatically speaking, six persons can perform an action: the first, second, and third persons, both singular and plural. Each personal pronoun has its own corresponding verb ending, which you can delve into in the section "Working with **Essere** and **Avere**," later in this chapter.

Table 4-1 lists the subject pronouns. *Note:* In Italian, when animals are referred to as possessing feelings and even a personality, you use pronouns usually reserved for human beings: **lui** (*he*), **lei** (*she*), and **loro** (*they*).

Table 4-1   Subject Pronouns

Person	Singular	Plural
First	**io** (*I*)	**noi** (*we*)
Second	**tu** (*you*, informal)	**voi** (*you [all]*)
Third	**lui** (*he*), **lei** (*she*)	**loro** (*they*)
Third (singular and plural, used to address people formally)	**Lei** (*you*, formal)	**Loro** (*you*, formal)

REMEMBER

Whenever I say *first person singular,* I mean the *I* (**io**) person and the first person singular of the verb; when I say the first person plural, I mean the *we* (**noi**) person of both the pronoun and the verb, and so forth.

REMEMBER

It might be silly for me to remind you that the plural of *I* is *we* (**io/noi**), the plural of *you* is *you all* (**tu/voi**) and the plural of *she* and *he* is *they* (**Lui** or **Lei/loro**), but I'm reminding you any way so that you can keep these six different persons in mind while you manipulate verb conjugations.

In certain areas of the United States, especially in inclusive schools and universities, people more frequently express their preferred pronoun according to the gender with which they identify (*she, her, hers; he, his, his; they, their, theirs*). Although this practice is not as common in Italy yet as it is in the United States, some schools have launched something called *carriera ALIAS,* which encourages students and faculty to declare their pronoun preference by choosing between **lui** and **lei** (but not **loro**). When my students choose *they, their, theirs* as pronouns, I ask them to choose between masculine and feminine endings in the Italian classroom because otherwise verb and adjective agreement just doesn't work. The asterisk * or the *schwa* that many Italianists in the United States use is an effective way to get around privileging one gender over the other when writing to a group of people.

Knowing when to use them

Even though you definitely have to know how the personal pronouns work, most of the time, you don't need personal pronouns in Italian because the verb conjugations indicate the subject. In the sentence **Guardano la televisione tutte le sere** (*They watch TV every night*), you know the subject is **loro** (*they*) because **guardano** (*they watch, they're watching*) is conjugated in the third-person plural form (and the *they* meaning is included in the verb itself). I cover verb conjugation details in the section "Working with **Essere** and **Avere**," later in this chapter.

REMEMBER

At times, you do need subject pronouns. You should use them whenever you're

» Emphasizing what a particular person is doing.

Io andrò alle Cinque Terre, non lei. (*I'm going to the Cinque Terre, not she.*)

» Emphasizing one subject over another (often inverting the word order).

Decido io, non tu, a che ora devi tornare a casa! (*I'm the one who decides what time you must come home, not you!*)

Using subject pronouns for informal and formal usage

You can address people either formally or informally in Italian, altering your pronoun and verb choice accordingly.

Being informal

Use the informal **tu** and **voi** only with the following:

» Friends

» Family

» Children

» Relatives

» Teenager and up to maybe 30 years old, generally with people your same age

Generally, when you use someone's first name, you use the **tu**. Informally, you address people with the following pronoun-verb combinations:

- **tu** (*you* singular) + the verb in the second-person singular

  [Tu] vieni alla partita, Andrea? (*Are you coming to the game, Andrea?*)

- **voi** (*you* plural) + the verb in the second-person plural

  [Voi] venite alla partita, Andrea e Giacomo? (*Are you coming to the game, Andrea and Giacomo?*)

Going formal

Use the formal **Lei** and **Loro** when addressing those you don't know well, people who are older than you, professors, waiters, salespeople, your friends' parents, and so forth.

You want to be respectful, so always use the formal when in doubt! If someone wants you to use the **tu** with them, they can invite you to do so (see Chapter 6, which presents the expressions **dare del tu/dare del Lei** – using the **tu**/using the **Lei**). Formally, you address people with the following pronoun-verb combinations:

> » **Lei** (*you*): With either a man or a woman + the verb in the third-person singular.
>
> **[Lei] viene alla partita, Signore/Signora?** (*Are you coming to the game, Sir/Madam?*)
>
> » **Loro** (*you* formal) + the verb in third-person plural.
>
> **[Loro] vengono alla partita Signori/Signore/Signori e Signore?** (*Are you coming to the game, Ladies and Gentlemen?*)
>
> Using **Loro** (*you* formal) is becoming less and less common.
>
> » **Voi** (*you* plural): Nowadays, you can use **voi** to address more than one person either informally or formally.
>
> **[Voi] venite alla partita Signori/Signore/Signori e Signore?** (*Are you coming to the game, ladies and gentlemen/people?*)

REMEMBER When you address someone formally, you can use his or her last name preceded by **Signor** (*Mr.*), **Signora** (*Mrs., Ms.*), **Signorina** (*Miss, Ms.*), **Dottor/Dottoressa** (*Dr.*, for all those with a **laurea** or university degree), **Ingegner** (*Engineer*), **Avvocato/Avvocata** (*Legal Counselor*), **Professor/Professoressa/Prof.**, (which is used also in secondary schools), and so on with specific professional titles.

TIP The comma that appears after someone's name or a term is a dead giveaway that you're dealing with a direct address and that you need **tu**, **voi**, or **Lei** — and the corresponding verb ending — according to context. You can find out more about subject verb agreement in Chapters 5 and 6.

For example:

Beppe, tu vieni alla festa? (*Beppe, are you coming to the party?*)

Dottor Husu, Lei viene alla festa? (*Dr. Husu, are you coming to the party?*)

TIP Italian has several sets of pronouns. In this book, you work with subject pronouns in this chapter, stressed pronouns in Chapter 6, and reflexive pronouns in Chapter 17.

PRACTICE Following the clues, fill in the blanks with the appropriate subject pronouns. In other words, what personal pronouns would you use to talk about the following?

Q. Marco,

A. tu (note that this is direct address)

1 Luisa _____

2 Giorgio _____

(3) Caterina e Margherita _____

(4) Vito e io _____

(5) Tu e Giulia _____

(6) Gli italiani _____

(7) Mia madre _____

(8) Ragazzi, _____

(9) Stefano, _____

(10) Dottor D'Angelo, _____

Working with Essere and Avere

Essere (*to be*) and **avere** (*to have*) are two important irregular verbs. The term *irregular* means that they don't follow any specific pattern in conjugation. Understanding the meaning and the usage of these two verbs is fundamental to learning Italian. (You can find many more irregular verbs in Chapter 6.)

Using essere (to be)

Essere o non essere. *To be or not to be.*

The following table shows the conjugation of the verb **essere**.

Essere (to be)

io sono	noi siamo
tu sei	voi siete
lui/lei/Lei è	loro/Loro

Sono stanca. (*I'm tired.*)

TIP

The verb **essere** in the present tense in Italian essentially has the same function as *to be* does in English.

So, when can you use **essere**? I guide you through your **essere** options in the following sections.

Essere with adjectives

You can use **essere** with adjectives, just like you can with *to be* in English — with one caveat. Most adjectives must agree in gender or in gender and number with the noun (depending on the type of adjective it is). See Chapter 7 for more on adjective agreement.

The following table shows you **essere** in action with the adjective **italiano** (*Italian*), which is an adjective that agrees in number and gender with the noun that it's modifying. So, a person who identifies as female would say, **"Io sono italiana."** and a person who identifies as male would say, **"Io sono italiano."**

Essere with Italiano	Translation
Io sono italiana/o.	I am Italian.
Noi siamo italiani/e.	We are Italian.
Tu sei italiana/o.	You are Italian.
Voi siete italiani/e.	You are Italian.
Lui/lei/Lei è italiano/a.	He/she is Italian./You all are Italian.
Loro/loro sono italiani/e.	They are Italian./You all are Italian.

REMEMBER

When you wish to negate something in the simplest way, just add **non** (*not*) in front of the verb.

Gaby, sei italiana? (*Gaby are you Italian?*)

No, Teresa, non sono italiana, sono uruguiana. (*No, Teresa, I am not Italian, I am Uruguayan.*)

PRACTICE

Include the correct form of **essere** in the blanks provided.

Q. Io _____ interessata.

A. Io sono interessata. (*I'm interested.*)

11 Eva _____ francese.

12 Egidio e Bruno _____ bravi studenti.

13 Stefania e Liliana _____ simpatiche.

14 Luca e io _____ buoni amici.

15 Tu ed Eleonora _____ divertenti.

Essere with ci

By itself, **ci** sometimes means *there*. You can combine it with **essere** to mean *there is* and *there are*, and to also ask the questions *is there?* and *are there?*

Use **c'è** for *there is/is there.*

Use **ci sono** for *there are/are there.*

Respond with the singular **c'è** or the plural **ci sono**, according to context. You can review indefi-nite articles, as well as noun gender and number (all in Chapter 2), if you need to. Follow the example.

Q. Quante matite ci sono?

A. Ci sono tre matite.

16 Quanti studenti ci sono?

17 C'è una macchina?

18 Quanti cani ci sono?

19 C'è una mela?

20 Ci sono quattro amiche?

Essere with dove (where) and come (how)

If someone says to you, **"Di dove sei?"** (*"Where are you from?"*), answer using **essere** with the word **dove** (*where*). For example, you might say, **"Sono di New York"** (*"I'm from New York"*) or **"Sono degli Stati Uniti"** (*"I'm from the United States"*).

Dove can also be combined with **essere**.

> **Dov'è Urbino?** (*Where is Urbino?*)
>
> **Dove sono le Dolomiti?** (*Where are the Dolomites?*)

You can also use **dove** by itself and without **essere**, such as saying, **"Dove mangi stasera?"** (*"Where are you eating tonight?"*)

REMEMBER You should not include **dove** in the response to these sorts of questions.

> **Urbino è nelle Marche.** (*Urbino is in the Marches region.*)
>
> **Le Dolomiti sono nelle Alpi.** (*The Dolomites are in the Alps.*)
>
> **Mangio a casa.** (*I'm eating at home.*)

Come means *how*, as in **Come stai?** (*How are you?*). You can also combine it with **essere** to ask how or what something is like.

> **Com'è la tua migliore amica?** (*What's your best friend like?*)
>
> **Come sono i tuoi nonni?** (*What are your grandparents like?*)

REMEMBER **Com'è**, **Come sei**, and **come sono** ask what something/someone is like, <u>not</u> how they are doing. So to answer the question **Com'è la tua migliore amica?** (*What's your best friend like?*), you might say: **La mia migliore amica è dolce, intelligente, e laboriosa.** (*My best friend is sweet, smart, and hard-working*).

Essere in agreement

Essere d'accordo (*to agree, to be in agreement*) is a common nifty phrase you hear frequently.

REMEMBER Here are a couple of examples.

> **"Quell'uomo è intelligente."** (*"That man is smart."*) **"Sono d'accordo."** (*"I agree."*)
>
> **"Siete d'accordo con me?"** (*"Do you agree with me?"*)

Using avere (to have)

The following table shows the conjugation of the verb **avere** (*to have*).

REMEMBER

The **h** is always silent in Italian: Just pretend it isn't there when you're speaking (and reading)!

avere (to have)

io ho	noi abbiamo
tu hai	voi avete
lui/lei/Lei ha	loro/Loro hanno

Hanno una casa a Pescara. (*They have a house in Pescara.*)

Note the following examples of the verb **avere**.

> **Quel ristorante ha dell'ottimo cibo.** (*The restaurant has great food.*)

> **Hai un cane o un gatto?** (*Do you have a dog or a cat?*)

> **Abbiamo qualche domanda.** (*We have some questions.*)

Avere has several idiomatic uses. Many, though not all, translate directly into English with the verb *to be*. For example: **Quanti anni hai?** (*How old are you?*) uses the verb **avere** rather than **essere**. These idiomatic uses need to be tucked away in your memory bank because they're quite common.

REMEMBER

All of the terms following the verb **avere** in Table 4-2 are nouns, and that explains why you use the verb **avere** rather than **essere**. So, you're literally saying *I have hunger* when you say **Ho fame**. And when you throw in an adjective, such as **molto**, you need to make it agree with the noun: **Ho molta fame** (literally, *I have much hunger* — meaning *I'm very hungry.*)

Table 4-2 lists the most common idiomatic expressions that use **avere,** but do not mean *to have*. It also provides you with a sample of each.

Table 4-2   Idiomatic Expressions That Use Avere

Expression	Example	Translation
avere...anni (*to be...years old*)	**Il mio cane ha dodici anni.**	*My dog is 12 years old.*
		(*Literally: My dog has 12 years.*)
avere bisogno di (*to need*)	**Ho bisogno di dormire.**	*I need to sleep.*
avere fame (*to be hungry*)	**Fatima ha fame.**	*Fatima is hungry.*
avere sete (*to be thirsty*)	**Connor, hai sete?**	*Connor, are you thirsty?*
avere caldo (*to be hot*)	**Abbiamo caldo!**	*We're hot!*
avere freddo (*to be cold*)	**Avete freddo?**	*Are you (all) cold?*
avere fretta (*to be in a rush*)	**È tardi e hanno fretta.**	*It's late and they're in a hurry.*
avere voglia di (*to feel like*)	**Ho voglia di un gelato.**	*I feel like having an ice-cream.*
avere sonno (*to be sleepy*)	**Ho sonno spesso a quest'ora.**	*I'm usually sleepy at this time.*

The preposition **di** will be followed by the infinitive of the verb when used with expressions such as **avere voglia di** and **avere bisogno di**, depending on context. (No infinitive is necessary with a noun!)

For example:

> **Chi ha voglia di giocare a bocce?** (*Who feels like playing bocce?*), but you would say **Chi ha voglia di gelato?** (*Who feels like having ice-cream?*)

> **Chi ha bisogno di studiare stasera?** (*Who needs to study tonight?*), but you would say Chi. **Ha bisogo di una pausa?** (*Who needs a break?*)

Complete the sentences with the correct form of **avere**. Also, try to translate each sentence.

PRACTICE

Q. Ci sono tre gradi oggi — _____ freddo! (noi)

A. Ci sono tre gradi oggi — abbiamo freddo! (*It's 3 degrees today — we're cold!*)

21 Per l'esame d'italiano tu _____ bisogno di un dizionario.

22 La bambina piccola _____ tre anni.

23 C'è acqua? Noi _____ sete.

24 Ahhh! Un ragno (spider)! Io _____ paura dei ragni!

25 Il martedì non fate colazione e poi alle undici (voi) _____ fame.

26 Sono le due di mattina e lui _____ molto sonno.

27 In estate loro _____ sempre voglia di gelato.

TIP

You may hear the term **avere bisogno di** (*to need*) with the following scenario: You walk into a shop and start to look around at the merchandise. The salesperson asks, **"Ha bisogno di aiuto?"** (*"Do you need anything?"*)

Answers to "Noting to Be or to Have with Essere and Avere" Practice Questions

1. lei
2. lui
3. loro
4. e io, noi
5. voi
6. loro
7. lei
8. voi
9. tu
10. lei
11. è; Eva è francese. (*Eva is French.*)
12. sono; Egidio e Bruno sono bravi studenti. (*Egidio and Bruno are good students.*)
13. sono; Stefania e Liliana sono simpatiche. (*Stefania and Lilliana are nice.*)
14. siamo; Luca e io siamo buoni amici. (*Luca and I are good friends.*)
15. siete; Tu ed Eleonora siete divertenti. (*You and Eleonora are fun.*)
16. C'è uno studente.
17. Ci sono due macchine.
18. C'è un cane.
19. Ci sono cinque mele.
20. C'è un'amica.
21. hai; Per l'esame d'italiano tu hai bisogno di un dizionario. (*You need a dictionary for the Italian exam.*)
22. ha; La bambina piccola ha tre anni. (*The little girl is three years old.*)

(23) **abbiamo; C'è acqua? Noi abbiamo sete.** (*Is there any water? We're thirsty.*)

(24) **ho; Ahhh! Un ragno** (*spider*)**! Io ho paura dei ragni!** (*Oh! A spider! I'm afraid of spiders!*)

(25) **avete; Il martedì non fate colazione e poi alle undici voi avete fame.** (*On Tuesday you don't have breakfast and then at eleven o'clock you're hungry.*)

(26) **ha; Sono le due di mattina e lui ha molto sonno.** (*It's two in the morning and I'm very sleepy.*)

(27) **hanno; In estate loro hanno sempre voglia di gelato. (***They always want ice-cream in the summer.*)

Chapter 5

Forming the Present

The present tense allows you to talk about the present (obviously!), such as **oggi** (*today*) or **stasera** (*this evening*), and sometimes about the future (not so obviously), such as **domani** (*tomorrow*). (I cover the future tense in Chapter 14.) The present tense takes two forms in Italian:

» **Present tense:** Also called the present indicative, this tense describes current situations, what's happening or what you're doing at a specific moment, recurring actions, and habits:

- **Noi viviamo in Italia.** (*We live in Italy.*)

- **Finisco i compiti e poi esco.** (*I'm going to finish my homework and then go out.*)

- **Giancarlo corre mentre io cammino.** (*Giancarlo is running while I'm walking./Giancarlo runs while I walk.*)

- **Io leggo il giornale ogni mattina.** (*I read the paper every morning.*)

- **Cosa fate questo fine settimana?** (*What are you all doing this weekend?*) **Andiamo a San Francisco.** (*We're going to San Francisco.*)

» **Present progressive tense:** Facilitates talking about what's happening or what you're doing only at a specific moment:

- **"Ciao Antonietta, cosa fai?" "Sto camminando."** (*"Hi Antonietta, what are you doing?" "I'm walking."*)

- **Lia sta parlando al telefono.** (*Lia is talking on the phone.*)

In this chapter, I show you how to form the present indicative of regular verbs, and of a few irregular verbs, simply by adding three sets of endings to the three different verb conjugations: –are verbs, –ere verbs and –ire verbs. I also show how to form the present progressive, which you create by using the verb **stare** (*to stay*, *to be*) in the present and adding the main verb in the gerund.

The Reliable Guys: Regular Verbs

You conjugate verbs in the present tense by using a verb stem and an ending. The infinitive — such as *to work*, *to play*, *to read*, and so forth — is the default form of the verb. In Italian, most infinitives end in **–are**, **–ere**, or **–ire**. When you take these endings out, you're left with the stem of the verb. So, first take the infinitive and cut off the stem. This table shows the three options, illustrated by three regular verbs.

Infinitive Ending	Example	Stem
–are	**guardare** (*to look at, to watch*)	**guard–**
–ere	**correre** (*to run*)	**corr–**
–ire	**sentire** (*to hear, to taste, to feel, to touch*)	**sent–**

TIP

To negate something, simply place the word **non** in front of the verb.

Balli bene? (*Do you dance well?*)

Non ballo bene. (*I don't dance well.*) or **No, non ballo bene.** (*No, I don't dance well.*) (The **no** is optional; the **non** is necessary).

–are verbs

Once you've determined your stem, to conjugate a verb you only have to figure out the conjugation pattern and apply it to each verb of that type. Table 5-1 shows you the regular –are verb endings.

Table 5-1   Present Tense Endings of –are Verbs

Person	–are Verb Endings
io	–o
tu	–i
lui/lei/Lei	–a
noi	–iamo
voi	–ate
loro/Loro	–ano

The following table conjugates the present indicative of **guardare** (*to look at, to watch*). Cut the verb at its stem (**guard–**) and add the endings.

Guardare Conjugations	Translations
io guardo	*I watch/am watching*
noi guardiamo	*we watch/are watching*
tu guardi	*you watch/are watching*
voi guardate	*you all watch/are watching*
lui/lei/Lei guarda	*he/she watches/is watching*
loro/Loro guardano	*they watch/are watching; you watch/are watching* (formal, pl); *you are watching* (formal, sing)

Here is an example of an –are verb in action. Notice that I do not use the pronoun **noi**, because **guardiamo** aleady means "*we are watching.*"

> **Guardiamo sempre la partita.** (*We always watch the game.*)

TIP

When you ask a question and then answer it, the words *do* and *does* are inferred.

> **Guardate sempre la partita?** (*Do you always watch the game?*)

> **Sì.** (*Yes* [we do].)

The English words *is* and *are* are also inferred in questions, as well as in declarative sentences.

> **Emilia mangia con voi stasera?** (*Is Emilia eating with you tonight?*)

> **Comprano i biglietti per Brindisi online.** (*They're buying the tickets for Brindisi online.*)

DIFFERENCES

Here are a few variations that occur with verbs ending in **–care**, **–gare**, **–ciare**, and **–giare**:

>> Just like the nouns in Chapter 2 and the adjectives in Chapter 7 that end in **–ca**, **–co**, **–ga**, and **–go**, you need to insert an **h** in some **–are** verbs.

>> In order to preserve the hard sound of the infinitive, verbs ending in **–care** and **–gare**, such as **giocare** (*to play*) and **pagare** (*to pay*), add an **h** before the verb ending beginning with **–i** (the **tu** and **noi** forms).

> Example: **paghi (tu)** → **paghiamo (noi)** (but **pago**, **paga**, **pagate**, and **pagano** do not take an **h**.)

> **Paghiamo l'affitto all'inizio del mese.** (*We pay rent at the beginning of the month*.)

>> Verbs ending in **–iare**, such as **studiare** (*to study*), **mangiare** (*to eat*), and **cominciare** (*to begin*) keep only one **i** when the ending begins with **–i** (the **tu** and **noi** forms).

> **Laura, mangi con noi stasera?** (*Laura, are you eating with us tonight?*)

> **Gigio e Riki, dove mangiate?** (*Gigio and Riki, where are you eating?*)

Although I can't really list every possible –are verb in this chapter (at least, not without a lot more paper), I'm going to list some of my favorites in this table.

Common –are Verbs	Translations
arrivare	*to arrive*
parlare	*to speak*
pagare	*to pay*
studiare	*to study*
cominciare	*to begin*
guidare	*to drive*
imparare	*to learn*
lavorare	*to work*
cercare	*to look for*
giocare	*to play* (a sport, cards)
suonare	*to play* (an instrument)
cenare	*to have dinner*
aspettare	*to wait for*
nuotare	*to swim*
ballare	*to dance*

REMEMBER

Suonare means *to play an instrument* (**uno strumento musicale**), such as **il pianoforte** (*piano*), **il violino** (*violin*), **la batteria** (*the drums*) and **la chitarra** (*guitar*).

Giocare means *to play a game* (**una partita**), and *a sport* (**uno sport**), such as **il calcio** (*soccer*), **la pallacanestro** (*basketball*), **la pallavolo** (*volleyball*) and **il tennis** (*tennis*). You also use **giocare** with **giocare a carte** (*to play cards*) and **giocare a bocce** (*to play bocce*).

PRACTICE

Conjugate the verbs listed in parentheses to match the subject.

Q. Io _____ a calcio. (giocare)

A. Io gioco a calcio. (*I play soccer.*)

1. Noi _____ alle 19:00. (arrivare)

2. Tu _____ l'università di tua figlia? (pagare)

3. Giulia, Caterina ed Elisabetta_____ ad Aspen in inverno. (sciare)

4. Mio padre _____ a Roma. (lavorare)

5. Tu e Guglielmo_____ a casa stasera. (mangiare).

6. I ragazzi _____ a basket. (giocare)

7. Nadia _____ bene l'inglese. (parlare)

(8) Olivia ed io _____ al mare. (nuotare)

(9) Io non _____ la carne. (mangiare)

(10) Gigio, dove _____ meglio, a casa o in biblioteca? (studiare)

The **noi** ending is always the same for **–are**, **–ere**, and **–ire** verbs: **iamo**.

REMEMBER The **voi** person always takes the vowel that's characteristic of the verb type: Illustrate this by underlining or highlighting the third to the last letter of the conjugated verb in the following three sentences:

>> **Mangiare = mangiate** (*You all eat./You all are eating.*)

>> **Ricevere = ricevete** (*You all receive./You all are receiving.*)

>> **Partire = partite** (*You all depart./You all are departing.*)

–ere verbs

Table 5-2 delineates the endings for the verbs of the second conjugation, **–ere** verbs. Compare these endings with the endings of **–are** verbs in Table 5-1.

Table 5-2   Present Tense Endings of –ere Verbs

Person	–ere Verb Endings
io	–o
tu	–i
lui/lei/Lei	–e
noi	–iamo
voi	–ete
loro/Loro	–ono

The following table conjugates the present indicative of **vedere** (*to see*). Cut the verb at its stem **ved–** and add the **–ere** verb endings.

Vedere Conjugations	Translations
io vedo	*I see*
noi vediamo	*we see*
tu vedi	*you see*
voi vedete	*you all see*
lui/lei/Lei vede	*he/she sees/is seeing*
loro/Loro vedono	*they see*

Any present tense verb can sound like a gerund, depending on the context, such as in the following example:

Vediamo Margherita sabato. (*We're seeing Margherita on Saturday.*)

Common –ere Verbs	Translations
scrivere	To write
leggere	To read
prendere	To take; to have (as in what you're having in a restaurant or bar)
perdere	to lose
vincere	To win
ripetere	to repeat
rispondere	to answer
correre	to run
vedere	to see
cadere	to fall
conoscere	to know
mettere	to put/to place
convincere	to convince
chiudere	to close
chiedere	to ask for

REMEMBER

The verb **bere** (*to drink*) is an exception to the standard **–ere** conjugation rules only because you have to alter the stem first, from **ber–** to **bev–**, and then add the **–ere** endings.

bere (to drink)

io bevo	noi beviamo
tu bevi	voi bevete
lui/lei/Lei beve	loro/Loro bevono

Bevono solo acqua. (*They drink only water.*)

PRACTICE

Translate the following six sentences with **–ere** verbs.

Q. Chiudiamo le finestre.

A. *We're closing the windows.*

11 Matteo scrive una poesia.

12 Leggo il giornale.

13 Gli studenti corrono dopo scuola.

14 Ricevo molte mail e messaggini ogni giorno.

15. Beviamo l'acqua minerale frizzante.

16. Maria, prendi un cappuccino o una spremuta d'arancia?

–ire verbs

There are two types of **–ire** verbs. The first kind follows a regular pattern without undergoing any change. The second type, what you can call the **–ire/isc** verbs, follows the exact same pattern, but you need to throw in an **–isc–** between the stem and the **–ire** endings, in all the persons except for **noi** and **voi**. Table 5-3 outlines the differences between an **–ire** verb and an **–ire/isc** verb. Create the stem first and then add on the endings (**aprire** becomes **apr–** and **capire** becomes **cap–**). Note that the endings (the last letters) are exactly the same in both types.

Table 5-3   Present Tense Endings of –ire and –ire/isc Verbs

–ire Verb Endings (for Aprire)	–ire/isc Verb Endings (for Capire)
io apro (*I'm opening/I open*)	**capisco** (*I understand*)
tu apri	**capisci**
lui/lei/Lei apre	**capisce**
noi apriamo	**capiamo**
voi aprite	**capite**
loro/Loro aprono	**capiscono**

REMEMBER

The pronunciation of the **c** sound in the **–ire/isc** verbs is odd in that it's both hard, like in **capisco/capiscono** (with a *k* sound) and soft, like in **capisci/capisce** (with a *shh* sound)

TIP

Students frequently wonder how to tell the difference between **–ire** verbs and **–ire/isc** verbs. Work to remember the **–ire/isc** verbs presented in this section, and then add on when you encounter more.

This table presents some common **–ire** and **–ire/isc** verbs.

–ire	–ire/isc
aprire (*to open*)	**capire** (*to understand*)
dormire (*to sleep*)	**finire** (*to finish*)
partire (*to leave/to depart*)	**preferire** (*to prefer*)
sentire (*to hear/to taste/to smell/to touch*)	**pulire** (*to clean*)
seguire (*to follow/to take a class*)	**costruire** (*to build*)

REMEMBER

Preferire (*to prefer*) is a special verb in that you can follow it with a noun.

Preferisci il pesce o la carne stasera? (*Do you prefer fish or meat this evening?*)

You can also follow **preferire** with an infinitive.

Mio padre preferisce restare a casa. (*My father prefers to stay home.*)

PRACTICE

Decide whether you need an –isc– in these following –ire verbs and conjugate the sentences.

Q. _____ questa pesca, è buonissima! (sentire, tu)

A. **Senti questa pesca, è buonissima!** (*Taste this peach, it's so good!*)

17 Tu _____ l'italiano? (capire)

18 Io _____ molto bene l'italiano. (capire)

19 Heather, _____ studiare il latino o l'italiano? (preferire)

20 Ragazzi, _____ i vostri libri a pagina 123. (aprire)

21 Beni e Samanta _____ i libri. (aprire)

22 Mio padre _____ Ravenna per la vacanza. (preferire)

23 Courtney, Anna e Chiara _____ gli sport. (preferire)

24 Liliana _____ sei classi questo semestre. (seguire)

25 A che ora _____ il treno? (partire)

26 Io _____ la mia camera oggi. (pulire)

What's Happening Right Now: The Present Progressive Tense

In Italian, you can convey that you're in the midst of doing something by using the present simple or the present progressive tense. For instance, if someone asks you **Che cosa stai facendo?** (*What are you doing?*), you can answer **Sto lavando la macchina** (*I'm washing the car*) or **Lavo la macchina** (*I'm washing the car*). Both are equally correct. And you should use the present progressive when you want to emphasize what's happening in that specific moment.

Chiudi la finestra. Non vedi che sta piovendo? (*Close the window. Don't you see it's raining?*)

Sta cominciando a piovere. (*It's beginning to rain.*)

REMEMBER

In Italian, you use only the present indicative tense, not the present progressive tense, with **essere** (*to be*) when you're talking about conditions in general, such as **Pietro è gentile con te** (*Pietro is being nice to you*). (See Chapter 4 for **essere**.)

You form the present progressive tense by adding the gerund to the present tense of the verb **stare** (*to be*), as in **Stiamo mangiando** (*We're eating*). The gerund is invariable in gender and number, so you don't have to make it agree with any other word. To form it, you add **–ando** to the stem of an **–are** verb, or add **–endo** to the stem of an **–ere** or **–ire** verb.

This table shows the slightly irregular conjugation of the verb **stare** (*to be*).

stare (to stay, to be)	
io sto	noi stiamo
tu stai	voi state
lui/lei/Lei sta	loro/Loro stanno
Come state? (*How are you?*) **Stiamo bene.** (*We're well.*)	

Table 5-4 illustrates the patterns for sample verbs of the three conjugations.

Table 5-4   Creating Gerunds

Verb Type	Infinitive	Gerund Ending	Gerund
–are	**guardare** (*to look at/to watch*)	**–ando**	**guardando** (*looking*)
	andare (*to go*)		**andando** (*going*)
–ere	**leggere** (*to read*)	**–endo**	**leggendo** (*reading*)
	vedere (*to see*)		**vedendo** (*seeing*)
–ire	**sentire** (*to hear/to taste/to smell/ to feel*)	**–endo**	**sentendo** (*hearing/tasting*)
	finire (*to finish*)		**finendo** (*finishing*)

Most verbs form the gerund regularly. Even the **–ire/isc** verbs, which add **–isc–** to some persons, follow a regular pattern. For instance, from the **–ire/isc** infinitive **finire** (*to finish*), you form the gerund as **finendo** (*finishing*).

Most of the verbs that form the gerund irregularly are verbs that add some letters to the stem, such as **bere** (*to drink*), which becomes **bev–** and has the gerund **bevendo** (*drinking*). The main irregular verbs appear in the following table.

Infinitive	Gerund
bere (*to drink*)	**bevendo** (*drinking*)
dire (*to say*)	**dicendo** (*saying*)
fare (*to do*)	**facendo** (*doing*)
produrre (*to produce*)	**producendo** (*producing*)

PRACTICE

Fill in the gaps in the following sentences with the appropriate form of the present progressive tense (**stare** + gerund) of the verb suggested in parentheses.

Q. Ciao Caterina, cosa _____? (fare)

A. Ciao Caterina, cosa stai facendo? (*Hi Caterina, what are you doing?*)

27 _____ per un esame. (studiare, io)

28 Mia madre _____ con mio padre. (parlare)

29 Bianca e Rosa _____ a fare i mosaici. (imparare)

30 Daniela, che cosa _____? (bere)

31 Il professore _____ che non c'è lezione domani. (dire)

32 Alessia ed io _____ le lasagne alla bolognese. (preparare)

33 Voi _____ un libro interessante. (leggere)

Answers to "Forming the Present" Practice Questions

1. **arriviamo; Noi arriviamo alle 19:00.** (*We arrive at 19:00.*)

2. **paghi; Tu paghi l'università di tua figlia?** (*Do you pay for your daughter's university?*)

3. **sciano; Giulia, Caterina ed Elisabetta sciano ad Aspen in inverno.** (*Giulia, Caterina, and Elisabetta ski in Aspen in the winter.*)

4. **lavora; Mio padre lavora a Roma.** (*My father works in Rome.*)

5. **mangiate; Tu e Guglielmo mangiate a casa stasera.** (*You and Guglielmo are eating at home tonight.*)

6. **giocano; I ragazzi giocano a basket.** (*The boys play basketball.*)

7. **parla; Nadia parla bene l'inglese.** (*Nadia speaks English well.*)

8. **nuotiamo; Olivia ed io nuotiamo al mare.** (*Olivia and I are swimming in the sea.*)

9. **mangio; Io non mangio la carne.** (*I don't eat meat.*)

10. **studi; Gigio, dove studi meglio, a casa o in biblioteca?** (*Gigio, where do you study best, at home or in the library?*)

11. **Matteo scrive una poesia.** (*Matteo is writing a poem.*)

12. **Leggo il giornale.** (*I read the paper./I'm reading the paper.*)

13. **Le ragazze corrono dopo scuola.** (*The girls run after school.*)

14. **Ricevo molte mail e messaggini ogni giorno.** (*I receive many e-mail and text messages every day.*)

15. **Beviamo l'acqua minerale frizzante.** (*We drink fizzy mineral water.*)

16. **Maria, prendi un cappuccino o una spremuta d'arancia?** (*Maria, are you having a cappuccino or a freshly squeezed orange juice?*)

17. **capisci; Tu capisci l'italiano?** (*Do you understand Italian?*)

18. **capisco; Io capisco molto bene l'italiano.** (*I understand Italian very well.*)

19. **preferisci; Heather, preferisci studiare il latino o l'italiano?** (*Heather, do you prefer to study Latin or Italian?*)

20. **aprite; Ragazzi, aprite i vostri libri a pagina 123.** (*Guys, open your books to page 123.*)

21. **aprono; Beni e Samanta aprono i libri.** (*Beni and Samanta open the books.*)

22. **preferisce; Mio padre preferisce Ravenna per la vacanza.** (*My father prefers Ravenna for the holiday.*)

(23) **peferiscono; Courtney, Anna e Chiara peferiscono gli sport.** (*Courtney, Anna and Chiara prefer sports.*)

(24) **segue; Liliana segue sei classi questo semestre.** (*Liliana follows six classes this semester.*)

(25) **parte; A che ora parte il treno?** (*What time does the train leave?*)

(26) **pulisco; Io pulisco la mia camera oggi.** (*I clean my room today.*)

(27) **Sto studiando; Sto studiando per un esame.** (*I am studying for an exam.*)

(28) **sta parlando; Mia madre sta parlando con mio padre.** (*My mother is speaking with my father.*)

(29) **stanno imparando; Bianca e Rosa stanno imparando a fare i mosaici.** (*Bianca and Rosa are learning how to make mosaics.*)

(30) **stai bevendo; Daniela, che cosa stai bevendo?** (*Daniela, what are you drinking?*)

(31) **sta dicendo; Il professore sta dicendo che non c'è lezione domani.** (*The professor is saying that there's no class tomorrow.*)

(32) **stiamo preparando; Alessia ed io stiamo preparando le lasagne alla bolognese.** (*Alessia and I are are preparing lasagne with Bolognese sauce.*)

(33) **state leggendo; Voi state leggendo un libro interessante.** (*You are reading an interesting book.*)

Chapter **6**

Going and Coming with Irregular Verbs

hat fun would Italian be if you didn't have to tackle some irregular verbs? It's time to face a slew of irregular verbs, most of which you use in your daily comings and goings.

In this chapter, I show you how to form the present tense of many irregular Italian verbs. Although some of them follow reliable patterns, which I share with you, others exist unto themselves. I also show you how to distinguish between the two verbs meaning *to know* — **sapere** and **conoscere**. I walk you through adding verbs in the infinitive to modal auxiliaries such as **potere** (*can/may*), **dovere** (*must/shall*) and **volere** (*to want*). Finally, I give you a new set of pronouns — the stressed, or tonic, pronouns — which you use frequently with the verbs **andare** (*to go*) and **venire** (*to come*).

Irregular–are Verbs

Andare (*to go*), **dare** (*to give*), **fare** (*to do/to make*), and **stare** (*to stay/to be*) (which I discuss in the context of the present progressive tense in Chapter 5) are the only irregular verbs of this conjugation, but they're quite important and very versatile. The following tables show you the conjugations of all four verbs. *Note:* These verbs have some similarities, such as the **i** in the **tu** person and the double **nn** in the **loro** person. Grouping these verbs together can help you remember their commonalities Throughout this chapter, I put an asterisk near the regular forms, to emphasize them.

andare (to go)

io vado	noi andiamo*
tu vai	voi andate*
lui/lei/Lei va	loro/Loro vanno

Andiamo sempre nello stesso ristorante. (*We always go to the same restaurant.*)

dare (to give)

io do*	noi diamo*
tu dai	voi date*
lui/lei/Lei dà (always accented)	loro/Loro danno

Dà un libro alla vicina. (*He/she gives the neighbor a book.*)

fare (to do/to make)

io faccio	noi facciamo
tu fai	voi fate*
lui/lei/Lei fa*	loro/Loro fanno

Faccio una torta. (*I'm making a cake.*)

stare (to stay/to be)

io sto*	noi stiamo*
tu stai	voi state*
lui/lei/Lei sta*	loro/Loro stanno

Stiamo bene. (*We're well.*)

Like always in Italian, there are idiomatic uses (exceptions) to these verbs that don't translate word for word into English. Here are several; some are intuitive (and others mean what they say):

>> **andare d'accordo** (*to get along*)

>> **andare al cinema** (*to go to the movies*)

>> **andare in vacanza** (*to go on vacation*)

>> **andare in macchina, in treno, in autobus, in aereo** (*to go by car, by train, by bus, by plane*)

>> **andare a cavallo, a piedi** (*to go by horse, on foot*)

>> **dare una mano** (*to give a hand/to help*)

>> **dare un esame** (*to take a test*)

>> **dare fastidio** (*to bother*)

>> **dare da mangiare** (*to feed*)

» **stare zittto** (*to be quiet*)

» **stare attento** (*to pay attention*)

» **stare bene/male** (*to be well/to be not well*)

» **fare una domanda** (*to ask a question*)

» **fare domanda** (*to apply*; for a job, to a school)

» **fare caldo** (*to be hot* as in, inside or outside; impersonal verb that uses only the third-person singular)

» **fare freddo** (*to be cold*; impersonal verb that uses only the third-person singular)

» **fare colazione** (*to have breakfast*)

» **fare una gita** (*to take an excursion/to take a day trip*)

» **fare una partita di carte** (*to play a game of cards*)

» **fare una foto** (*to take a picture*)

» **Non fa niente** (*it doesn't matter*)

REMEMBER

When you talk about weather, you use the third person of the verb, such as **Fa caldo!** (*It's hot!*) or **Piove!** (*It's raining!*)

Choose the most appropriate verb, according to context — **andare, dare, fare,** and **stare** — and conjugate it in the blanks provided.

PRACTICE

Q. Tu _____ male?

A. **Tu stai male?** (*Are you not feeling well?*)

1. _____ noi qualcosa da mangiare al gatto.

2. _____ tu all'ufficio postale?

3. I miei genitori _____ bene.

4. Riccardo _____ in panetteria a comprare il pane.

5. I miei amici _____ una partita a carte.

6. Dove _____ in vacanza di solito? (tu)

7. Come andate in Maine? _____ in aereo.

8. _____ colazione al bar di solito. (io)

9. Alana é timida e _____ sempre zitta.

10. Tu _____ l'esame di storia fra tre ore.

11. Claudio è gentile: _____ d'accordo con tutti.

12 Il cane _____ fastidio al gatto.

13 _____ domanda alla Stanford University. (io)

14 _____ molto caldo in Sicilia in estate.

Irregular –ere Verbs:

Most irregular verbs are **-ere** verbs, so it's impossible to list them all here. I walk you through some of the most commonly used ones.

The modal auxiliaries

Modal verbs, which provide different nuances to what you're saying, also act as auxiliaries; they're followed by the infinitive of the main verb. The modals include **dovere** (*to have to/must/ to need to/ought to*), **potere** (*can/may*), and **volere** (*to want to*). (Italian also uses **sapere** as a modal auxiliary, meaning *to know how to*. I discuss **sapere** in the section "Sapere versus conoscere," later in this chapter.)

Here are some common uses of **dovere**, **potere**, and **volere**:

>> **Dovere** translates as *to have to/must/to need to/ought to*. And you can use **dovere** by itself, meaning *to owe*.

- **Devo parlargli.** (*I have to talk to him.*)

- **Quanto Le devo?** (*How much do I owe you?*)

>> **Potere** means both *can* and *may*.

- **Posso entrare?** (*May I come in?*)

- **Puoi fare tu la spesa?** (*Can you do the shopping?*).

When expressing the meaning of *being able to* or *being successful at completing something* (such as buying a ticket to the opera), Italian uses either **potere** (*can*) or **riuscire a** (*to be able to/to manage to*).

- **Puoi studiare con questo caldo?/Riesci a studiare con questo caldo?** (*Are you able to study in this heat?*)

- **Può riparare la TV Ugo?/Riesce a riparare la TV Ugo?** (*Is Ugo able to repair the TV?*)

The verb **riuscire** (*to be able to/to manage to*) is conjugated exactly like the irregular verb **uscire** (*to go out*), which I discuss in the section "Irregular **–ire** Verbs," later in this chapter.

REMEMBER

>> **Volere** can be translated sometimes as *will*, as in the proverb: **Volere è potere.** (*Where there's a will, there's a way.*)

Italian **volere** generally corresponds to *to want* or *to want to*, and can be followed by a noun or followed by an infinitive, as in the following examples.

● **Voglio un altro biscotto.** (*I want another cookie.*)

● **Voglio parlare con lei.** (*I want to talk to her.*)

REMEMBER

It sounds just as boorish to say **Voglio un gelato** in Italian as it does in English (*I want an ice cream*). So, keep in mind that you use the conditional tense (see Chapter 16) **vorrei** (*I would like*), when you want to be polite and that **per favore** (*please*) always goes a long way.

The following tables show conjugations of each of the modal auxiliary verbs. Notice that for some of the persons, **dovere** takes the stem **dev–** with the **–ere** endings.

dovere (must/to have to/to need to/ought)

io devo	noi dobbiamo
tu devi	voi dovete*
lui/lei/Lei deve	loro/Loro devono

Devono andare a casa. (*They have to go home.*)

potere (can/may)

io posso	noi possiamo
tu puoi	voi potete*
lui/lei/Lei può	loro/Loro possono

Può giocare con noi. (*He/she can play with us.*)

volere (to want)

io voglio	noi vogliamo
tu vuoi	voi volete
lui/lei/Lei vuole	loro/Loro vogliono

Vogliono vederti. (*They want to see you.*)

REMEMBER

Volere in the third person singular and plural (**ci vuole** and **ci vogliono**) can also mean *to take*, as in with time and abstract comments.

Use **ci vuole** for singular things.

> **Quanto tempo ci vuole per arrivare a casa?** (*How much time does it take to arrive home?*)

Use **ci vogliono** with plural items.

> **Quanti minuti ci vogliono per arrivare a casa?** (*How many minutes does it take to get home?*)

PRACTICE Conjugate the verbs in the blanks in the following sentences.

Q. Cristoforo _____ diventare un uomo di affari. (volere)

A. **Cristoforo vuole diventare un uomo di affari.** (*Christopher wants to become a businessman.*)

15 Gigia e Gianni, _____ andare a prendere un gelato? (volere)

16 Totò _____ lavorare con Alfredo. (volere)

17 I miei amici _____ fare i compiti stasera. (dovere)

18 Mariapaola non _____ venire al concerto con noi. (potere)

19 La mia mamma ed io _____ visitare Capri la prossima estate. (volere)

20 Yasmin, _____ ripetere, per favore? (potere)

21 Io e Mandiaye _____ andare a Roma domani. (dovere)

Sapere versus conoscere

Both the verbs **sapere** and **conoscere** mean *to know* in Italian, whereas English uses only one verb. **Sapere** is irregular, and **conoscere** is regular — but if you learn them side by side, you can more easily keep their meaning and usage separate. At times, it can be difficult to decide when to use **sapere** or **conoscere**. Use the following rules of thumb to help you identify when to use each.

Sapere can generally be followed by a verb in the infinitive or an *interrogative* word — meaning a word that you use to ask a question. (See Chapter 11 for more on interrogatives.)

> **Sai andare in barca a vela?** (*Do you know how to sail?*)

> **Sai chi ha vinto le elezioni?** (*Do you know who won the election?*)

And **conoscere** means *to know* someone or something, as in to be acquainted with.

> **Conosci Davide?** (*Do you know Davide?*)

The samples following and the practice exercise will illustrate these differences.

sapere (to know)

io so	noi sappiamo
tu sai	voi sapete
lui/lei/Lei sa	loro/Loro sanno
Sai giocare a scacchi? (*Do you know how to play chess?*)	
Sai quanto costa una Lamborghini? (*Do you know how much a Lamborghini costs?*)	

conoscere (to know)

io conosco	noi conosciamo
tu conosci	voi conoscete
lui/lei/Lei conosce	loro/Loro conoscono

Conosci un buon ristorante qui vicino? (*Do you know a good restaurant near here?*)

"Conosci Lucy?" "No, ma so chi è?" (*"Do you know Lucy?" "No, but I know who she is."*)

PRACTICE

Decide whether you need **sapere** or **conoscere**, and conjugate the appropriate verb in the blanks provided.

Q. Marco, _____ Ermanna?

A. Marco, conosci Ermanna? (*Marco, do you know Ermanna?*)

22 Non _____ suonare il pianoforte. (io)

23 Noi _____ bene Roma.

24 Voi _____ quanti abitanti ci sono a Castellaneta?

25 _____ bene Giovanni? (tu)

26 Loro _____ parlare italiano molto bene.

27 Scusi, _____ dov'è il Colosseo? (Lei)

28 Giacomo _____ quante regioni ci sono in Italia.

Piacere and dispiacere

The frequently used verbs **piacere** (*to like; literally, to be pleasing to*) and **dispiacere** (*to be sorry/ to mind*) number among verbs ending in **–cere**. *Note:* Piacere is used primarily in third-person singular and plural forms, and **dispiace** is used in the third-person singular.

> **Mi dispiace non essere là.** (*I'm sorry not to be there.*)

> **Ti dispiace se mi siedo qui?** (*Do you mind if I sit here?*)

Piacere and **dispiacere**, while different in meaning, share a similar conjugation. Both also use indirect object pronouns instead of subject pronouns.

You probably want to say *I like* (**mi piace**) or *I do not like* (**non mi piace**) practically every day, maybe even multiple times a day. So you need to be equipped to express your likes and dislikes easily and promptly in Italian.

In this book, I talk about only two persons of **piacere** (third person singular and third persona plural), since they are the easiest to use:

>> **piace** (third-person singular): Use if what you like (or what anyone else likes) is singular or an infinitive.

>>> **Mi piace la pizza. Ti, gli/le, ci, vi, gli piace la pizza.** (*I like pizza. You, he/she, we, you all, they like pizza*) **Pizza** is singular.

>>> **Mi piace dormire. Ti, gli/le, ci, vi, gli piazza piace.** (*I like to sleep. You, he/she, we, you all, they like to sleep.*) **Dormire** is an infinitive.

>> **piacciono** (third-person plural): Use if what you like is plural.

>>> **Mi piacciono le lasagne. Ti, gli/le, ci, vi, gli piacciono le lasagne.** (*I like lasagna. You, he/she, we, you all, they like lasagna.*) **Lasagne** is plural.

The other forms are reserved for more advanced study, but you might like to use the following example anyway: **"Ti piaccio?" "Sì, mi piaci tanto!"** (*"Do you like me?" "Yes. I like you a lot!"*)

Check out these examples for additional usage:

>>> **Ti piace Pesaro?** (*Do you like Pesaro?*)

>>> **Sì, mi piace.** (*Yes, I do.*)/**No, non mi piace.** (*No, I don't./No, I don't like it.*)

>>> **Che cosa ti piace fare nel tempo libero?** (*What do you like to do in your free time?*)

>>> **Mi piace leggere e camminare.** (*I like to read and walk.*)

>>> **Ti piacciono gli gnocchi al gorgonzola?** (*Do you like gnocchi with Gorgonzola sauce?*)

>>> **Mi piacciono molto!** (*I like it a lot!*)

 Note that the *do* and the *it* are implied.

REMEMBER **Piacere** needs indirect object pronouns to accompany it. These indirect object pronouns pair with **piace** and **piacciono**. The only thing that changes is the indirect object pronoun, which varies based on who is doing the liking.

 Decide whether you need the singular **piace** or the plural **piacciono** in each sentence and fill in the blanks.

PRACTICE

Q. Silvia, ti _____ nuotare?

A. piace (*Silvia, do you like to swim?*)

29 Mi _____ i biscotti.

30 Ti _____ viaggiare?

31 Gli _____ gli spaghetti al pomodoro.

32 Non le _____ il pesce crudo.

33 Vi _____ le fragole?

Use **dispiace** when saying *you're sorry*: It is generally preceded by the indirect object pronouns: **Mi (ti, gli, le, ci, vi gli) dispiace!** (*I'm you're, he's, she's, we're, you all are, they're sorry!*). Might you use **dispiace** without an indirect object pronoun? Yes, of course: **A John dispiace molto.** (*John is very sorry.*) This book does not go into replacing indirect objects with indirect object pronouns, though.

Irregular–ire Verbs

The **–ire** verbs have fewer irregular verbs. I illustrate some basic patterns in this section while walking you through some practical examples and practice exercises.

TIP

The most frequent and essential **–ire** verbs are **dire** (*to say*), **venire** (*to come*), and **uscire** (*to go out*). To commit this set of verbs to memory, as well as other grammatical points in this book, drill with them on sites such as Conjuguemos (www.conjuguemos.com) or Quizlet (www.quizlet.com). Some people find hand-written flash cards more effective when learning a language: Whatever works for you!

REMEMBER

Notice that the verb **dire** (*to say/to tell*) takes **dic–** as its stem in some persons, but the endings are the regular **–ire** endings (see Chapter 5).

dire (to say/to tell)

io dico	noi diciamo
tu dici	voi dite*
lui/lei/Lei dice	loro/Loro dicono

Maria e Lee dicono che stanno per comprare una casa nuova. (*Maria and Lee say they're buying a new house.*)

REMEMBER

Be careful with your pronunciation of the **c** in **dire**: **dico** and **dicono** have a *k* sound; but **dici**, **dice**, and **diciamo** have a *ch* sound.

The verb **venire** (*to come*) undergoes a stem change in some persons and also adds a **g** in others, while keeping two regular persons. Even though it's all over the place, it follows a pattern.

venire (to come)

io vengo	noi veniamo*
tu vieni	voi venite*
lui/lei/Lei viene	loro/Loro vengono

Veniamo a Livorno il diciotto giugno. (*We're coming to Livorno on June eighteenth.*)

The verb **uscire** takes **esc–** as its stem for its irregular persons and keeps the regular **–ire** endings for all of its persons. The **c** in **esco** and **escono** and **escono have** a hard c (k) sound, and the **c** in **esci**, **esce**, **usciamo** and **uscite** has a *sh* sound. Practice reading this verb aloud.

uscire (to go out)	
io esco	noi usciamo*
tu esci	voi uscite*
lui/lei/Lei esce	loro/Loro escono
Marcella esce con Tram da molti anni. (*Marcella's been going out with Tram for many years.*)	

PRACTICE

Conjugate the verbs in parentheses in the following sentences.

Q. Pinocchio non _____ la verità. (dire)

A. Pinocchio non dice la verità. (*Pinocchio does not tell the truth.*)

34. _____ "salute" quando qualcuno starnutisce (sneezes). (dire, io)

35. I miei amici _____ a casa mia stasera. (venire)

36. Antonio, _____ domani sera? (uscire)

37. Sofia, _____ con noi in Italia a marzo? (venire)

38. Che cosa _____ al babbo? (dire, noi)

39. Io non _____ con quel ragazzo perché è antipatico! (uscire)

40. Che cosa _____ Salvatore a Elena? (dire)

41. Elena _____ al Cinema Paradiso per vedere Salvatore. (venire)

42. Ragazzi, a che ora _____ sabato? (uscire)

43. Michele e Bruno _____ sabato. (uscire)

44. La Pimpa _____ "Buongiorno!" all'ippopotamo. (dire)

Stressed Pronouns

Stressed pronouns are most often placed after a preposition. I'm including these pronouns in this chapter because they're frequently used with the verbs **andare** (*to go*), which you can read about in the section "Irregular **–are** Verbs," earlier in this chapter, and **venire** (*to come*), which pops up in the "Irregular **–ire** Verbs," section earlier in this chapter.

Note the following examples.

Vieni con me al mercato. (*Come to the market with me.*)

But you also can use them directly after a verb without a preposition for emphasis.

La mamma vuole te. (*Mom wants you.*).

At this stage, to make your life simpler, use the stressed pronoun only when you have a preposition.

Qualcuno ha lasciato un messaggio per te. (*Someone left a message for you.*)

Table 6-1 demonstrates the forms of the stressed pronouns. As you can see, the only forms that change from the subject pronouns are the forms for **io** (**me**) and **tu** (**te**). Although I show only four prepositions **a/con/di/per**, you can combine any preposition with a stressed pronoun.

Table 6-1 Stressed Pronouns

Pronoun	Prepositions	Translation
me (*me*)	**a/con/di/per me**	*to/with/about/for me*
te (*you*, singular informal)	**a/con/di/per te**	*to/with/about/for you*
lui (*him*), **lei** (*her*)	**a/con/di/per lui/lei**	*to/with/about/for him/her/it*
Lei (*you*, singular formal)	**a/con/di/per Lei**	*to/with/about/for you*
noi (*us*)	**a/con/di/per noi**	*to/with/about/for us*
voi (*you*, plural informal)	**a/con/di/per voi**	*to/with/about/for you all*
loro (*them*)	**a/con/di/per loro**	*to/with/about/for them*
Loro (*you*, plural formal)	**a/con/di/per Loro**	*to/with/about/for you*

PRACTICE

Fill in the blanks in the following sentences by substituting stressed pronouns for the words in parentheses.

Q. Non mi piace lavorare con _____. (Gianluca)

A. Non mi piace lavorare con lui. (*I don't like working with him.*)

45 Volete venire con _____ a cena? (me e Mario)

46 Giovanni va con _____ al mare. (i figli)

47 Gioco a carte con _____. (te e i tuoi cugini)

48 Gix viene con _____. (io)

49 Veniamo da_____? (tu)

Answers to "Going and Coming with Irregular Verbs" Practice Questions

1. **Diamo/Facciamo; Diamo/Facciamo noi qualcosa da mangiare al gatto.** (*Let's give the cat something to eat.*)

2. **Vai; Vai tu all'ufficio postale** (*Are you going to go to the post office?*)

3. **stanno; I miei genitori stanno bene.** (*My parents are well.*)

4. **va; Riccardo va in panetteria a comprare il pane.** (*Riccardo is going to the breadshop to buy bread.*)

5. **fanno; I miei amici fanno una partita a carte.** (*My friends are playing a game of cards.*)

6. **vai; Dove vai in vacanza di solito?** (*Where do you usually go on vacation?*)

7. **Andiamo; Come andate in Maine? Andiamo in aereo.** (*How are you going to Maine? We're going by plane.*)

8. **Faccio; Faccio colazione al bar di solito.** (*I usually have breakfast at the bar.*)

9. **sta; Alana è timida e sta sempre zitta.** (*Alana is shy and is always quiet.*)

10. **dai; Tu dai l'esame di storia fra tre ore.** (*You're taking the History exam three hours.*)

11. **Va; Claudio è gentile: Va d'accordo con tutti.** (*Claudio is kind: he gets along with everyone.*)

12. **dà; Il cane dà fastidio al gatto.** (*The dog is bothering the cat.*)

13. **Faccio; Faccio domanda alla Stanford University.** (*I'm applying to Stanford University.*)

14. **Fa; Fa molto caldo in Sicilia in estate.** (*It's very hot in Sicily in the summer.*)

15. **volete; Gigia e Gianni, volete andare a prendere un gelato?** (*Gigia and Gianni, do you want to go for an ice cream?*)

16. **vuole; Totò vuole lavorare con Alfredo.** (*Totò wants to work with Alfredo.*)

17. **devono; I miei amici devono fare i compiti stasera.** (*My friends need to do homework tonight.*)

18. **può; Mariapaola non può venire al concerto con noi.** (*Mariapaola can't come to the concert with us.*)

19. **vogliamo; La mia mamma ed io vogliamo visitare Capri la prossima estate.** (*My mom and I want to visit Capri next summer.*)

20. **puoi; Yasmin, puoi ripetere, per favore?** (*Yasmin, can you please repeat?*)

21. **dobbiamo; Io e Mandiaye dobbiamo andare a Roma domani.** (*Mandiaye and I need to go to Rome tomorrow.*)

22. **so; Non so suonare il pianoforte.** (*I don't know how to play the piano.*)

23. **conosciamo; Noi conosciamo bene Roma.** (*We know Rome well.*)

(24) **sapete; Voi sapete quanti abitanti ci sono a Castellaneta?** *(Do you know how many inhabitants Castellaneta has?)*

(25) **Conosci; Conosci bene Giovanni?** *(Do you know Giovanni well?)*

(26) **sanno; Loro sanno parlare italiano molto bene.** *(They know how to speak Italian well.)*

(27) **sa; Scusi, sa dov'è il Colosseo?** *(Excuse me, do you know where the Colosseum is?)*

(28) **sa; Giacomo sa quante regioni ci sono in Italia.** *(Giacomo knows how many regions there are in Italy.)*

(29) **piacciono; Mi piacciono i biscotti.** *(I like cookies.)*

(30) **piace; Ti piace viaggiare?** *(Do you like to travel?)*

(31) **piacciono; Gli piacciono gli spaghetti al pomodoro.** *(He likes spaghetti with tomato sauce.)*

(32) **piace; Non le piace il pesce crudo.** *(She doesn't like raw fish.)*

(33) **piacciono; Vi piacciono le fragole?** *(Do you all like strawberries?)*

(34) **Dico; Dico "salute" quando qualcuno starnutisce.** *(I say "God bless you" when someone sneezes.)*

(35) **vengono; I miei amici vengono a casa mia stasera.** *(My friends are coming to my house tonight.)*

(36) **esci; Antonio, esci domani sera?** *(Antonio, are you going out tomorrow evening?)*

(37) **vieni; Sofia, vieni con noi in Italia a marzo?** *(Sofia, will you be coming to Italy with us in March?)*

(38) **diciamo; Che cosa diciamo al babbo?** *(What are we going to say to Dad?)*

(39) **esco; Io non esco con quel ragazzo perché è antipatico!** *(I'm not going out with that boy because he is unpleasant!)*

(40) **dice; Che cosa dice Salvatore a Elena?** *(What does Salvatore say to Elena?)*

(41) **viene; Elena viene al Cinema Paradiso per vedere Salvatore.** *(Elena comes to Cinema Paradiso to see Salvatore.)*

(42) **uscite; Ragazzi, a che ora uscite sabato?** *(Guys, what time are you going out on Saturday?)*

(43) **escono; Michele e Bruno escono sabato** *(Michele and Bruno are going out on Saturday.)*

(44) **dice; La Pimpa dice "Buongiorno!" all'ippopotamo.** *(Pimpa says "good morning!" to the hippopotamus.)*

(45) **noi; Volete venire con noi a cena?** *(Do you all want to come with us to dinner?)*

(46) **loro; Giovanni va con loro al mare.** *(Giovanni is going with them to the beach.)*

(47) **voi; Gioco a carte con voi.** *(I'm going to play cards with you.)*

(48) **me; Gix viene con me.** *(Gix is coming with me.)*

(49) **te; Veniamo da te?** *(Are we coming to your place?)*

3

Building Beautiful Sentences: Parts of Speech

Uncover the ins and outs of adverbs and adjectives. Make adjectives agree in gender and number with nouns. Also, see how you can create an adverb out of an adjective, and get to know some adverbs that don't derive from adjectives.

Find out how to make different comparisons as well as how to form the superlatives.

Discover all you need to know about prepositions: how to contract them, how to make them agree in gender and number, and when you need to use them.

Understand the possessive adjectives and how to talk about your favorite things and family.

Get up to speed on asking questions to keep the conversation moving.

Chapter **7**

Enriching Adjectives and Adverbs

f you say **Marina ha una casa grande** (*Marina has a big house*) or **Marina ha una casa piccola** (*Marina has a small house*), all you've changed is one word, but you've said two very different things. **Grande** (*big*) and **piccola** (*small*) are adjectives, which convey qualities of people, animals, objects, and situations. In Italian, like in English, you employ adjectives to describe nouns, names, and pronouns. Most adjectives agree in number and gender with what they're describing, and then there are the ones that have a mind of their own.

Adverbs are another important way of enriching language. In Italian, adverbs are invariable, which means that you don't need to make them agree with the words they modify. You can add an adverb to qualify a verb, an adjective, and even another adverb. For example, if you say **È molto presto** (*It's very early*), you're using two adverbs — **molto** (*very*) and **presto** (*early*) — together.

In this chapter, I explain the various endings that adjectives can have, as well as the differences between masculine and feminine, singular and plural adjectives and how to match them to the words that they refer to. As for adverbs, I give you some common adverbs, and how to form the kind that are derived from nouns.

Making Adjectives Agree

Adjectives make language rich and varied. In Italian, you must match adjectives in gender and number to the nouns that they modify. You need a masculine singular adjective to modify a masculine singular noun, a feminine singular adjective to modify a feminine singular noun, and so forth. For example, you say, **"Mario è bello"** because **bello** is masculine, and you say, **"Maria è bella"** (*"Maria is beautiful"*), and **bella** here is feminine.

A few adjectives are *invariable*, meaning they have only one form. I list the most commonly used invariable adjectives in the section "Invariable adjectives," later in this chapter.

Regular adjectives vary in their endings, depending on gender (masculine or feminine):

>> Four endings: **–o** (m/sing.), **–a** (f/sing.), **–i** (m/pl.), **–e** (f/pl.)

>> Two endings: **–e** (m/f/sing.), **–i** (m/f/pl.)

Regular adjectives

Regular adjectives are those that modify only the last letter to change either gender and number (see Table 7-1) or only number (shown in Table 7-2).

Table 7-1   Four-Ending Adjectives

Ending	Gender and Number	Example Adjective	Example Phrase
–o	Masculine singular (m/sing.)	**italiano**	**il ragazzo italiano** (*the Italian boy*)
–a	Feminine singular (f/sing.)	**italiana**	**la ragazza italiana** (*the Italian girl*)
–i	Masculine plural (m/pl.)	**italiani**	**i ragazzi italiani** (*the Italian boys*)
–e	Feminine plural (f/pl.)	**italiane**	**le ragazze italiane** (*the Italian girls*)

Note that the nouns I use in the examples in Table 7-2 — **cane** (m) and **madre** (f) — end in an **–e** but have their specific gender. (See Chapter 2 for the details on this type of noun that ends in **–e**.)

Table 7-2   Two-Ending Adjectives

Ending	Number	Example Adjective	Example Phrase
–e	Singular	intelligente	il cane intelligente (m/sing.)
			(the smart dog)
			la madre intelligente (f/sing.)
			(the smart mother)
–i	Plural	intelligenti	i cani intelligenti (m/pl.)
			(the smart dogs)
			la madri intelligenti (f/pl.) (the smart mothers)

Here are a couple of examples of a very common adjective with four endings, **preferito** (*favorite*).

Chi è la tua attrice preferita? (*Who is your favorite actress?*)

Chi sono i tuoi scrittori preferiti? (*Who are your favorite authors?*)

Table 7-3 shows common adjectives that end in –o and –e. This list is not exhaustive, but if you understand how to make these adjectives agree, you'll know what to do with all the other ones you encounter. I note which adjectives are invariable — they remain the same whether singular or plural.

Table 7-3   Common Adjectives (Color and Origin)

Colors	Nationalities	Italian Provenances (Regions/Cities)
arancione (*orange*)	albanese (*Albanian*)	bolognese (*from Bologna*)
azzurro (*light blue*)	americano (*American*)	genovese (*from Genoa*)
bianco (*white*)	australiano (*Australian*)	lombardo (*from Lombardy*)
blu (*dark blue*, inv.)	cinese (*Chinese*)	marchigiano (*from the Marche*)
grigio (*grey*)	giapponese (*Japanese*)	milanese (*from Milano*)
marrone (*brown*)	indiano (*Indian*)	napoletano (*from Naples*)
nero (*black*)	italiano (*Italian*)	pugliese (*from Puglia*)
rosa (*pink*, inv.)	messicano (*Mexican*)	romano (*Roman*)
rosso (*red*)	rumeno (*Romanian*)	siciliano (*from Sicily*)
verde (*green*)	russo (*Russian*)	
viola (*purple*, inv.)	tedesco (*German*)	

A good way to remember adjectives is to categorize them with their opposite meaning, as shown in Table 7-4.

Table 7-4   Adjectives with Opposites

Adjective	Opposite
basso (*short,* as in stature)	alto (*tall*) of
bello (*beautiful*)	brutto (*ugly*)
biondo (*blond*)	bruno (*brunette*)
buono (*good*)	cattivo (*bad/mean*)
carino (*cute*)	brutto (*ugly*)
contento/felice (*happy*)	triste (*sad*)
corto (*short*; as in hair or a dress)	lungo (*long*)
costoso/caro (*expensive*)	economico (*cheap*)
divertente (*fun*)	noioso (*boring*)
facile (*easy*)	difficile (*difficult/hard*)
generoso (*generous*)	avaro (*stingy*)
gentile (*kind*)	crudele (*cruel/mean*)
grasso (*fat*)	magro (*thin*)
inclusivo (*inclusive*)	esclusivo (*exclusive*)
intelligente (*intelligent/smart*)	stupido (*stupid*)
interessante (*interesting*)	noioso (*boring*)
onesto (*honest*)	disonesto (*dishonest*)
ricco (*rich*)	povero (*poor*)
simpatico (*nice*)	antipatico (*unpleasant*)
stesso (*same*)	diverso (*different*)
timido (*shy*)	socievole (*outgoing*)

Regular adjectives with a twist: Bello and buono

Bello (*beautiful*) and **buono** (*good*) are common regular adjectives in Italian. When used after a noun, they're regular adjectives that have four possible endings (see Table 7-1). However, when used before a noun, they become variable depending on the gender and number of the noun they modify.

Beginning of Noun	Singular (m/f)	Plural (m/f)
s- + consonant; or z-	bello/bella	begli/belle
other consonants	bel/bella	bei/belle
vowels	bell'/bell'	begli/belle

Buono follows the rules of the indefinite article (see Chapter 2). Note the similarities in the following two tables:

DIFFERENCES

un amico	un'amica
uno zoo	una persona

buon amico	buon'amica
buono zio	buona persona

Irregular adjectives

Some irregular adjectives undergo a spelling modification, usually to preserve the soft or hard sound of the singular masculine, as in **bianco, bianca, bianchi, bianche** (*white*). But many times, the variations from the norm are accidents of history, for which I can't give you any reason. Table 7-5 breaks down the ending changes for irregular adjectives, with examples.

Table 7-5   Variations of Irregular Adjective Endings

Type of Adjective	Singular Ending Change	Plural Ending Change	Singular Examples	Plural Examples
–ista	**–ista** (m/f)	**–isti** (m); **–iste** (f)	**ottimista** (m/f)	**ottimisti** (m); **ottimiste** (f)
Two-syllable adjective	**–co, –go, –ca**, or **–ga**	**–chi, –che, –ghi**, or **–ghe**	**bianco** (m); **bianca** (f)	**bianchi** (m); **bianche** (f)
			lungo (m); **lunga** (f)	**lunghi** (m); **lunghe** (f)
Multi-syllable adjective	**–co** or **–ca**	**–ci** or **–che**	**simpatico** (m); **simpatica** (f)	**simpatici** (m); **simpatiche** (f)

Invariable adjectives

A few adjectives are invariable, meaning that the ending remains the same regardless of what the noun's gender or number is. Key invariable adjectives include the following:

» Adjectives for color: **blu** (*blue*), **beige** (*beige*), **rosa** (*pink*), **turchese** (*turquoise*), and **viola** (*violet/mauve*)

» Mathematical qualifiers: **pari** (*even*) and **dispari** (*odd*)

» Adjectives taken from other languages: **snob** (*snobbish*), **chic** (*chic*), **trendy** (*trendy*), and **bordeaux** (*burgundy*)

Insert the correct form of the adjective in the space provided.

Q. limoni _____ (*yellow*)

A. **limoni gialli** (*yellow lemons*)

1. spaghetti (good) _____

2. uomo (English) _____

3. macchine (German) _____

4. esame (difficult) _____

5. ristorante (Roman) _____

6. pantaloni (black) _____

7. occhi (blue) _____

8. amica (Italian) _____

9. capelli (long) _____

Choose the adjective in the gender and number appropriate for the word that it describes. Both the adjective ending and the meaning of the sentence should help you choose the right word from the options provided.

Q. Il film era (lunga/interessanti/noioso).

A. **Il film era noioso.** (*The movie was boring.*)

10. La canzone è (bello/interessante/lunghe).

11. Paolo compra una macchina (nuova/rosso/grandi).

12. Giuliana è (intelligenti/noioso/simpatica).

13. [Loro] sono (giovani/importante/bella).

14. Le mie sorelle sono (giovane/vecchi/stanche).

15. Le arance non sono (mature/buona/cattivi).

16. I biglietti dell'aereo erano (economiche/costosi/saporiti).

17. Mio padre è nato in Irlanda, è (inglese/scozzese/irlandese).

PRACTICE

Complete the following sentences by making the adjective in parentheses agree with the noun it's modifying. (*Hint:* Remind yourself whether it is a regular adjective with four endings or two endings, or is an **–ista** adjective, a spelling exception adjective, or an invariable adjective, even before you begin.)

Q. I miei amici _____ vengono a cena. (romano)

A. I miei amici romani vengono a cena. (*My Roman friends are coming to dinner.*)

18. La pizza è _____ ! (delizioso)

19. Indosso i pantaloni _____ stasera. (lungo)

20. Stasera vengono a cena le mie amiche _____. (pugliese)

21. Siamo _____ per la situazione politica. (pessimista)

22. Devo cercare le scarpe _____. (bianco)

23. Elena è una _____ amica. (buono)

24. Com'è il libro che stai leggendo? _____ (buono)

25. Mia madre è _____ e_____. (simpatico, intelligente)

26. Ho i capelli _____. (rosso)

27. Gli sport invernali sono _____. (divertente)

28. Alcune pizzerie_____ sono _____. (napoletano, famoso)

Putting Adjectives in Their Place

DIFFERENCES

In English, as in Italian, you place adjectives after verbs that indicate a status or a condition, such as *to be* or *to feel*; for example, **Olivia è contenta** (*Olivia is happy*). More importantly however, when you match an adjective to a noun, in English you place it before the noun to which it refers, as in a *blue sky*. In Italian, you usually do the opposite, and the adjective comes *after* the noun, as in **cielo azzurro** (which translates as *blue sky*) and **libri importanti** (translates as *important books*).

However, you place some commonly used adjectives before the noun in Italian. For example, the correct way to say, *"They have a beautiful house"* is **"Hanno una bella casa,"** even though everyone will understand you if you say, **"Hanno una casa bella."** Here's a list of the most important adjectives that take this placement:

» **bello** (*beautiful*)

» **brutto** (*ugly*)

>> **buono** (*good*)

>> **cattivo** (*nasty/evil*)

>> **breve** (*short*)

>> **lungo** (*long*)

In a few cases, the adjective changes meaning depending on whether you place it before or after the noun.

"**È un grand'uomo.**" (*"He's a great man."*)

"**È un uomo grande.**" (*"He's a big man."*)

Forming Adverbs the Italian Way

In Italian, adverbs add details and nuances by modifying verbs, adjectives, nouns, entire sentences, and other adverbs. Adverbs change the meaning of what you're saying.

Lia si comporta bene. (*Lia behaves well.*)

Lia si comporta male. (*Lia behaves badly.*)

Adverbs are invariable in the sense that they have neither gender nor number, so you don't have to worry about making them agree with the words they modify.

In Italian, adverbs fall into two categories:

>> **Original:** These adverbs aren't derived from other words. For example: **bene** (*well*)

>> **Derived:** These adverbs are derived from adjectives. For example: **fortunatamente** (*fortunately*), from the adjective **fortunato** (*lucky, fortunate*)

Original adverbs

Original adverbs don't have a fixed form, so you're forced to simply learn them while you go. Here are some important adverbs to remember:

>> **abbastanza** (*enough*)

>> **adesso/ora** (*now*)

>> **anche** (*also*)

>> **ancora** (*still/yet*)

>> **bene** (*well*)

>> **davvero** (*really*)

>> **domani** (*tomorrow*)

>> **fa** (*ago*)

>> **già** (*already*)

>> **ieri** (*yesterday*)

>> **mai/non . . . mai** (*ever/never*)

>> **male** (*badly*)

- » **no** (*no*)
- » **non** (*not*)
- » **oggi** (*today*)
- » **presto** (*soon/early*)
- » **purtroppo** (*unfortunately*)

- » **sempre** (*always*)
- » **spesso** (*often*)
- » **subito** (*at once/right away*)
- » **tardi** (*late*)

Key adjectives that you can use as adverbs include:

- » **comodo** (*comfortable*)
- » **chiaro** (*clear*)
- » **duro** (*hard/tough*)
- » **forte** (*strong*)
- » **giusto** (*just/correct*)
- » **leggero** (*light*)
- » **molto** (*very/much*)
- » **parecchio** (*a lot*)

- » **poco** (*too little*)
- » **quanto** (*how/how much*)
- » **sicuro** (*sure*)
- » **solo** (*alone*)
- » **tanto** (*so/so much*)
- » **troppo** (*too*)
- » **veloce** (*fast*)
- » **vicino** (*near*)

TIP

I may be giving you an abundance of new vocabulary in this book. Choose which words are the most useful to you and commit them to memory with whatever method works best for you. Some people prefer to make a Quizlet; others look for games on a site such as Kahoot; others opt for flashcards.

MOLTO: ADJECTIVE AND ADVERB

Molto is an adjective meaning *much/many/a lot of*; it's also an adverb (invariable) meaning *very*.

Here are examples of **molto** as an adjective:

molta acqua (*a lot of water*)

molti ravioli (*many ravioli*)

molto pane (*a lot of bread*)

molte lasagne (*a lot of lasagna*)

And here's **molto** playing the role of adverb:

Anna, sei molto bella. (*Anna, you are very beautiful.*)

Mangiamo molto. (*We eat a lot.*)

Derived adverbs

You form most derived adverbs in Italian by taking the singular form of an adjective and adding −**mente** (the equivalent of −*ly* in English) to it. Here are the basic rules for forming these adverbs, followed by some examples:

>> Adjectives that ends in −**o**: Add −**mente** to the feminine singular form of the adjective.

For example, **curioso** (*curious*) becomes **curiosamente** (*curiously*).

>> Adjectives that end in −**e**: Add −**mente** to that adjective.

For example, **dolce** (*sweet*) becomes **dolcemente** (*sweetly*).

>> Adjectives that end in −**le** or −**re**: Drop the −**e** before adding −**mente**.

For example, **normale** (*normal*) becomes **normalmente** (*normally*); **regolare** (*regular/usual*) becomes **regolarmente** (*usually*).

Form adverbs from the following adjectives, and then translate them into English.

PRACTICE

Q. **puntuale**

A. **puntualmente** (*punctually*)

29 certo: _____

30 diligente: _____

31 generale: _____

32 gentile: _____

33 lento: _____

34 veloce: _____

Complete each sentence by providing the Italian equivalent of the word in parentheses.

PRACTICE

Q. **Risolveremo quel problema _____.** (*easily*)

A. **Risolveremo quel problema facilmente.** (*We'll solve that problem easily.*)

35 A due anni, suo figlio parla _____. (*well*)

36 Mi dispiace, ma costa _____. (*too much*)

37 Ha risposto _____ alle domande. (*often*)

38 Mangiamo _____ stasera. (*light*)

39 [Tu] lavori _____. (hard)

40 È _____ interessante. (really)

41 Cliente: "Ci porta il conto, per favore?" Cameriere "_____ !"
(right away)

PRACTICE

Molto is so common and so important, it deserves a little exercise all to itself. Complete each sentence by deciding whether you need an adjective or an adverb and insert the correct form.

Q. Risolveremo quel problema _____ facilmente.

A. Risolveremo quel problema molto facilmente. (*We'll solve that problem very easily.*)

42 Ci sono _____ macchine per strada.

43 Parli _____ bene l'italiano!

44 Vedono _____ film italiani.

45 Ho _____ paura di volare.

46 Parlano _____ rapidamente.

47 Lei parla _____.

48 Loro sono _____ gentili.

Finding a Place for Adverbs in a Sentence

In general, you place most adverbs close to the words that they modify — that is, before the adjective and the noun, or after the verb. Here are a couple of examples (note that the adverbs are **spesso** and **molto**).

> **Roberto gioca spesso a golf.** (*Roberto plays golf often.*)

> **Mi è piaciuto molto il concerto.** (*I liked the concert a lot.*)

Exceptions to the general rule are these simple adverbs:

>> **appena** (*just*)

>> **ancora** (*yet/still*)

>> **già** (*already*)

>> **mai** (*ever*)

These compound adverbs are also exceptions:

>> **non . . . mai** (*ever/never*)

>> **non . . . ancora** (*not yet*)

>> **non . . . più** (*no more/no longer*)

The following guidelines explain where to place them:

>> **Compound verbs:** With a compound verb composed of an auxiliary and a past participle (see Chapter 12), you place the simple adverbs between the auxiliary and the past participle.

Il film è già finito. (*The film has ended already.*)

>> **Negations:** When negating with adverbs, **non** precedes the verb, and **mai**, **ancora**, or **più** follows it.

Non mangio più il sushi. (*I don't eat sushi anymore.*)

REMEMBER

Ancora means *yet* or *still*, but it also means *some more* or *again*. Regardless of meaning, its placement after a verb remains the same. Here are a couple of examples.

È ancora presto per telefonargli. (*It's still too early to call him.*)

Vuoi ancora del gelato? (*Do you want some more ice cream?*)

The adverb **sempre**, however, can go before or after the verb without any change in meaning. For example, **Ha sempre giocato con lei** and **Ha giocato sempre con lei** both mean *He's always played with her.*

Answers to "Enriching Adjectives and Adverbs" Practice Questions

1. **buoni spaghetti** (*good spaghetti*)

2. **uomo inglese** (*Englishman*)

3. **macchine tedesche** (*German cars*)

4. **esame difficile** (*difficult exam*)

5. **ristorante romano** (*Roman restaurant*)

6. **pantaloni neri** (*black trousers*)

7. **occhi blu** (*blue eyes*)

8. **amica italiana** (*Italian female friend*)

9. **capelli lunghi** (*long hair*)

10. **interessante; La canzone è interessante.** (*The song is interesting.*)

11. **nuova; Paolo compra una macchina nuova.** (*Paolo is buying a new car.*)

12. **simpatica; Giuliana è simpatica.** (*Giuliana is nice.*)

13. **giovani; Loro sono giovani.** (*They are young.*)

14. **stanche; Le mie sorelle sono stanche.** (*My sisters are tired.*)

15. **mature; Le arance non sono mature.** (*The oranges aren't ripe.*)

16. **costosi; I biglietti dell'aereo erano costosi.** (*The airplane tickets were expensive.*)

17. **irlandese; Mio padre è nato in Irlanda, è irlandese.** (*My father was born in Ireland, he's Irish.*)

18. **deliziosa; La pizza è deliziosa!** (*The pizza is delicious!*)

19. **lunghi; Indosso i pantaloni lunghi stasera.** (*I'm wearing long pants tonight.*)

20. **pugliesi; Stasera vengono a cena le mie amiche pugliesi.** (*My (girl)friends from Puglia are coming to dinner tonight.*)

21. **pessimisti** (m)/**pessimiste** (f); **Siamo pessimisti/pessimiste per la situazione politica.** (*We are pessimistic about the political situation.*)

22. **bianche; Devo cercare le scarpe bianche.** (*I have to look for white shoes.*)

23. **buon'; Elena è una buon'amica.** (*Elena is a good friend.*)

24. **Buono; Com'è il libro che stai leggendo?** (*How is the book you're reading?*) **Buono.** (*Good.*)

25. **simpatica, intelligente; Mia madre è simpatica e intelligente.** (*My mother is nice and smart.*)

26. **rossi; Ho i capelli rossi.** (*I have red hair.*)

27. **divertenti; Gli sport invernali sono divertenti.** (*Winter sports are fun.*)

28. **napoletane, famose; Alcune pizzerie napoletane sono famose.** (*Some Neapolitan pizzerias are famous.*)

29. **certamente** (*certainly*)

30. **diligentemente** (*diligently*)

31. **generalmente** (*generally*)

32. **gentilmente** (*kindly*)

33. **lentamente** (*slowly*)

34. **velocemente** (*quickly*)

35. **bene; A due anni, suo figlio parla bene.** (*At 2 years old, his son speaks well.*)

36. **troppo; Mi dispiace, ma costa troppo.** (*I'm sorry, but it costs too much.*)

37. **spesso; Ha risposto spesso alle domande.** (*He often answered the questions.*)

38. **leggero; Mangiamo leggero stasera.** (*Let's eat light tonight.*)

39. **duro; [Tu] lavori duro.** (*[You] work hard.*)

40. **davvero; È davvero interessante.** (*It's really interesting.*)

41. **Subito; Cliente: "Ci porta il conto, per favore?"** (*Customer: "Can you bring us the bill, please?"*)
    Cameriere: "Subito!" (*Waiter: "Right away!"*)

42. Adjective, **molte; Ci sono molte macchine per strada.** (*There are many cars on the street.*)

43. Adverb, **molto; Parli molto bene l'italiano!** (*You speak Italian very well!*)

44. Adjective, **molti; Vedono molti film italiani.** (*They see a lot of Italian films.*)

45. Adjective, **molta; Ho molta paura di volare.** (*I am very afraid of flying.*)

46. Adverb, **molto; Parlano molto rapidamente.** (*They speak very quickly.*)

47. Adverb, **molto; Lei parla molto.** (*She talks a lot.*)

48. Adverb, **molto; Loro sono molto gentili.** (*They are very kind.*)

Chapter **8**

Comparisons and Superlatives

n this chapter, I explore the different ways you can make comparisons and express super-latives by using adjectives and adverbs for just that purpose. I've divided this chapter into three kinds of comparisons:

» **Comparative:** The comparative of equality (=), the comparative of greater than (+), and the comparative of less than (–)

» **Superlative:** The relative superlative (**superlativo relativo**) and the absolute superlative (**superlativo assoluto**)

» **Irregular:** The irregular comparatives and superlatives of specific adjectives and adverbs

Making Comparisons with the Comparative

In both English and Italian, you use a comparative adjective to compare things in one of three ways:

» **The comparative of equality:** Describing two similar items (*as much as*); I indicate a comparative of equality with an equal sign (=) in this chapter.

>> **The comparative of greater than:** Say something is more than (*bigger, better, faster, prettier than*), using the word **più** (*more*); indicated with a plus sign (+) in this chapter.

>> **The comparative of less than:** Say something is less than (*smaller, worse, slower, uglier than*), using the word **meno** (*less*); denoted throughout this chapter with a negative sign (–).

You can convey the comparative in relation to names, nouns, pronouns, adjectives, infinitives, prepositional phrases, adverbs, and verbs.

The following sections discuss the rules for establishing comparisons in Italian.

Comparison of equality

To say that one object possesses a quality equal to another object, you use these expressions:

>> **così ... come** (*as ... as*)

>> **tanto ... quanto** (*as much ... as/as many ... as*)

You must use **tanto ... quanto** when comparing a quantity.

For example:

Gina è (così) studiosa come Lisa. (*Gina is as studious as Lisa.*) (The **così** is considered redundant and can be omitted, as is the **tanto**, hence it is indicated in parentheses.)

Bianca è (tanto) intelligente quanto Silvia. (*Bianca is as intelligent as Silvia.*)

Compriamo tante pere quante mele. (*We'll buy as many pears as apples.*)

A Gianni piace tanto nuotare quanto sciare. (*Gianni likes swimming as much as skiing.*)

"Come sono quei cappelletti? Sono (così) buoni come quelli del babbo?" (*"How are those cappelletti? Are they as good as your dad's?"*)

Non è (così) caldo come ieri. (*It's not as hot as yesterday.*)

Comparisons of greater than or less than

Unlike English, Italian doesn't add endings to adjectives or adverbs to create comparisons. For example, **vecchio** (*old*) remains the same, and you add the words **più** (**più vecchio**, *older*) or **meno** (**meno vecchio**, *less old*) before it.

Io sono più vecchia della mia amica Laura. (*I am older than my friend Laura.*)

There are two ways of saying that one object has a quality more than or less than another object:

>> **più** (+) or **meno** (–) + **di** (*than*)

>> **più** (+) or **meno** (–) + **che** (*than*)

Be careful! Both **di** and **che** translate as *than*. Remember these tips to help you identify which version you need and use these terms in context:

>> **di:** When the second term in a comparison is a name, a pronoun without a preposition, a noun, or an adverb. (See Chapter 9 for how to contract the preposition **di**.)

>> **che:** When you're comparing two identical parts of speech (two adjectives, two adverbs, two prepositional phrases, or two verbs).

Here are some examples of sentences that use **di** and what term is being compared:

>> Name (**Bianca**): **Silvia è più intelligente di Bianca.** (*Silvia is more intelligent/smarter than Bianca.*)

>> Preposition with stressed pronoun (**te**): **Mangio più di te.** (*I eat more than you.*)

>> Noun (**ieri**): **Sembri meno nervoso di ieri.** (*You seem less nervous than yesterday.*)

>> Pronoun (**altro**): **Come sono carini questi bambini; uno è più carino dell'altro.** (*How cute these children are; one is cuter than the other.*)

>> Noun (**treni**): **I treni in Italia sono più veloci dei treni negli Stati Uniti.** (*The trains in Italy are faster than the trains in the United States.*)

>> Noun (**cappuccino**): **Un caffè costa un euro e un cappuccino costa 1.50 Euro: Il caffè costa meno del cappuccino.** (*An espresso costs one euro, and a cappuccino costs one and a half euros: the espresso costs less than the cappuccino.*)

You must use **che** if you're comparing two identical parts of syntax (direct or indirect objects):

>> Nouns (**pere; mele**): **Compriamo meno pere che mele.** (*We buy fewer pears than apples.*)

>> Nouns (**montagna; mare**): **Vorrei andare più in montagna che al mare.** (*I'd rather go to the mountains than the beach.*)

>> Verbs (**sciare; nuotare**): **Gli piace più sciare che nuotare.** (*He likes skiing more than swimming.*)

>> Nouns (**carne; pesce**): **Mangi meno carne che pesce.** (*You eat less meat than fish.*)

TIP

When you want to say that something keeps increasing or decreasing – as in *more and more tired*, *taller and taller*, and *less and less ready* — in Italian, you use the always-invariable **sempre più** (literally, *always more*) and **sempre meno** (literally, *always less*) + an adjective, an adverb, or a noun.

Fa sempre più freddo. (*It's getting colder and colder.*)

Abbiamo sempre meno vacanze. (*We have fewer and fewer vacation days.*)

Diventi sempre più saggia. (*You're becoming wiser and wiser.*)

PRACTICE

In the following exercise, use the cues to compare two cities in the Emilia-Romagna region, Ravenna and Ferrara, by either filling in the blank or choosing the correct response.

Q. Ferrara ha _____ studenti universitari _____ Ravenna. (+)

A. Ferrara ha più studenti universitari di Ravenna. (*Ferrara has more university students than Ravenna.*)

1 Ravenna è considerata la _____ bella città dell'Emilia-Romagna. (+)

2 Ferrara è chiamata la "città delle biciclette" perché ci sono più biciclette _____ macchine in centro. (+)

3 Ferrara ha _____ abitanti di Ravenna. (−)

4 I lidi ferraresi sono (così) belli _____ le spiagge della riviera romagnola. (=)

5 Mi piacciono più i cappelletti di Ravenna dei/che i tortelli di zucca di Ferrara.

6 Questa città ha più arte di/che quella.

7 Recenti sondaggi (surveys) mostrano che la qualità della vita in entrambe le città diventa _____ alta. (higher and higher)

Designating the Best and the Worst: The Superlatives

Just like in English, in Italian, you can rank objects to establish which one is the highest or the lowest in a series or group. The relative superlative and the absolute superlative allow you to express comparisons between two or more things and to describe the level of intensity of some qualities.

The relative superlative

The relative superlative is the first of the two kinds of superlatives in this chapter. When you say **È il mare più inquinato del mondo** (*It's the most polluted sea in the world*), you're using the relative superlative; the item of comparison (*the sea*) is the most something (*polluted*) relative to a whole (*the world*).

Not to jump ahead too much, but for the sake of simplifying this explanation, an example of the absolute superlative (see the following section) comes in handy: **Il mare è inquinatissimo!** (*The sea is very polluted!*)

In order to say something is superlative, but relative to a whole, you use **il/la più/il/la meno. . . di/in** (*the most/the least. . . of/in*). The adjective should agree with the noun that it refers to, as in the two following examples.

Luciano è il più alto dei figli. (*Luciano is the tallest of the children.*)

Marta è la meno brava nella squadra. (*Marta is the least capable on the team.*)

Or, you can also add on. Here's a formula that usually works:

subject + verb + object + **più/meno** + adjective + **di** (contracted, if necessary) + whole

So, for example, if you want to say something like *Pepe's has the best pizza in New Haven*, you do the following: **Pepe's ha la pizza più buona di New Haven**.

Amalfi ha gli scorci più affascinanti della costiera amalfitana. (*Amalfi has the most fascinating views in the Amalfi Coast.*)

Ferrara ha il numero di biciclette in uso tra i più alti in Europa. (*Ferrara has the highest number of bicycles in use in Europe.*)

PRACTICE

Write these sentences using the relative superlative with the given cues. Remember to make the adjectives agree and pay attention to the (+) and (−) signs.

Q. Mocca/cane/(+) docile/casa

A. Mocca è il cane più docile della casa. (*Mocca is the tamest dog in the house.*)

8. Nadia/studentessa/(+) simpatico/ classe

9. Questi spettacoli/(−) noioso/ stagione

10. L'italiano/lingua/(+) divertente/università

11. Quest'isola/(+) bello/mondo

12. Io/(−) atletico/famiglia

The absolute superlative

The absolute superlative expresses a lot of something, often translated as *very*, or even as *very very*, as in **I ragazzi sono veloci** (*The boys are very quick*).

Using the absolute superlative expresses the same thing as saying **I ragazzi sono molto lenti**. (*The boys are very slow.*) **Molto** acts like an adverb in this sentence and means *very*. In English, you convey it by adding *very*, *much*, *by far*, *incredibly*, *amazingly*, and so on to an adjective or an adverb.

To express the absolute superlative in Italian, you can simply add the adverb **molto** to an adjective or adverb. Or you can add even more enthusiasm to your language by modifying adjectives by dropping the final vowel and adding **–issimo**, **–issima**, **–issimi**, or **–issime**, which agrees in gender and number with the noun.

For example:

>> **ragazzo gentile** (*kind boy*) becomes **ragazzo gentilissimo** (*very kind boy*)

>> **esami facili** (*easy exams*) becomes **esami facilissimi** (*very easy exams*)

When an adjective or adverb ends in **–i**, it only adds **–ssimo**. For example, **È tardi!** (*It's late!*) becomes **È tardissimo** (*It's very late!*)

As usual, you coordinate the adjective to the noun in gender and number.

Quei vestiti sono carissimi. (*Those dresses are very expensive.*)

Torno a casa prestissimo. (*I'll be coming home very early.*)

For some emphasis, you also have the option of repeating a short adjective or adverb with no comma between them, such as **grande grande** (*really big*) or **veloci veloci** (*really fast*). You typically don't do repeat long words in this way because it doesn't sound right.

Mi ha dato un abbraccio forte forte. (*She gave me a really strong hug.*)

PRACTICE

Transform the following adjectives and adverbs into the absolute superlative.

Q. È un concetto importante. (adj.)

A. È un concetto importantissimo. (*It's a very important concept.*)

13 È tardi! (adv.)

14 Sei bella! (adj.)

15 I mosaici sono famosi. (adj.)

16 La professoressa è contenta. (adj.)

17 Siamo felici per te! (adj.)

18 Le mucche mangiano molto. (adv.)

19 L'esame è difficile. (adj.)

20 Il coro canta bene. (adv.)

21 Come stai? Male! (adv.)

22 Sono fresche queste uova? _____! (adj.)

23 Sono molto molto stanca. Sono _____. (adj.)

Making Irregular Comparisons

In Italian, you have two ways of saying that someone or something is better or worse by using the adjectives **buono/migliore** (*good*) or **cattivo/peggiore** (*bad*). Similarly, you have two ways of saying if someone is **grande/maggiore** (*old/big*) or **piccolo/minore** (*young/little*). You can add **più** (*more*) or **meno** (*less*) to the adjective; or use special words as listed in Table 8-1.

Table 8-1   Comparatives and Superlatives of Adjectives with Special Forms

Adjective	Comparative	Relative Superlative	Absolute Superlative
buono (*good*)	**più buono/migliore** (*better*)	**il più buono** (*the best*)	**buonissimo/ottimo** (*very good*)
cattivo (*bad*)	**più cattivo/peggiore** (*worse*)	**il più cattivo** (*the worst*)	**cattivissimo/pessimo** (*very bad*)
grande/maggiore (*old*)	**più grande/maggiore** (*older*)	**il più grande/il maggiore** (*the oldest/the biggest*)	**maggiore** (*very old*)
piccolo (*small*)	**piu piccolo/minore** (*smaller*)	**il piu piccolo/il minore** (*the smallest*)	**picolissimo/minimo** (*very small*)

In all other respects, you use these special forms in the same way that you use the other comparatives.

> **Umberto è il più grande dei fratelli./Umberto è il fratello maggiore.** (*Umberto is the oldest of the siblings.*)
>
> **Penso che il parmigiano sia migliore della fontina./Penso che il parmigiano sia più buono della fontina.** (*I think that parmesan is better than fontina.*)

Note: **Migliore** (+) and **peggiore** (–) are –**e** adjectives, and thus only have two forms. (Check out Chapter 7 for a discussion of the types of adjectives.)

Gender and Number	Forms of migliore	Forms of peggiore
m/f, sing.	**Migliore**	**peggiore**
m/f, pl.	**Migliori**	**peggiori**

Here are a couple of examples using the appropriate forms of **migliore** and **peggiore**.

> **Chi sono le tue migliori amiche?** (*Who are your best [girl]friends?*)
>
> **Qual è stato il peggiore film dell'anno?** (*What was the worst film of the year?*)

With the adverbs **bene** (*well*) and **male** (*badly*), you have special forms only to express the comparatives and absolute superlatives of these qualities. I list them in Table 8-2.

Table 8-2   Comparatives and Superlatives of Adverbs with Special Forms

Adverb	Comparative	Absolute Superlative
bene (*well*)	**meglio** (*better*)	**benissimo** (*very well*)
male (*badly*)	**peggio** (*worse*)	**malissimo** (*very badly*)

This example puts these forms into practice.

> **Mio marito dice che gli italiani guidano meglio degli americani, ma non sono d'accordo. Guidano malissimo!** (*My husband says that Italians drive better than Americans, but I don't agree. They drive terribly!*)

REMEMBER

In this section, focus on recognizing the differences between using an adjective or an adverb to say *better* (**migliore/meglio**) and *worse* (**peggiore/peggio**).

Decide whether you need an adjective or an adverb, and then complete the following lines by using **migliore/meglio** or **peggiore/peggio**. Use the hints in parentheses to fill in the blanks.

PRACTICE

Q. La tua squadra sta giocando _____ della nostra quest'anno. (*better than*)

A. La tua squadra sta giocando meglio della nostra quest'anno. (*Your team is playing better than ours this year.*) (The adverb **meglio** here is modifying the verb **giocare**.)

24 Ma certo, abbiamo dei _____ giocatori. (*better*)

25 Chi canta _____ tu o tua sorella? (*better*)

26 Cucino bene, ma le mie lasagne sono _____ di quelle di mia madre. (*worse than*)

27 Questo è il _____ film dell'anno. (*worst*)

28 Giulia si sente _____ di prima. (*worse*)

Use the most appropriate irregular comparative or superlative for the sentences in this exercise.

PRACTICE

Q. Paola, come stai? _____ (*Very well!*)

A. Benissimo!

29 Ragazzi, avete fatto un _____ lavoro all'esame! (*very good*)

30 Direi che è il poeta _____ del secolo. (*best*)

31 Quel treno è _____. (*very bad*)

32 Giovanni è il _____ della nostra famiglia. (*youngest*)

Answers to "Comparisons and Superlatives" Practice Questions

1. **più; Ravenna è considerata la più bella città dell'Emilia-Romagna.** (*Ravenna is considered the most beautiful city in Emilia-Romagna.*)

2. **che; Ferrara è chiamata la "città delle biciclette" perché ci sono più biciclette che macchine in centro.** (*Ferrara is called the "city of bicycles" because there are more bicycles than cars in the center.*)

3. **meno; Ferrara ha meno abitanti di Ravenna.** (*Ferrara has fewer inhabitants than Ravenna.*)

4. **come; I lidi ferraresi sono (così) belli come le spiagge della riviera romagnola.** (*The Ferrara beaches are as beautiful as the beaches of the Romagna Riviera.*)

5. **che; Mi piacciono più i cappelletti di Ravenna che i tortelli di zucca di Ferrara.** (*I prefer the Ravenna cappelletti more than the pumpkin tortelli from Ferrara.*)

6. **di; Questa città ha più arte di quella.** (*This city has more art than that.*)

7. **più; Recenti sondaggi mostrano che la qualità della vita in entrambe le città diventa sempre più alta.** (*Recent surveys show that the quality of life in both cities is getting higher and higher.*)

8. **Nadia è la studentessa più simpatica della classe.** (*Nadia is the nicest student in the class.*) (Note that **simpatica** is agreeing with **studentessa** and that **di** + **la** contracts before **classe**.)

9. **Questi spettacoli sono i meno noiosi della stagione.** (*These shows are the least boring of the season.*) (**Stagione** is a feminine noun, therefore **di** + **la** = **della**)

10. **L'italiano è la lingua più divertente dell'università.** (*Italian is the most fun language at the university.*)

11. **Quest'isola è la più bella del mondo.** (*This island is the most beautiful in the world.*)

12. **Io sono la meno atletica della famiglia.** (*I am the least athletic of the family.*)

13. **tardissimo; È tardissimo.** (*It is very late.*)

14. **bellissima; Sei bellissima!** (*You are very beautiful!*)

15. **famosissimi; I mosaici sono famosissimi.** (*The mosaics are very famous.*)

16. **contentissima; La professoressa è contentissima.** (*The teacher is delighted.*)

17. **felicissimi; Siamo felicissimi per te!** (*We are delighted for you!*)

18. **moltissimo; Le mucche mangiano moltissimo.** (*Cows eat a lot.*)

19. **difficilissimo; L'esame è difficilissimo.** (*The exam is very difficult.*)

20. **benissimo; Il coro canta benissimo.** (*The choir sings wonderfully.*)

21. **malissimo; Come stai? Malissimo!** (*How are you? Very bad!*)

22. **freschissime; Sono fresche queste uova? Freschissime!** (*Are these eggs fresh? Very fresh!*)

(23) **stanchissima; Sono molto molto stanca. Sono stanchissima.** (*I'm very, very tired. I'm so very tired.*)

(24) Adj., **migliori; Ma certo, abbiamo dei migliori giocatori.** (*Of course, we have some better players.*)

(25) Adv., **meglio; Chi canta meglio, tu o tua sorella?** (*Who sings better, you or your sister?*)

(26) Adj., **peggiori; Cucino bene, ma le mie lasagne sono peggiori di quelle di mia madre.** (*I cook well, but my lasagna is worse than my mom's.*)

(27) Adj., **peggiore; Questo è il peggiore film dell'anno.** (*This is the worst movie of the year.*)

(28) Adv., **peggio; Giulia si sente peggio di prima.** (*Giulia feels worse than before.*)

(29) Absolute superlative, **ottimo; Ragazzi, avete fatto un ottimo lavoro all'esame!** (*Kids, you did a great job on the exam!*)

(30) Relative superlative, **migliore; Direi che è il poeta migliore del secolo.** (*I would say he's the best poet of the century.*)

(31) Absolute superlative, **pessimo; Quel treno è pessimo.** (*That train is terrible/really bad.*)

(32) Relative superlative, **minore/il più piccolo; Giovanni è il minore/il più piccolo della nostra famiglia.** (*Giovanni is the youngest of our family.*)

Chapter 9

Prepositions, and Then Some

Prepositions are words that you need to link other words in a sentence in order to create fuller sentences. For example, *I'm going school* is not a complete sentence. You need to say, *I'm going to school*. And similarly in Italian, you say **Vado a scuola** (a means *to* here). Choosing one preposition over another leads you to say different things, such as *I'm speaking to you* or *I'm speaking about you*. One preposition can play different functions and convey several meanings.

Prepositions are difficult to learn in any language because their use is often *idiomatic* meaning native to the language but not obvious in translation. The basic rule, therefore, is practice, practice, and more practice.

In this chapter, I give you some preposition guidelines. I show you the main Italian prepositions (called **preposizioni semplici** or *simple prepositions*). Then, I show you how to combine (or contract) five simple prepositions with the definite articles in what's called **la preposizione articolata** (*the articulated preposition*, what I call the contracted preposition in this chapter).

I also show you how to choose the preposition that corresponds to the one you'd use in English in the same situation. And I walk you through some very common exceptions and idiomatic uses for when literal translation just won't do. For example, the preposition **da** usually translates as *from*, but in the expression **Vado da Renzo stasera** (*I'm going to Renzo's tonight*), **da** means *to* someone's place/house.

Prepositions can also introduce infinitives, but then their meaning is slightly altered. The prepositions **a** (*to/at*) and **di** (*of/about/some*) are the most common in Italian, as in the examples **Comincia a piovere** (*It's starting to rain*) and **Penso di visitare la Corsica** (*I'm thinking about visiting Corsica*).

Getting Familiar with Simple Prepositions

Italian has eight basic prepositions, corresponding to the basic prepositions used in English. I list them here, starting with the most-frequently used. I give you the English translations that reflect the Italian prepositions' meanings, but remember that you can't assume that you'll use the same preposition in Italian and English every time.

REMEMBER

Italian has many more prepositions than I cover in this book. Consider this list a greatest hits of prepositions:

>> **di** (*of/about/some*)

>> **a** (*at/to*)

>> **da** (*from/by*)

>> **in** (*in/into/to/by*)

>> **su** (*on/onto*)

>> **con** (*with*)

>> **per** (*for/through/in order to*)

>> **fra/tra** (*between/among*)

Sometimes, the prepositions do translate neatly into English, as in this practice set. Fill in the blank with the requested simple preposition.

PRACTICE

Q. Flavia abita _____ Italia. (*in*)

A. Flavia abita in Italia. (*Flavia lives in Italy.*)

1 Ricevo una mail _____ mia madre. (from)

2 Vado a scuola _____ Rachele. (with)

3 Questo regalo (gift) è _____ te! (for)

4 Il numero 5 è _____ 4 e 6. (between)

5 Questo è il libro _____ Paolo. (of)

6 Andiamo _____ casa! (to)

REMEMBER

The stressed pronouns (which you can read about in Chapter 6) generally follow prepositions.

Penso a te! (*I'm thinking about you!*)

Hai qualcosa per me? (*Do you have something for me?*)

By the way, a great song by Lucio Battisti ("Penso a te") can help you embed this structure in your mind, and you can practice your listening and speaking at the same time.

Contracting Prepositions with Articles and Nouns

In this section, I show you how to contract the five most common prepositions with the seven definite articles (check out Chapter 2 for more on definite articles). Each definite article agrees with a noun in gender and number. So, for example, you definitely need to remember whether a noun is masculine singular or plural, and what article it takes. These contracted prepositions all follow a pattern, which you can see in Table 9-1. You have to get this pattern down before we jump into usage, practice, and exceptions (which I cover later in this chapter).

For example, contract **di** + a definite article:

>> **di + il = del**

   Del becomes the stem for you to carry through for the other six articles, as in the first column in Table 9-1. Read these aloud to yourself to help yourself remember them, and to connect them to the other prepositions.

>> **in + il = nel**

   Nel then becomes the stem that you can combine with the other six articles, as in the fourth column in Table 9-1. (Read these aloud to yourself to help with memorizing them.)

You can see how the other prepositions are combined with the articles in Table 9-1; read them aloud here as well.

Table 9-1   Prepositions Combined with Articles

Definite Article	di	a	da	in	su
il	del	al	dal	nel	sul
lo	dello	allo	dallo	nello	sullo
la	della	alla	dalla	nella	sulla
l'	dell'	all'	dall'	nell'	sull'
I	dei	ai	dai	nei	sui
gli	degli	agli	dagli	negli	sugli
le	delle	alle	dalle	nelle	sulle

Some common prepositions, such as **con** (*with*), **per** (*for*), and **fra/tra** (*between*), are hardly ever contracted. Keep them in mind!

General rules of thumb can help you familiarize yourself with prepositions regarding usage. Some verbs are typically followed by specific prepositions. In the sections that follow, I combine practice exercises with individual prepositions, and I throw in some hints and exceptions along the way.

Going places: a or in

The following guidelines show you when to use the preposition **a** or the preposition **in** when talking about going somewhere:

>> **a:** In front of **isole piccole** (*small islands*), **città** (*cities*)

- Small island: **Andiamo a Capri.** (*Let's go to Capri.*)
- City: **Vado a New Orleans per il fine settimana**. (*I'm going to New Orleans for the weekend*).

>> **in:** In front of **paesi** (*countries*), **regioni** (*regions*), **stati** (*states*), **isole grandi** (*large islands*)

- Large island and region: **Andiamo in Sardegna.** (*Let's go to Sardegna.*)
- Country: **Beatrice e Francesca abitano in Italia**. (*Beatrice and Francesca live in Italy*).

In is almost never contracted with the article in front of a country.

Abito in Russia. (*I live in Russia.*)

Vado in Brasile (*I'm going to Brazil.*)

MORE USES FOR A

Certain verbs are generally followed by the preposition **a** (*to/at*):

scrivere (*to write*)

telefonare (*to phone*)

dare (*to give*); as in **dare un regalo** (*to give a present to*)

rispondere (*to answer/respond*)

For holidays or named days and months, use **a** (*at/in*). For example:

a Pasqua (*at Easter*)

a Ferragosto (*at Ferragosto* [on August 15])

ad aprile (*in April*). (Use **ad** if the noun starts with a vowel.)

But if the country name is plural, you use an article:

Abitiamo negli Stati Unitit. (*We live in the United States.*)

Andiamo negli Emirati Arabi Uniti. (*We're going to the United Arab Emirates.*)

Working with andare

I mention in the preceding section the difference between using **andare a** (*to go to*) in front of cities and **andare in** (*to go to*) in front of countries. But the verb **andare** (*to go*) can be followed by several prepositions, depending on what you're trying to say.

The following four examples use each of the four prepositions. These prepositions aren't contracted.

Vado a casa. (*I'm going home.*)

Vado in Argentina. (*I'm going to Argentina.*)

Vado da Stefania. (*I'm going to Stefania's place.*)

Vado con Stefania. (*I'm going with Stefania.*)

PRACTICE

In the following exercise, decide which of the four prepositions you need. I've put an asterisk by the ones in which you need to add a definite article and contract the preposition and article. *Note:* cinema in the practice is masculine singular.

Each of the sentences begins with **Elena va . . .**

Q. Elena va _____ partita di calcio.*

A. Elena va alla partita di calcio.* (*Elena is going to the soccer game.*)

7　_____ Mirco per cena. (Mirco's place)

8　_____ Roma.

9　_____ Francia.

10　_____ Sicilia.

11　_____ cinema di Salvatore*.

12　_____ Stati Uniti*.

13　_____ mangiare

14　_____ oceano*

15　_____ festa*

16　_____ gli amici al parco. (with)

Noting the many uses of da

You frequently use **da** with the verb **ricevere** (*to receive*). Here's the formula for using **da** with **ricevere**.

> **ricevere una mail/una telefonata/un bacio/un regalo. . . da** = *to receive an e-mail, a phone call, a kiss, a present . . . from.*

PRACTICE

Contract the preposition **da** with the following nouns. I put an asterisk by the nouns that don't take a definite article. Also keep in mind that singular family relatives generally do not take an article with possessive adjectives (see Chapter 10) and proper nouns do not take an article.

The beginning of each sentence is **Riceviamo una mail . . .**

Q. Riceviamo una mail _____ mio fratello.*

A. Riceviamo una mail **da mio fratello.** (*We receive an email from my brother*).

17 _____ mia madre.*

18 _____ italiani.

19 _____ moglie (f/s) di Alfredo.

20 _____ Totò*

21 _____ zio Franco.

22 _____ amica di mia madre.

23 _____ mie sorelle.

24 _____ ragazzi italiani.

25 _____ studente.

In Chapter 3, I show you how to contract the preposition **a** in the context of saying **a che ora** (*at what time* something happens). Here are some examples that demonstrate more on how to say what time you do things. When you use the preposition **da** in the context of time (and place) it means *from*, just as it does in English.

> **Prendo il treno da Genova a Torino.** (*I'm taking the train from Genova to Torino*).
>
> **Ceniamo dalle 20:00 alle 21:00.** (*Let's have supper from 8:00 to 9:00 p.m.*)

REMEMBER

When telling time, use the definite articles:

>> **l'** if the hour is singular (such as 1 p.m.)

>> **le** if the hour is plural (such as 3 a.m.)

>> Don't use any definite article if you're talking about **mezzogiorno** (*noon*) or **mezzanotte** (*midnight*).

Studio dall'una alle sette di sera. (*I study from 1 to 7 in the evening*).

Lavora dalle otto a mezzogiorno. (*He/she works from 8 until noon.*)

Use the prepositions **da** or **a**, according to context, and contract them if necessary.

PRACTICE

Q. Il mio cane Toby dorme _____ 10:00 di sera _____ 6:00 di mattina.

A. Il mio cane Toby dorme dale 10:00 di sera alle 6:00 di mattina. (*My dog Toby sleeps from 10:00 p.m. until 6:00 a.m.*)

Studio (26) _____ 19:00 (27 _____ 21:00 ogni sera.

(28) _____ che ora vai (29) _____ dormire?

Vado a letto (30) _____ 23:00 o (31) _____ mezzanotte. Dormiamo (32) _____ 10:00 di sera (33) _____ 6:30 di mattina.

(34) _____ che ora inizia la lezione?

La lezione inizia (35) _____ 2:30.

Da can also translate as *for* when asking for how long something has been happening.

Use **da** + the present indicative (which you can read about in Chapter 5).

Da quanto tempo abiti a Miami? (*For how long have you been living in Miami?*)

Da trenta anni. (*For 30 years.*)

Figuring out the Italian ins

The preposition **in** (*in*) contracts with the Italian definite article to translate as *in/in the*. We have one way of saying that in English, but Italian has seven! The verb **mettere** (*to put/to place*) is frequently used with the preposition **in**.

Contract the preposition **in** with the following nouns by following the example provided. Each of these practice questions need a definite article.

PRACTICE

Each of your sentences will begin as follows: **Metto lo zucchero . . .**

Q. Metto lo zucchero _____ tè.

A. Metto lo zucchero nel tè. (*I'm putting/I put sugar in [the] tea.*)

36 _____ limonata.

37 _____ biscotti.

38 _____ paste. (pastries)

39 _____ aranciata.

40 _____ pane.

41 _____ struffoli.

Using di for possession or the partitive

Di has two prominent uses: to show possession of something and to show an indefinite quantity (known as a *partitive* construction), translated as *some.*

Showing possession

If you say that something belongs to someone or something, you use the preposition **di**, as in the following examples:

>> **il succo di mela** (literally, *the juice of the apple; apple juice*)

>> **le foto del matrimonio** (*the photos of the wedding*)

DIFFERENCES

In English, for possession, you add an apostrophe and *s* to a noun or a name. **Il libro di Teresa** literally translates as *the book of Teresa,* but common English usage translates as *Teresa's book.* You also use a possessive adjective, such as *his* or *her.* Here's how Italian works: To convey ownership, use possessive adjectives and pronouns (**il suo gatto** translates as *his/her cat*). (See Chapter 10 for more on possessive adjectives.) And use **di** followed by the thing owned, as in **il gatto di Marta** (literally, *the cat of Marta,* or *Marta's cat*) or **la padrona del gatto** (literally, *the owner of the cat,* or *the cat's owner*).

PRACTICE

Get a handle on the possessive **di** in the following practice set. To help you out, I place an asterisk by the nouns that don't take any definite article.

Q. Questo è il libro _____ ragazzo.

A. **Questo è il libro del ragazzo.** (*This is the boy's book.*)

42 _____ Luigi.*

43 _____ spagnolo.*

44 _____ studenti.

45 _____ miei studenti.

46 _____ altra classe.

47 _____ studente.

48 _____ studentesse italiane.

(49) _____ mia madre.*

(50) _____ mia mamma.

REMEMBER

When talking about subjects and books, you don't use an article, just **di** + the noun:

> » **il professore di biologia,** (literally, *the professor of biology; the biology professor*)

> » **il libro di biologia** (literally, *the book of biology; the biology book*)

Using the partitive

Italian commonly uses the preposition **di** + definite article + noun as the partitive, which simply means *some*. So, if you say, "**prendi dell'olio d'oliva,**" it translates as, "*Get some olive oil.*" Like always, you need to know noun number and gender to effectively use this structure. Use the singular partitive for uncountable things (**del, dell', della, dello**), and the plural partitive for countable things (**dei, degli, delle**). The singular partitive identifies an indeterminate amount of something, such as water and bread.

REMEMBER

You can also form the partitive in a few other common ways: **un po' di** (*a little bit of*), **qualche** (*some*), **alcuni/alcune** (*some*). I don't cover these partitive options in this workbook, simply because they fall out of its grammatical scope.

PRACTICE

Pretend that you're at the market, listing the things that you need to buy. Use **di** + the article + the noun. *Note:* The noun for *egg* is an exception in that it's masculine in the singular (**l'uovo**) and feminine in the plural (**le uova**).

Q. Vado al mercato e prendo _____ uova.

A. Vado al mercato e prendo **delle uova.** (*I go to the market and get some eggs.*)

Vado al mercato e compro

(51) _____ zucchero

(52) _____ pane

(53) _____ lasagne

(54) _____ spaghetti

(55) _____ gnocchi

(56) _____ acqua minerale

(57) _____ frutta

(58) _____ pizzette

Putting su on the spot

The preposition **su** usually means *on*. It generally translates literally into English. (Okay, **su** also has an idiomatic meaning that doesn't translate, which I talk about in the following section.) So, if you want to say *The cat is on the car* in Italian, you'd say **Il gatto è sulla macchina**.

You do not use **su** to talk about days of the week. If you do something on a certain day of the week, in Italian, you use the name of that day with the article, without a preposition.

> **Giochiamo a tennis il sabato.** (*We play tennis every Saturday/on Saturdays.*)

If you're talking about doing something on a certain day, use the name of the day, as you do in English.

> **Giochi a tennis sabato?** (*Are you going to play tennis on Saturday?*)

PRACTICE

Start each of the following sentences with the phrase **Le farfalle sono** (*The butterflies are*), and then fill in **su** + the preposition.

Q. Le farfalle sono _____ albero.

A. Le farfalle sono sull'albero. (*The butterflies are on the tree.*)

59 _____ alberi.

60 _____ fiori notturni. (night flowers, m/pl.)

61 _____ sedia (chair).

62 _____ zaino.

63 _____ fiore. (flower, m/sing.)

64 _____ foglie. (leaves, f/pl.)

Finding the Exceptions to the Rule

Italian has so many idiomatic uses of prepositions that I can't list them all. These oddball forms don't follow the same contracted preposition guidelines that are discussed in the section "Contracting Prepositions with Articles and Nouns," earlier in this chapter, and therefore you must memorize them. Of course, you can look for patterns, and also create some of your own to help you remember.

For example, most means of transportation take the preposition **in** and no definite article, when conveying the notion *by*.

> **Vado in traghetto.** (*I'm going by ferry.*)

Some specific places also take **in** and no definite article.

> **Vado in biblioteca.** (*I'm going to the library.*)
>
> **Sono in biblioteca.** (*I'm in the library.*)

See the following exceptions:

- » **in macchina** (*by car*)
- » **in treno** (*by train*)
- » **in bici/in bicicletta** (*by bike*)
- » **in autobus** (*by bus*)
- » **in barca** (*by boat*)
- » **a cavallo** (*by horse*)
- » **a piedi** (*on foot*)
- » **a casa** (*to/at home*)
- » **in biblioteca** (*in/to the library*)
- » **in cucina** (*in/to the kitchen*)
- » **in centro** (*to/in the center of town*)
- » **in banca** (*to/in the bank*)
- » **in vacanza** (*on vacation*)
- » **a letto** (*to bed*)
- » **a teatro** (*to the theater*)
- » **a scuola** (*to school*)
- » **in montagna** (*to/in the mountains*)
- » **a tavola** (*to/at the table*)
- » **al cinema** (*to the movies*)
- » **a mezzanotte** (*at midnight*)
- » **sul giornale** (*in the newspaper*)
- » **su Internet** (*on the Internet*)
- » **alla radio** (*on the radio*)
- » **alla televisione** (*on the television*)

TIP

You might want to make yourself a Quizlet or flashcards out of these exceptions to really get them down.

Note the difference between the verbs and the prepositions in the phrases *to come from* versus *to be from*. Use **venire** (*to come*) with **da** and **essere** (*to be*) with **di**.

DIFFERENCES

Vengo da Ravenna. (*I come/I'm coming from Ravenna.*)

Sono di Roma. (*I'm from Rome.*)

Here are a couple more useful phrases that don't quite fit in the other sections in this chapter:

REMEMBER

>> **contare + su + di** + stressed pronoun (read about stressed pronouns in Chapter 6) translates to *to count on* [*pronoun*]

Conto su di te. (*I'm counting on you.*)

>> **dipende + da** + stressed pronoun translates to *it depends on* [*pronoun*]/*it's up to* [*pronoun*]

Passo subito o più tardi? (*Should I stop by now or later?*)

Dipende da te. (*That's up to you.*)

Answers to "Prepositions, and Then Some" Practice Questions

(1) **da; Ricevo una mail da mia madre.** (*I get an e-mail from my mother.*)

(2) **con; Vado a scuola con Rachele.** (*I go to school with Rachele.*)

(3) **per; Questo regalo è per te!** (*This gift is for you!*)

(4) **tra; Il numero 5 è tra 4 e 6.** (*The number 5 is between 4 and 6.*)

(5) **di; Questo è il libro di Paolo.** (*This is Paul's book.*)

(6) **a; Andiamo a casa!** (*Let's go home!*)

(7) **da; Elena va da Mirco per cena.** (*Elena is going to Mirco's for dinner.*)

(8) **a; Elena va a Roma.** (*Elena is going to Rome.*)

(9) **in; Elena va in Francia.** (*Elena is going to France.*)

(10) **in; Elena va in Sicilia.** (*Elena goes to Sicily.*)

(11) **al; Elena va al cinema di Salvatore.** (*Elena goes to the cinema with Salvatore.*)

(12) **negli; Elena va negli Stati Uniti.** (*Elena goes to the United States.*)

(13) **a; Elena va a mangiare.** (*Elena goes to eat.*)

(14) **nell'; Elena va all'oceano/al mare.** (*Elena goes to the ocean.*)

(15) **alla; Elena va alla festa.** (*Elena is going to the party.*)

(16) **con; Elena va con gli amici al parco.** (*Elena is going to the park with friends.*)

(17) **da; Riceviamo una mail da mia madre.** (*We get an e-mail from my mother.*)

(18) **dagli; Riceviamo una mail dagli italiani.** (*We get an e-mail from the Italians.*)

(19) **dalla; Riceviamo una mail dalla moglie di Alfredo.** (*We get an e-mail from Alfredo's wife.*)

(20) **da; Riceviamo una mail da Totò.** (*We get an e-mail from Totò.*)

(21) **dallo; Riceviamo una mail dallo zio Franco.** (*We get an e-mail from Uncle Franco.*)

(22) **dall'; Riceviamo una mail dall'amica di mia madre.** (*We get an e-mail from my mother's friend.*)

(23) **dalle; Riceviamo una mail dalle mie sorelle.** (*We get an e-mail from my sisters.*)

(24) **dai; Riceviamo una mail dai ragazzi italiani.** (*We get an e-mail from the Italian boys.*)

(25) **dallo; Riceviamo una mail dallo studente.** (*We get an e-mail from the student.*)

Studio (26) dalle 19:00 (27) alle 21:00 ogni sera. (*I study from 7pm to 9pm every evening.*)

(28) A che ora vai (29) a dormire? (*What time do you go to sleep?*)

Vado a letto (30) alle 23:00 o (31) a mezzanotte. Dormiamo (32) dalle 10:00 di sera (33) alle 6:30 di mattina. (*I go to bed at 11pm or midnight. We sleep from 10 in the evening to 6:30 in the morning.*)

(34) **A che ora inizia la lezione?** (*What time does the lesson start?*)

La lezione inizia (35) **alle 2:30.** (*The lesson starts at 2:30.*)

(36) **nella; Metto lo zucchero nella limonata.** (*I put sugar in the lemonade.*)

(37) **nei; Metto lo zucchero nei biscotti.** (*I put sugar in the cookies.*)

(38) **nelle; Metto lo zucchero nelle paste.** (*I put sugar in the pastry.*)

(39) **nell'; Metto lo zucchero nell'aranciata.** (*I put sugar in the orangeade.*)

(40) **nel; Metto lo zucchero nel pane.** (*I put sugar in the bread.*)

(41) **negli; Metto lo zucchero negli struffoli.** (*I put sugar in the struffoli.*)

(42) **di; Questo è il libro di Luigi.** (*This is Luigi's book.*)

(43) **di; Questo è il libro di spagnolo.** (*This is the Spanish book.*)

(44) **degli; Questo è il libro degli studenti.** (*This is the students' book.*)

(45) **dei; Questo è il libro dei miei studenti.** (*This is my student's book.*)

(46) **dell'; Questo è il libro dell'altra classe.** (*This is the other class's book.*)

(47) **dello; Questo è il libro dello studente.** (*This is the student's book.*)

(48) **delle; Questo è il libro delle studentesse italiane.** (*This is the Italian students' book.*)

(49) **di; Questo è il libro di mia madre.** (*This is my mother's book.*)

(50) **della; Questo è il libro della mia mamma.** (*This is my mom's book.*)

(51) **dello zucchero** (*some sugar*)

(52) **del pane** (*some bread*)

(53) **delle lasagne** (*some lasagna*)

(54) **degli spaghetti** (*some spaghetti*)

(55) **degli gnocchi** (*some gnocchi*)

(56) **dell'acqua minerale** (*some mineral water*)

(57) **della frutta** (*some fruit*)

(58) **delle pizzette** (*some pizza*)

(59) **sugli; Le farfalle sono sugli alberi.** (*The butterflies are on the trees.*)

(60) **sui; Le farfalle sono sui fiori notturni.** (*The butterflies are on the night flowers.*)

(61) **sulla; Le farfalle sono sulla sedia.** (*The butterflies are on the chair.*)

(62) **sullo; Le farfalle sono sullo zaino.** (*The butterflies are on the backpack.*)

(63) **sul; Le farfalle sono sul fiore.** (*The butterflies are on the flower.*)

(64) **sulle; Le farfalle sono sulle foglie.** (*The butterflies are on the leaves.*)

Chapter **10**

La Mia Famiglia: Possessive Adjectives and Pronouns

When you want to denote ownership or possession while referring to someone or something, you can use possessive adjectives and pronouns, which help you be more specific: **il mio, la mia, i miei, le mie** (*my/mine*), **il tuo, la tua, i tuoi, le tue** (*your/yours*), and so forth. The possessive adjectives precede a noun, and the possessive pronouns stand by themselves. The main difference between possessives in English and Italian is that the Italian possessives must agree in number and in gender with what's being possessed (hence the four forms for *my* and *your*).

This chapter points out similarities and differences between Italian and English in the use of possessives. It also tells you how to match the Italian possessives to the nouns to which they refer and touches on how to express the fact that you're talking about part of a larger set.

> **Molti dei miei studenti sono ammalati.** (*Many of my students are sick.*)
>
> **Un mio amico ha detto . . .** (*A friend of mine said . . .*)

This chapter also introduces you to the vocabulary, as well as the possessives, associated with family members.

Possessing with Adjectives

In Italian, possessive adjectives must agree in number and gender with the noun they're modifying.

> **Jenny ha portato i suoi sci.** (*Jenny brought her skis.*)

In this example, the possessive **i suoi** (*her*) agrees with the masculine plural noun **sci** (*skis*).

In English, you assign ownership by simply adding an apostrophe and the letter *s* (or just the apostrophe), as in *Mary's cat*, which in Italian becomes **Il gatto di Maria** (literally, *the cat of Mary*). You never use an apostrophe to denote ownership in Italian.

In Italian you have three options to express possession. Context and intent can guide you in deciding which option is more appropriate for each situation:

>> Add a possessive adjective to the owner.

   il suo gatto (*his/her cat*)

>> Introduce the owner by using the preposition **di** (*of*).

   l'università di Lilly (*Lilly's university*); **il cibo della mensa** (*the dining hall's food*)

>> Use the idiomatic expression **essere di** [*owner's name*], which means something like *to belong to*.

   "**Di chi è questo spazzolino?**" (*Whose toothbrush is this?*) "**È di Emilia**". (*It's Emilia's.*)

TIP

Contract the **di** if necessary. See Chapter 9 for more on when and how to combine **di** + a definite article when they precede a noun.

REMEMBER

The formula for possessive adjectives, when not talking about exceptions to rules, is as follows:

> definite article (**il/la/i/le**) + possessive adjective + noun

Note how each possessive adjective in this list of examples follows the formula and agrees with the noun being possessed:

>> **il mio professore** (*my professor*)

>> **la mia penna** (*my pen*)

>> **i miei professori** (*my professors*)

>> **le mie penne** (*my pens*)

Unlike in the English *his/her*, in the third-person singular Italian **il suo/la sua/i suoi/le sue** (*his/her*) the possessive adjective or pronoun doesn't convey whether the owner is male or female. That information is clarified only by the context of the sentence; for example, **la sua barca** can mean *his boat* or *her boat*: **la sua** is agreeing with **barca**. The context lets us know that we are saying his boat in the following sentence: **Davide porta la sua barca in Croazia.** (*Davide is taking his boat to Croatia.*)

Here's an exception where the possessive comes after the noun, and the sentence doesn't contain a definite article:

Sono a casa mia. (*I'm at my house.*)

Andiamo a casa sua. (*Let's go to his/her house.*)

Table 10-1 lists possessive adjectives and pronouns, which are identical in Italian, along with the corresponding definite articles.

Table 10-1   Possessive Adjectives and Pronouns

Translation	Masculine Singular	Masculine Plural	Feminine Singular	Feminine Plural
my/mine	**il mio**	**i miei**	**la mia**	**le mie**
your/yours (singular)	**il tuo**	**i tuoi**	**la tua**	**le tue**
his/hers/its *your/yours* (formal)	**il suo**	**i suoi**	**la sua**	**le sue**
our/ours	**il nostro**	**i nostri**	**la nostra**	**le nostre**
your/yours (plural)	**il vostro**	**i vostri**	**la vostra**	**le vostre**
their/theirs	**il loro**	**i loro**	**la loro**	**le loro**

REMEMBER

The possessive adjective **loro** (*their*) doesn't change, regardless of the noun. The only indicator of the gender and number of the noun is the definite article, which is always used with **loro**.

PRACTICE

Practice making the possessive adjectives agree. Fill in the blanks with the appropriate singular or plural form of each possessive adjective. See Chapter 2 if you need a brush-up on gender and number. *Note:* **Bici** is one of those nouns that can be either singular or plural; context tells you which it is.

Q. **il mio/la mia/i miei/le mie**

_____ letto

_____ amiche italiane

_____ problemi

_____ bici

A. **il mio letto** (*my bed*)

le mie amiche italiane (*my Italian friends*)

i miei problem (*my problems*)

la mia/le mie bici (*my bike/my bikes*)

1 il tuo/la tua/i tuoi/le tue

_____ squadra

_____ volo

_____ attrici preferite

_____ attori preferiti

2 il suo/la sua/i suoi/ le sue

_____ zuppa

_____ crostate

_____ biscotti

_____ pane

3 il nostro/la nostra/i nostri/le nostre

_____ città (f/sing. + f/pl.)

_____ vie

_____ negozio

_____ luoghi

4 il vostro/la vostra/i vostri/ le vostre

_____ cane

_____ gatta

_____ compagni

_____ partite di calcio

⑤ il loro/la loro/i loro/le loro

_____ gatti

_____ migliori amici

_____ arte

_____ galleries

Talking about family

In order to talk about possession within a family unit, you need to know some vocabulary associated with family members:

>> **la madre** (*mother*)

>> **il padre** (*father*)

>> **la mamma** (*mom/mommy*)

>> **il papà** (*pop/dad/daddy*)

>> **il babbo** (*pop, dad, daddy; in some regions*)

>> **i genitori** (*parents*)

>> **la sorella** (*sister*)

>> **le sorelle** (*sisters*)

>> **il fratello** (*brother*)

>> **i fratelli** (*brothers/siblings*)

>> **il marito** (*husband*)

>> **la moglie** (*wife*)

>> **il nonno** (*grandfather*)

>> **la nonna** (*grandmother*)

>> **i nonni** (*grandparents*)

>> **la zia** (*aunt*)

>> **lo zio** (*uncle*)

>> **gli zii** (*aunts and uncles*)

>> **la cugina** (*cousin*, f)

>> **il cugino** (*cousin*, m)

>> **il figlio** (*son*)

>> **la figlia** (*daughter*)

>> **i figli** (*children/sons*)

>> **il nipote** (*nephew/grandson*)

>> **la nipote** (*niece/granddaughter*)

>> **i nipoti** (*nieces and nephews/grandchildren*)

You can also say **le mie nipoti** if you're referring to *my nieces* and *my granddaughters*.

TIP

In Italian, gender still defaults to the masculine, even if you're talking about a room of eight women and one man. This gender usage is changing, slowly, in the classroom and outside of it, while some people use the feminine default gender when referring to or addressing a group of mixed gender. See Chapter 1 for more on gender in Italian.

PRACTICE

Take a look at the family tree of **La famiglia Abbat.**

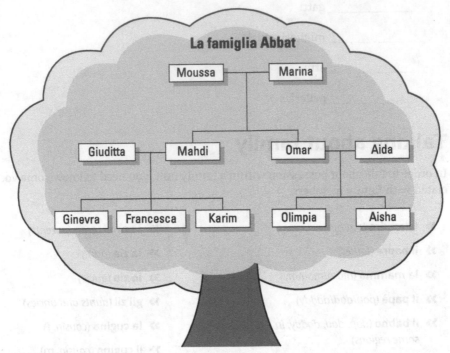

La famiglia Abbat

Moussa — Marina

Giuditta — Mahdi   Omar — Aida

Ginevra Francesca Karim   Olimpia Aisha

Use family-related vocabulary to complete the following sentences to talk about how these people are related to each other. The **di** denotes possession.

Q. Marina è _____ di Moussa.

A. Marina è la moglie di Moussa. (*Marina is Moussa's wife.*)

6   Moussa è _____ di Marina.

7   Moussa e Marina sono _____ di Mahdi e Omar.

8   Ginevra, Francesca e Karim sono _____ di Giuditta e Mahdi.

9   Olimpia e Aisha sono _____ di Francesca.

10 Omar e Aida sono _____ di Karim.

11 Karim e Olimpia sono _____ di Moussa e Marina.

TIP

For extra practice, sketch out your own family tree and describe as many relationships as you can!

Using possessive adjectives with family

When using possessive adjectives with singular family members, remember that you never use the definite article. (Except for a few informal exceptions: **mamma**, **papà**, and **babbo**.)

So, you would say

> » **Mio fratello** (*my brother*) but **i miei fratelli** (*my brothers/my siblings*)
>
> » **Tua zia** (*your aunt*) but **le tue zie** (*your aunts*)
>
> » **Sua cugina** (*his/her cousin*, f) but **le sue cugine** (*his/her cousins*, f)

Follow this rule with all family members except for the informal **mamma**, **papà**, and **babbo**, which always take an article. They are endearing shortened forms. (The formal **madre** and **padre** don't take an article; they follow the standard rule.)

For example, you say **la mia mamma** (*my mom*) but **mia madre** (*my mother*).

The Italian pronoun **loro** (*their*) always takes an article, whether you're saying **la loro mamma** (*their mom*) or **la loro madre** (*their mother*).

PRACTICE Check your understanding on how to use possessive adjectives with family members by translating the following phrases.

Q. *My dad*

A. **Il mio papà/Il mio babbo**

12 Our father/our parents

13 Your mother

14 Her uncle

15 My grandmother

16 My sisters

17 Your (sing./informal) grandchildren

18 Their cousin (m)/their cousins

PRACTICE Read how Maria describes her family in the following paragraph, and then answer the questions by selecting the correct response.

Questa è la mia famiglia. Mio marito si chiama Domenico ed io mi chiamo Maria. Abbiamo tre figli: Annamaria, Teresa e Giovanni. Annamaria ha tre figli: si chiamano Giancarlo, Daniele, e Maria Francesca. Teresa ha una figlia che si chiama Emilia. Giovanni ha due figlie che si chiamano Jenny e Lucia. Ho anche un pronipote, Nico (il figlio di Giancarlo), ma lui non è nella foto!

BODY PARTS AND CLOTHING

When you talk about body parts and clothing, in Italian, you generally don't use a possessive adjective (whereas you do in English). Frequently, you accompany this vocabulary with reflexive verbs (see Chapter 12 for more on those types of verbs).

Here are some examples:

- **farsi male a** (*to hurt one's*)

  Mi sono fatta male al polpaccio. (*I've hurt my calf.*)

- **fare male** (*to hurt*)

  Mi fa male la testa. (*My head hurts.*)

- **mettersi** (*to wear, to put on*)

  Mi metto le lenti a contatto prima di uscire. (*I put on my contact lenses before leaving.*)

Q: How is Maria related to Daniele?

(A) Figlio

(B) Mamma

(C) Nonna

(D) Nipoti

A: C. **Nonna** (*grandmother*)

19 How are Emilia and Lucia related to Domenico and Maria?

(A) Figli

(B) Genitori

(C) Sorelle

(D) Nipoti

20 What's the relationship between Annamaria, Teresa, and Giovanni?

(A) Figli

(B) Genitori

(C) Fratelli

(D) Nipoti

Using Possessive Pronouns

Use possessive pronouns to refer to something already mentioned or implied. Possessive pronouns agree in number and gender with whatever they're substituting. Sometimes, you use the possessive pronouns to emphasize ownership.

"Questo è il mio problema, non il tuo." (*This is my problem, not yours."*)

In Italian, you use the definite article with possessive pronouns, except for when you use a possessive word after the verb **essere** (*to be*). In those instances, you can use the article or skip it, whichever comes easier.

> **Quell'automobile è la mia.** (*That car is mine.*)
>
> **Quell'automobile è mia.** (*That car is mine.*)

Table 10-2 lists possessive pronouns, which are identical in Italian to the possessive adjectives, along with the corresponding definite articles.

Table 10-2 Possessive Pronouns

Translation	Masculine Singular	Masculine Plural	Feminine Singular	Feminine Plural
mine	**(il) mio**	**(i) miei**	**(la) mia**	**(le) mie**
yours	**(il) tuo**	**(i) tuoi**	**(la) tua**	**(le) tue**
your/his/hers/its	**Suo/il suo**	**Suoi/i suoi**	**Sua/la sua**	**Sue/le sue**
ours	**(il) nostro**	**(i) nostri**	**(la) nostra**	**(le) nostre**
yours	**(il) vostro**	**(i) vostri**	**(la) vostra**	**(le) vostre**
Your/theirs	**Loro/il loro**	**Loro/i loro**	**Loro/la loro**	**Loro/le loro**

REMEMBER

You can use the possessive pronouns also to express the concept *my parents* (**i miei**) and *your parents* (**i tuoi**).

> **Dove sono i tuoi?** (*Where are your parents?*)
>
> **Mi fermo dai miei.** (*I'm stopping at my parents' house.*)

PRACTICE

Complete the following sentences with the appropriate possessive pronoun.

Q. Non ho fatto il compito, mi dai _____?

A. Non ho fatto il compito, mi dai il tuo? (*I didn't do my homework, will you give me yours?*)

21 Non vengo in macchina, ma Emilia porta _____. (hers)

22 Il nostro volo è in ritardo. E _____? (yours, voi)

23 Porto i miei figli. Tu porti _____? (yours, tu)

24 Roberta andrà con sua moglie alla festa e John andrà con _____. (his)

25 Di chi è questo libro? È _____. (mine)

Answers to "La Mia Famiglia: Possessive Adjectives and Pronouns" Practice Questions

(1) **la tua squadra** (*your team*)

  il tuo volo (*your flight*)

  le tue attrici preferite (*your favorite actresses*)

  i tuoi attori preferiti (*your favorite actors*)

(2) **la sua zuppa** (*his/her soup*)

  le sue crostate (*his/her piess*)

  i suoi biscotti (*his/her cookies*)

  il suo pane (*his/her bread*)

(3) **la nostra città/le nostre città** (*our city*)

  le nostre vie (*our streets*)

  il nostro negozio (*our shop*)

  i nostri luoghi (*our places*)

(4) **il vostro cane** (*your dog*)

  la vostra gatta (*your cat*)

  i vostri compagni (*your companions*)

  le vostre partite di calcio (*your soccer matches*)

(5) **i loro gatti** (*their cats*)

  i loro migliori amici (*their best friends*)

  la loro arte (*their art*)

  le loro gallerie (*their galleries*)

(6) **il marito; Moussa è il marito di Marina.** (*Moussa is Marina's husband.*)

(7) **i genitori; Moussa e Marina sono i genitori di Mahdi e Omar.** (*Moussa and Marina are Mahdi and Omar's parents.*)

(8) **i figli; Ginevra, Francesca e Karim sono i figli di Giuditta e Mahdi.** (*Ginevra, Francesca, and Karim are the children of Giuditta and Mahdi.*)

(9) **le cugine; Olimpia e Aisha sono le cugine di Francesca.** (*Olimpia and Aisha are Francesca's cousins.*)

(10) **gli zii; Omar e Aida sono gli zii di Karim.** (*Omar and Aida are Karim's uncle and aunt.*)

(11) **i nipoti; Karim e Olimpia sono i nipoti di Moussa e Marina.** (*Karim and Olimpia are the grandchildren of Moussa e Marina.*)

(12) **nostro padre/i nostri genitori**

(13) **tua madre** (inf)/**sua madre** (f); both are correct, which one you use depends on whether you're speaking formally or informally to someone.

(14) **suo zio**

(15) **mia nonna**

(16) **le mie sorelle**

(17) **i tuoi nipoti**

(18) **il loro cugino/i loro cugini**

(19) D. **Nipoti**; Emilia and Lucia are the granddaughters of Domenico and Maria.

(20) C. **Fratelli**; Annamaria, Teresa, and Giovanni are siblings.

(21) **la sua; Non vengo in macchina, ma Emilia porta la sua.** (*I don't come by car, but Emilia brings hers.*)

(22) **il vostro; Il nostro volo è in ritardo. E il vostro?** (*Our flight is delayed. And yours?*)

(23) **i tuoi; Porto i miei figli. Tu porti i tuoi?** (*I take my children. Do you bring yours?*)

(24) **la sua; Roberta andrà con sua moglie alla festa e John andrà con la sua.** (*Roberta will go with her wife to the party and John will go with his.*)

(25) **(il) mio; Di chi è questo libro? È (il) mio.** (*Whose book is this? It's mine.*)

Chapter **11**

Asking with Interrogatives; Pointing Out with Demonstratives

C ommunication and interaction are key elements to language construction, and so for this reason, I devote this chapter primarily to showing you how to ask questions using *interrogative adjectives* (or question words) and how to answer questions affirmatively or negatively. You never know when you're going to strike up a conversation with your recently acquired Italian pen pal, look for a partner on a dating app, or meet your new neighbors.

And, because people frequently point things out to ask a question, in this chapter, I also introduce the demonstrative adjectives **questo** (*this/these*) and **quello** (*that/those*).

Asking and Answering Questions

You can ask a question quite simply by changing the inflection of your voice without changing any word order. For example: **Sei stanca** translates as *You're tired*, but if you say, **"Sei stanca?"** and change the inflection of your voice, the meaning shifts to the question, *"Are you tired?"*

Italian has a whole group of question words that can help you to ask, and understand, questions. Most of these words are invariable, such as **chi?** (*who?*). Some interrogative adjectives, such as **dove** (*where*), **come** (*how*), and **quale** (*which/what*), are frequently combined with the verb **essere** (*to be*), and undergo a modification.

> For example, **Dov'è Francesca?** (*Where is Francesca?*)

Table 11-1 lists the interrogative adjectives and pronouns, as well as their meanings.

Table 11-1   Interrogative Adjectives and Pronouns

Interrogative	Meaning	Example
Chi	*Who*	**Chi è quello?** (*Who's that* (man)*?*)
Quando	*When*	**Quando torni?** (*When are you coming back?*)
Perché	*Why*	**Perché studi l'italiano?** (*Why are you studying Italian?*)
Quanto	*How much*	**Quanto costa una Ferrari?** (*How much does a Ferrari cost?*)
Quanti/Quante	*How many*	**Quanti anni hai?** (*How old are you? Literally, How many years do you have?*)
		Quante persone vengono? (*How many people are coming?*)
Cosa	*What*	**Cosa dici?** (*What are you saying?*)
Che cosa	*What*	**Che cosa è questo?** (*What is this?*)
Che + noun	*What*	**Che giorno è oggi?** (*What day is today?*)
Dove	*Where*	**Dove vivi?** (*Where do you live?*)
Dov'è	*Where is*	**Dov'è Piazza Garibaldi?** (*Where is Piazza Garibaldi?*)
		Dove sei?/Dove siete? (*Where are you?*)
		Di dove sei?/Di dove siete? (*Where are you from?*)
Dove sono	*Where are*	**Dove sono le chiavi?** (*Where are the keys?*)
Come	*How*	**Come stai?** (*How are you?*)
		Come si dice *peach* **in italiano?** (*How do you say peach in Italian?*)
Com'è	*How is/What is something like*	**Com'è il tuo uomo ideale?** (*What's your ideal man like?*)
		Come sei? (*What are you like?*)
		Come sono? (*How are/what is something like.*)
		Come sono gli spaghetti? (*How's the spaghetti?*)
Quale	*What/Which*	**Quale dei due preferisci?** (*Which of the two do you prefer?*)
Qual è	*What is*	**Qual è il tuo ristorante preferito?** (*What's your favorite restaurant?*)
Quali sono	*What are*	**Quali sono i giorni della settimana?** (*What are the days of the week?*)

REMEMBER

Che, che cosa, and **cosa** are interchangeable when they mean *what* and are followed by a verb. For example, these three sentences all translate as *"What do you do in your free time?"*:

>> **Che cosa fai nel tempo libero?**

>> **Che fai nel tempo libero?**

>> **Cosa fai nel tempo libero?**

You never include the interrogative adjective or pronoun in your answer (just like you don't in English).

> **Dove vai dopo la lezione?** (*Where are you going after the library?*)

> **Vado a casa.** (*I'm going home.*)

No **dove** needed in the preceding response!

The one exception, although it's not really an exception, is when you use **perché**, which means both *why* and *because.*

> **"Perché non vai al mare?"** (*"Why don't you go to the beach?"*)

> **"Perché non mi va."** (*"Because I don't feel like it."*)

When you say **perché non . . . ?**, it means you're also making a suggestion. Think of how, in English, you would use the words, *"Why don't . . . ?"*

> **"Cosa facciamo?"** (*"What should we do?"*)

> **"Perché non andiamo a prendere un gelato?"** (*"Why don't we go get an ice cream?"*)

But, if someone says, **Andiamo al cinema?** (*Should we go to the movies?*), you can answer, **"Perché no?"** (*Why not?*)

Table 11-2 shows some sample answers to questions. I'll put some optional words in parentheses; this means that the sentence makes sense without them, but you could/should add them for clarification or for the sake of writing a complete sentence. See Chapters 4, 5, and 6 if you need a refresher on present tense verb conjugations.

REMEMBER

Use **quale** (*what/which*) in the singular and **quali** (*what/which*) in the plural, regardless of gender.

TIP

You might need some possessive adjectives — **il mio** (*my*) or **il tuo** (*your*) — to formulate a complete response when answering questions: Check out Chapter 10 for all your possessive adjective needs.

Table 11-2   Answering Questions

Question	Translation	Answer	Translation
Chi è quello?	Who is that?	(Lui) È mio cugino.	He's my cousin.
Quando torni?	When are you coming back?	(Torno) A settembre.	(I'm coming back) in September.
Perché studi l'italiano?	Why do you study Italian?	(Studio l'italiano) Perché mi piace.	(I study Italian) because I like it.
Quanto costa una Ferrari?	How much does a Ferrari cost?	(Una Ferrari) Costa 275.000 euro.	(A Ferrari) costs 275,000 euros.
Quanti anni hai?	How old are you?	Ho venticinque anni.	I'm 25.
Quante persone vengono?	How many people are coming?	Vengono diciassette persone.	Seventeen people are coming.
Che cosa/Che/Cosa è questo?	What is this?	È un pesce.	It's a fish.
Che giorno è oggi?	What day is today?	(Oggi) È sabato.	(Today) is Saturday.
Dove vivi?	Where do you live?	(Vivo) A Fairfield.	(I live) in Fairfield.
Dov'è Piazza Garibaldi?	Where is Piazza Garibaldi?	È in centro.	It's downtown.
Dove sei?	Where are you?	(Sono) In macchina.	(I'm) in the car.
Di dove sei?	Where are you from?	(Sono di) Frosinone.	(I'm from) Frosinone.
Dove sono le chiavi?	Where are the keys?	(Le chiavi sono) Sul tavolo.	(The keys are) on the table.
Come stai?	How are you?	Sto benissimo, grazie! E tu?	I'm super, thanks! And you?
Come si dice *peach* in italiano?	How do you say peach in Italian?	Si dice pesca.	You say pesca.
Com'è il tuo uomo ideale?	What is your ideal man?	(Il mio uomo ideale) È onesto, moro, gentile, sportivo e intelligente.	(My ideal man) is honest, dark-haired, kind, athletic, and smart.
Come sei?	What are you like?	Sono bassa e pigra.	I'm short and lazy.
Come sono gli spaghetti?	How is the spaghetti?	(Gli spaghetti sono) Ottimi!	(The spaghetti is) great!
Quale dei due preferisci?	Which of the two do you prefer?	(Preferisco) Quello.	(I prefer) that one.
Qual è il tuo ristorante preferito?	What's your favorite restaurant?	(Il mio ristorante preferito è) La Ca' de Vèn.	(My favorite restaurant is) La Ca' de Vèn.
Quali sono i giorni della settimana?	What are the days of the week?	(I giorni della settimana sono) Lunedì, martedì. . .	(The days of the week are) Monday, Tuesday. . .

PRACTICE

You're getting to know someone new, but they don't want to get too personal. Answer the following questions using a complete sentence. I've modeled the response for you in the Answer Key.

Q. Chi è il tuo migliore amico? (*Who is your best friend* [m]?)

A. Il mio migliore amico è Gix. (*Gix is my best friend* [m].)

(1) Dove abiti?

(2) Quanti anni hai?

(3) Chi è la tua migliore amica?

(4) Di dove sei?

(5) Che lavoro fai?

(6) Che cosa fai per le vacanze?

(7) Che giorno è oggi?

(8) Qual è il tuo cibo italiano preferito?

(9) Che cosa fai nel tempo libero?

(10) Come si chiama la tua mamma?

(11) Dove vai stasera?

(12) Quante volte hai visitato l'Italia?

Fill in the blank in these questions with the interrogative that makes the most sense. Table 11-1 gives you the interrogatives you need.

PRACTICE

Q. _____ ti chiami?

A. **Come ti chiami?** (*What's your name?*)

(13) _____ il tuo numero di telefono?

(14) Di _____ sei?

(15) _____ abiti?

(16) _____ anni hai?

(17) _____ studi? (what)

(18) Con _____ abiti?

(19) _____ lingue parli?

(20) _____ fai nel tempo libero?

(21) _____ stai?

(22) _____ non vieni all amia festa?

Pointing to Something with Questo and Quello

The demonstrative adjectives and pronouns **questo** (*this/these*) or **quello** (*that/those*) are versatile words that you use to point to people, things, and situations. You can use them to ask questions and to point things out.

You can use them as adjectives or pronouns:

>> **Adjectives:** When you add a noun after **questo** or **quello**

>> **Pronouns:** When they refer to a noun, name, or pronoun that you've already mentioned

When you use either **questo** or **quello**, make it agree in gender and number with the person or thing to which it refers.

Questo (this/these)

Questo (*this/these*) acts like an adjective that has four possible endings, but it actually has five forms. Use **quest'** in front of a singular noun beginning with a vowel.

m sing.	questo (this)
f sing.	questa (this)
m pl.	questi (these)
f pl.	queste (these)
m/f sing. with noun beginning with vowel	quest' (this)

Here are a couple of example sentences:

Questo cantante è fantastico! (*This singer is fantastic!*)

Prendo questi stivali. (*I'm going to take these boots.*)

As a pronoun, **questo** replaces the noun as well, while agreeing with it. It has four forms: **questo, questa, questi,** and **queste.** For example: **"Quali stivali prendi?" "Prendo questi."** (*"What boots are you getting?" "I'm getting these."*)

You can add an adjective to **questo** instead of repeating a noun and an adjective.

Provide the correct form of **questo** in the following sentences.

PRACTICE

Q. _____ lasagne sono deliziose!

A. **Queste lasagne sono deliziose!** (*This lasagna is delicious!*) (**Lasagne** is almost always plural in Italian.)

23 _____ è mia madre.

24 _____ studenti sono molto bravi.

25 Chi è _____ studente? Chi sono _____ ragazze?

26 Che cos'è _____? (_What's this?_)

27 Purtroppo, _____ albero è morto.

Quello (that/those)

Quello (_that/those_) has seven forms when preceding a noun, which correspond to the seven definite articles when combined with a preposition (which you can read about in Chapter 9). The **quello** you use should agree in number and gender with the noun.

The following table gives the forms for **quello** when used as a demonstrative adjective.

that	quel
that	quello
that	quell'
that	quella
those	quei
those	quegli
those	quelle

Take a look at a couple of examples:

> **Quanto è alto quell'edificio.** (_That building is so tall._)

> **Mi porti quei giornali, per favore**? (_Will you bring me those newspapers please?_)

When acting as a pronoun, **quello** behaves like the adjectives that have four endings: It agrees in number and gender with whatever it's substituting.

m sing.	quello (that)
f sing.	quella (that)
m pl.	quelli (those)
f pl.	quelle (those)

REMEMBER

You use the form **quelli** (_those ones/those who_) only as a pronoun.

> **Quelli non vogliono pagare il conto.** (_Those_ [people] _don't want to pay the bill._)

When you refer to a group of only females, you use **quelle** (_those ones_), which is the plural of **quella**.

Similar to **questo**, you can add an adjective instead of repeating a noun and an adjective.

> **"Vuoi la giacca blu o quella verde?"** ("Do you want the blue or the green jacket?")
>
> **"Quella verde."** (*The green one."*)

This practice is a quick check of your understanding of the demonstrative **quello**. Fill in the blanks with one of the seven forms.

Q.   Di chi è _____ cane?

A.   Di chi è quel cane? (*Whose dog is that?*)

28   Chi è _____ uomo?

29   Chi è _____ bell'uomo?

30   È tuo_____ zaino?

31   Come sono belli _____ ravioli.

32   _____ amica è una buon'amica.

Answers to "Asking with Interrogatives; Pointing Out with Demonstratives" Practice Questions

1. **Dove abiti?** (*Where do you live?*) **Abito a Ravenna.** (*I live in Ravenna.*)

2. **Quanti anni hai?** (*How old are you?*) **Ho sessantaquattro anni.** (*I am 64 years old.*)

3. **Chi è la tua migliore amica?** (*Who is you best friend?*) **La mia migliore amica è Barbara.** (*My best friend is Barbara.*)

4. **Di dove sei?** (*Where are you from?*) **Sono di Parma.** (*I'm from Parma.*)

5. **Che lavoro fai?** (*What job do you do?*) **Faccio l'impiegato./Faccio l'insegnante.** (*I'm a clerk./I'm a teacher.*)

6. **Che cosa fai per la vacanza?** (*What do you do for vacation?*) **Vado al mare./Vado a sciare.** (*I go to the beach./I go skiing.*)

7. **Che giorno è oggi?** (*What day is today?*) **Oggi è lunedì.** (*Today is Monday.*)

8. **Qual è il tuo cibo italiano preferito?** (*What is your favorite Italian food?*) **Il mio cibo italiano preferito è la pizza.** (*My favorite Italian food is pizza.*)

9. **Che cosa fai nel tempo libero?** (*What do you do in your spare time?*) **Nel tempo libero gioco a ping pong.** (*In my spare time I play table tennis.*)

10. **Come si chiama la tua mamma?** (*What is your mom's name?*) **La mia mamma si chiama Rosa.** (*My mom's name is Rosa.*)

11. **Dove vai stasera?** (*Where are you going tonight?*) **Stasera vado al cinema.** (*I'm going to the movies tonight.*)

12. **Quante volte hai visitato l'Italia?** (*How many times have you visited Italy?*) **Ho visitato l'Italia dodici volte.** (*I have visited Italy 12 times.*)

13. **Qual è; Qual è il tuo numero di telefono?** (*What's your telephone number?*)

14. **dove; Di dove sei?** (*Where are you from?*)

15. **Dove; Dove abiti?** (*Where do you live?*)

16. **Quanti; Quanti anni hai?** (*How old are you?*)

17. **Che cosa; Che cosa studi?** (*What do you study?*)

18. **chi; Con chi abiti?** (*Who do you live with?*)

19. **Quali/quante; Quali/quante lingue parli?** (*What/How many languages do you speak?*)

20. **Che cosa; Che cosa fai nel tempo libero?** (*What do you do in your free time?*)

21. **Come; Come stai?** (*How are you?*)

22 **Perché; Perché non vieni alla mia festa?** (*Why don't you come to my party?*)

23 **Questa; Questa è mia madre.** (*This is my mother.*)

24 **Questi; Questi studenti sono molto bravi.** (*These students are very good.*)

25 **questo, queste; Chi è questo studente?** (*Who is this student?*) **Chi sono queste ragazze?** (*Who are these girls?*)

26 **questo; Che cos'è questo?** (*What's this?*)

27 **quest'; Purtroppo, quest'albero è morto.** (*Unfortunately, this tree is dead.*)

28 **quell'; Chi è quell' uomo?** (*Who is that man?*)

29 **quel; Chi è quel bell'uomo?** (*Who is that handsome man?*)

30 **quello; È tuo quello zaino?** (*Is that backpack yours?*)

31 **quei; Come sono belli quei ravioli.** (*How beautiful these ravioli are.*)

32 **Quell'; Quell'amica è una buon'amica.** (*That friend is a good friend.*)

4

More Verb Tenses

Incorporate the past in your speaking and writing by using two important tenses, the **passato prossimo** and the **imperfetto**, and figure out when to use which.

Look ahead and find out how to use the simple form and the compound form of the future tense.

Get a little bossy, using formal and informal commands with the imperative.

Express yourself with the present conditional and past conditional tense.

Explore reflexive verbs across most of the tenses that you can encounter in this book (as well as reflexive pronouns) and incorporate them in your daily routine.

Chapter **12**

Glancing Back at the Past: The Passato Prossimo

n Italian, when you talk or write about the past, you mostly use the present perfect tense, or **passato prossimo** (literally, *near past*), which is the term I use in this book. For example, the sentence **Sono andata a casa** (*I went home*) is in the **passato prossimo**. When you talk or write about the past in English you use the simple past, which is similar. You say *I went home*, no matter whether you went home two minutes ago or two months ago.

Italian has two other past forms: the **imperfetto** (*imperfect*) and the **passato remote** (known as the preterit in English). In this chapter, I focus on the **passato prossimo**, which is the most common past tense form. In Chapter 13, I cover the **imperfetto**. I don't include the **passato remoto**, which is used primarily in historical narratives, because it lies outside the scope of this book.

The most important thing you need to know about the **passato prossimo** is that it's a compound tense, which means that it always has two parts.

an auxiliary (or helping) verb + a past participle

More specifically, you form the **passato prossimo** with

> **avere** (*to have*) or **essere** (*to be*) + past participle

In other words, the **passato prossimo** is made of the present indicative of either **avere** or **essere**, plus the past participle of the main verb.

> **Ho mangiato il gelato** (*I ate the ice cream*).

See Chapter 4 for **avere** and **essere** in the present tense.

Turning a Verb into a Past Participle

Words such as **amato** (*loved*), **andato** (*gone*), **tenuto** (*kept*), **visto** (*seen*), and **studiato** (*studied*) are past participles. They're forms of the verbs used in several compound tenses.

Forming the past participle of regular verbs

When it comes to the past participle, most verbs — even those that are irregular in other tenses — form the past participle according to the rules that I spell out in this section.

To form a regular past participle, follow these steps.

1. **Take the infinitive of the verb.**

   For example, **parlare** (*to speak*), **vedere** (*to see*), **dormire** (*to sleep*)

2. **Cut the infinitive at its stem.**

   parl–, **ved–**, **dorm–**.

3. **Add the appropriate ending.**

   For **–are** verbs, use **–ato**; for **–ere** verbs, use **–uto**; and for **–ire** verbs, use **–ito**.

   parlato (*spoke/spoken*), **veduto** (*saw/seen*), **dormito** (*slept/slept*).

TIP

The past participle of the verb **fare** (*to do/to make*) keeps only the **f–** of the infinitive and doubles the **–t–** to become **fatto**. In that case, it's a little bit irregular. When answering a question, such as in the following example, you don't need **fatto** in your response.

> **"Cosa hai fatto ieri sera?"** (*"What did you do last night?"*)

> **"Ieri sera sono andata a cena al mare con gli amici."** (*"Last night, I went to dinner at the beach with my friends."*)

The past participle of the verb **dare** (*to give*) is quite regular: It keeps the **d–** and becomes **dato**.

> **Hai dato i soldi alla mamma?** (*Did you give mom the money?/Did you give the money to mom?*)

Forming the past participle of irregular verbs

Even with irregular verbs, the endings of the past participles never change. But the stem of the verb does change, in most cases losing some letters — really, it contracts.

Irregular -ere verbs

Most irregular past participles are in the conjugation of **-ere** verbs. Most of them form the past participle by contracting the infinitive before adding the endings. For example, **rimanere** (*to stay*) drops **-nere** and becomes **rimasto**. **Dipingere** (*to paint*) drops the **-gere** and becomes **dipinto**.

Table 12-1 lists the most common irregular verbs ending in **-ere**. As you go through the table, look for patterns in these irregular past participles that you can easily remember. If that doesn't work, learn them by heart when you encounter them by drilling with them on a site such as Quizlet or by creating your own flashcards (and check a dictionary when in doubt).

Table 12-1   The Irregular Past Participle of Verbs Ending in -ere

Infinitive	Past Participle	Infinitive	Past Participle
accendere (*to light/to turn on*)	**acceso** (*lighted/turned on*)	**nascere** (*to be born/to rise*)	**nato** (*born*)
nascondere (*to hide*)	**nascosto** (*hid*)	**bere** (*to drink*)	**bevuto** (*drunk*)
perdere (*to lose*)	**perduto/perso** (*lost*)	**chiedere** (*to ask*)	**chiesto** (*asked*)
piangere (*to cry*)	**pianto** (*cried*)	**chiudere** (*to close*)	**chiuso** (*closed*)
prendere (*to take*)	**preso** (*taken*)	**rispondere** (*to answer*)	**risposto** (*answered*)
correre (*to run*)	**corso** (*ran*)	**scegliere** (*to choose*)	**scelto** (*chose*)
cuocere (*to cook*)	**cotto** (*cooked*)	**scendere** (*to go down*)	**sceso** (*went down*)
discutere (*to discuss*)	**discusso** (*discussed*)	**scrivere** (*to write*)	**scritto** (*written*)
dividere (*to divide*)	**diviso** (*divided*)	**spegnere** (*to extinguish*)	**spento** (*extinguished*)
fingere (*to pretend*)	**finto** (*pretended*)	**spingere** (*to push*)	**spinto** (*pushed*)
leggere (*to read*)	**letto** (*read*)	**vedere** (*to see*)	**veduto/visto** (*seen*)
mettere (*to put*)	**messo** (*put*)	**vincere** (*to win*)	**vinto** (*won*)
vivere (*to live*)	**vissuto** (*lived*)	**piacere** (*to like*)	**piaciuto** (*liked*)
rimanere (*to stay*)	**rimasto** (*stayed*)	**dipingere** (*to paint*)	**dipinto** (*painted*)

REMEMBER

Verbs formed by adding prefixes to the main verb take the same ending as the basic verb when it comes to the past participle. So **rompere** (*to break*) becomes **rotto** (*broken*), and **corrompere** (*to corrupt*) becomes **corrotto** (*corrupted*).

Most verbs ending in **-scere** add an **i** before the past participle ending in order to preserve the soft (shh) sound of the infinitive. For example, **conoscere** (*to know*) becomes **conosciuto** (*known*), and **crescere** (*to grow/to raise*) becomes **cresciuto** (*grown/raised*). But not **nascere** (*to be born*), which is **nato** (*born*).

Verbs ending in –**cere**, like **piacere** (*to like*), also take an i before adding the past participle ending, in order to keep a *ch* sound, as in **piaciuto** (*liked*).

Irregular –ire verbs

A few verbs that end in –**ire** are irregular. They behave similarly to the verbs that drop pieces of the infinitive before adding the endings of the past participle. Table 12-2 lists the most important irregular –**ire** verbs.

Table 12-2   Irregular Verbs Ending in –ire

Infinitive	Past Participle
apparire (*to appear*)	**apparso** (*appeared*)
aprire (*to open*)	**aperto** (*opened*)
dire (*to say*)	**detto** (*said*)
morire (*to die*)	**morto** (*died*)
offrire (*to offer*)	**offerto** (*offered*)
soffrire (*to suffer*)	**sofferto** (*suffered*)
venire (*to come*)	**venuto** (*came*)

Form the regular or irregular past participle of the following verbs in the default masculine singular form. (I put an asterisk at the end of the irregular ones for this first practice exercise.)

PRACTICE

Q. guardare

A. guardato

1   mangiare: _____

2   vincere*: _____

3   perdere*: _____ (+ regular form)

4   venire*: _____

5   ripetere: _____

6   visitare: _____

7   dormire: _____

8   dire*: _____

9   vedere*: _____ (+ regular form)

10   stare: _____

(11) aprire*: _____

(12) chiudere*: _____

(13) prendere*: _____

Figuring Out Which Auxiliary to Use

When you want to form any compound tense that requires the past participle, you need to choose between the auxiliaries **avere** and **essere**.

In order to form the **passato prossimo** of a particular verb, you need to follow these steps:

1. **Choose an auxiliary verb.**

   You use either **avere** (*to have*) or **essere** (*to be*), depending on whether the verb is transitive or intransitive.

2. **Change the verb's infinitive into a past participle.**

   Check out the sections on forming past participles earlier in this chapter, for details on making that change.

3. **Choose the ending of the past participle.**

   The past participle takes an **o** ending with the **avere** (or transitive) verbs.

   With **essere** (or intransitive) verbs the past participle must agree in gender and number with the subject of the sentence, and therefore have four endings **o, a, i, e** (just like the adjectives that have four endings, which I talk about in Chapter 7).

Looking at transitive versus intransitive

The distinction between transitive (**avere**) and intransitive (**essere**) verbs is clear-cut in Italian.

When a verb may be followed directly by the direct object, it's transitive.

> **Ho suonato il pianoforte per un'ora.** (*I played the piano for an hour.*).

So, *transitive* means that the verb's action may be transferred to an object directly, without adding any other part of speech (in particular, a preposition).

When you have a preposition plus a person, the noun is an *indirect object*. For example, in the sentence **Ho scritto a Mirko** (*I wrote to Mirko*), **a Mirko** is the indirect object. The direct object — what you wrote — is implied, but doesn't have to be present in order for the verb to be transitive.

Intransitive verbs may take a preposition, but the preposition is usually coupled with a place.

Sono andata in ufficio. (*I went to the office.*)

REMEMBER

A direct object can follow a transitive verb, but it can't follow an intransitive verb. But you can use a transitive verb by itself, without expressing the object.

Le ho scritto (*I wrote to her./I've written to her./I did write to her.*)

And you can use an intransitive verb by itself, without a preposition.

Sono arrivata! (*I've arrived!/I'm here!*)

When in doubt, any Italian dictionary can tell you whether the verb is transitive (v. tr.) or intransitive (v. intr.).

Using avere in the passato prossimo

To create the **passato prossimo** with **avere** (*to have*), you need its present tense: **ho, hai, ha, abbiamo, avete, hanno** + the past participle

Use this structure:

Avere + the past participle of a transitive verb

REMEMBER

For the purposes of this book, the past participle of transitive verbs ends in **o**. In Italian, a direct object pronoun can change the ending of the past participle. I don't want you to worry about that now because keeping the **o** ending in mind can help you differentiate and navigate between the transitive and intransitive verbs.

TIP

Transitive verbs may take a direct object. Direct objects always answer the questions who? or what?

A few intransitive verbs, such as **dormire** (*to sleep*), **pranzare/cenare** (*to dine*), **parlare** (*to speak*), and **telefonare** (*to phone*) always take **avere**.

Ho dormito poco. (*I slept very little.*)

The following table lists some common expressions that use the **passato prossimo**.

Expression that Uses the Passato Prossimo	Translation	Examples
Ieri	*yesterday*	
ieri sera	*yesterday evening*	
fa	*ago*	**due settimane fa** (*two weeks ago*), **due giorni fa** (*two days ago*), **due ore fa** (*two hours ago*), **due anni fa** (*two years ago*), **due mesi fa** (*two months ago*)
scorso/a/i/e	*last*	**la settimana scorsa** (*last week*), **l'anno scorso** (*last year*), **il mese scorso** (*last month*)

PRACTICE

Practice your understanding of transitive verbs in the **passato prossimo** by conjugating the infinitives in parentheses. You need both parts: the auxiliary **avere** (*to have*) + the past participle, which ends in **o**.

Q. Buongiorno! _____ bene? (**dormire, tu**).

A. Buongiorno! **Hai dormito bene?** (*Good morning! Did you sleep well?*)

14 Egidio _____ le lasagne ieri sera. (preparare)

15 Eva e Stefania _____ un cappuccino al bar stamattina. (prendere)

16 Bruno, che cosa _____ sabato scorso? (fare)

17 Io non _____ il miele nel tè oggi. (mettere)

18 Liliana ed io _____ il nostro libro due giorni fa! (perdere)

19 Tu ed Elena _____ Catcher in the Rye nella classe d'inglese sei mesi fa. (leggere)

20 Massimo e Carlo _____ la partita di calcio la settimana scorsa. (vincere)

21 Silvia _____ molta acqua ieri. (bere)

22 Amelia, _____ tuo padre oggi? (vedere)

Using essere in the passato prossimo

You need the auxiliary **essere** (*to be*) with intransitive verbs.

> **essere** (in the present tense) + the past participle

DIFFERENCES

The main difference between using **essere** and **avere** verbs in the **passato prossimo** lies in the ending of the past participle. The preceding section shows you that transitive (**avere**) verbs in the **passato prossimo** end in **o**. The past participles that use intransitive (**essere**) verbs must agree in gender and number with the subject. They function like adjectives and have one of four endings: **o, a, i, e**.

> **Io** (f) **sono andata dal dentista.** (*I went to the dentist.*)

I review the structure for intransitive verbs in the **passato prossimo** in Table 12-3, using the very common intransitive verb **arrivare** (*to arrive*). Note that the endings of the first three persons are singular, and the endings for the plural persons are, well, plural.

Table 12-3   Intransitive Verbs in the Passato Prossimo

Form of essere	Passato Prossimo of arrivare (agrees with subject)	Example
sono	arrivata/o	**Sono** (f) **arrivata alle 5:00.** *I arrived at 5:00.*
sei	arrivata/o	**Sauro** (m), **a che ora sei arrivato?** *Sauro, what time did you arrive?*
è	arrivata/o	**Danila** (f) **è arrivata in anticipo.** *Danila arrived early.*
siamo	arrivate/i	**Siamo** (m) **arrivate insieme.** (*We arrived together.*)
siete	arrivate/i	**Siete** (f) **arrivati troppo tardi.** (*You all arrived/got here too late.*)
sono	arrivate/i	**Sono** (m) **arrivate in orario.** (*They arrived on time.*)

Here is a list of common intransitive verbs, verbs that take **essere**. I provide you with the irregular past participles:

- **venire venuto/a/i/e** *(to come)*
- **arrivare** *(to arrive)*
- **andare** *(to go)*
- **stare** *(to be/to stay)*
- **essere stato/a/i/e** *(to be)*
- **restare** *(to stay)*
- **rimanere rimasto/a/i/e** *(to remain)*
- **diventare** *(to become)*
- **morire morto/a/i/e** *(to die)*
- **nascere nato/a/i/e** *(to be born)*
- **ritornare** *(to return)*
- **partire** *(to leave/to depart)*
- **uscire** *(to go out)*
- **salire** *(to go up)*
- **scendere sceso/a/i/e** *(to go down)*
- **cadere** *(to fall)*

The following shows some very common usages of intransitive (**essere**) verbs:

- **stare** (*to stay/to be* in set phrases, such as **stare bene/male** [*to be well/unwell*]), takes the same past participle as **essere: stato, stata, stati, state** (*stayed/felt*).

  Lucio è stato male. (*Lucio was ill.*)

- Most verbs of motion, used literally or metaphorically.

  Siamo arrivati a Hong Kong. (*We arrived at Hong Kong.*)

  Il dollaro è sceso rispetto all'euro. (*The dollar has fallen against the euro.*)

- Verbs conveying a change of status in the subject, such as **invecchiare** (*to age*), **nascere** (*to be born*), **crescere** (*to grow up*), and **morire** (*to die*).

  Mio padre è nato nel 1963. (*My father was born in 1963.*)

- All reflexive verbs, such as **svegliarsi** (*to wake up*) and **rompersi** (to break). See Chapter 17 for more on reflexive verbs.

  Mi sono svegliato. (*I woke up.*)

- **Mi sono rotto un dito.** (*I broke my finger.*)

Provide the past participles for these very common intransitive **essere** verbs.

PRACTICE

Q: rimanere

A: rimasto/a/i/e

23. venire

24. nascere

25. salire

26. partire

27. (ri)tornare

28. essere

29. stare

30. morire

31. scendere

32. andare

33. uscire

34. diventare

Now, conjugate the verbs in the **passato prossimo**. I've put an asterisk near the infinitives that have irregular past participles (so do look them up if you need to). *Remember:* The past participle has four endings (**o, a, i, e**).

PRACTICE

Q. Giancarlo e Francesca _____ dall'aereo. (scendere)

A. Giancarlo e Francesca sono scesi dall'aereo. (*Giancarlo and Francesca got off the plane.*)

35. Antonio e Margherita _____ in Porto Rico per le vacanze. (andare)

36. Chiara _____ per la festa alle 8:00 di sera. (partire)

37. Owen, a che ora _____ a scuola oggi? (venire)*

38. Olivia e Maria Caterina non _____ sabato sera. (uscire)

39. Mio nonno _____ 30 anni fa. (morire)*

40 Ragazzi, quando _____? (nascere)*

41 La settimana scorsa Sophia ed io _____ a casa tutta la sera. (rimanere)*

42 La gatta _____ dalla finestra! (cadere)

43 Tu (m) e tua sorella _____ alti questo anno! (diventare)

44 9 mesi fa, i nuovi studenti _____ (arrivare) all'università.

Using piacere

Because **piacere** is such a common verb, it deserves its own section in this chapter. You can see how the verb **piacere** (*to like*) works in the present in Chapter 6.

REMEMBER

Piacere takes **essere** in the **passato prossimo**. Also, **piacere** always uses indirect object pronouns (not the subject pronouns), or, when you have a proper noun, you need to precede that subject with the preposition **a** (to): so you always write it as **a** + a proper noun + third person singular or third person plural form of **piacere**.

> **A Maria piace Pepe.** (*Maria likes Pepe.*)
>
> **Le piace Pepe.** (*She likes Pepe*; literally, *Pepe is pleasing to her.*)

TIP

Piacere aways agrees with what's being liked.

Table 12-4 illustrates piacere.

Table 12-4 Piacere in the Present and the Passato Prossimo

Presente Singular and Present Plural	Passato Prossimo Singular and Plural
piace	
Mi piace la pizza. (*I like pizza.*)	**Mi è piaciuta la pizza.** (*I liked the pizza.*) **piaciuta** here has to agree with **pizza**.
Piacciono	
Mi piacciono le fragole. (*I like strawberries.*)	**Mi sono piaciute le fragole.** (*I liked the strawberries.*) **piaciute** here agrees with **fragole**.

Here is another way of visualizing **piacere** in the **passato prossimo**. Use the indirect object pronoun (or indirect object) + third person of the verb **essere** and make the form of piacere agree with what's being liked.

> indirect object pronoun + **essere** + **piaciuto/piaciuta/piaciuti/piaciute**

mi _____ è	piaciuto
mi	piaciuta
ti	
gli/le	
ci	
vi	
gli/loro	
_____ sono mi	piaciuti
ti	piaciute
gli/le	
ci	
vi	
gli/loro	

PRACTICE

Complete the sentences by conjugating the verb **piacere** in the **passato prossimo**. First add the indirect object pronouns.

Q. (io) _____ il film.

A. **Mi è piaciuto il film.** (*I liked the film*)

45 (io) _____ la pizza.

46 (tu) _____ il gelato?

47 (lei) _____ gli spaghetti alla carbonara.

48 (lui) _____ le melanzane alla parmigiana.

49 (noi) _____ vedere il film Cinema Paradiso.

50 (voi) _____ il film?

Expanding meaning with adverbs

You use some essential adverbs frequently in the present tense and **passato prossimo**. For a more complete discussion of adverbs, see Chapter 7.

Many adverbs, such as **bene** (*well*) always follow the verb.

> **Mangi bene a casa?** *Do you eat well at home?*
>
> **Hai mangiato bene a casa?** *Did you eat well at home?*

Exceptions to the general rule about adverbs following the verb include these simple and compound adverbs:

>> **appena** (*just*)

>> **ancora** (*yet/still*)

>> **già** (*already*)

>> **sempre** (*always*)

>> **mai** (*ever*)

>> **non . . . mai** (*never*)

>> **non . . . ancora** (*not yet*)

>> **non . . . più** (*no more/no longer*)

The following guidelines explain where to place these exceptions:

>> If you have a compound verb composed of an auxiliary and a past participle, place the simple adverbs listed previously between the auxiliary and the past participle.

Il bambino ha già mangiato. (*The child has already eaten.*)

Sei mai stato in Italia? (*Have you ever been to Italy?*)

>> If the verb is in a compound tense, such as the **passato prossimo**, place the second word of the adverb between the two verbs.

Non ho <u>ancora</u> mangiato il dolce. (*I haven't eaten dessert yet.*)

PRACTICE Translate the following sentences by using the adverbs listed in this section.

Q. Hai mai visitato Ravello?

A. *Have you ever visited Ravello?*

51 Tu hai già fatto il compito?

52 Mia figlia non ha mai visitato Lecce.

53 Hai visto Susanna? Non l'ho più vista.

54 Non abbiamo ancora mangiato l'anguilla.

55 I miei sono sempre venuti per Natale.

Answers to "Glancing Back at the Past: The Passato Prossimo" Practice Questions

1. mangiato

2. vissuto

3. perduto/perso

4. venuto

5. ripetuto

6. visitato

7. dormito

8. detto

9. veduto/visto

10. stato

11. aperto

12. chiuso

13. preso

14. ha preparato; Egidio ha preparato le lasagne ieri sera. (*Egidio prepared lasagna last night*).

15. hanno preso; Eva e Stefania hanno preso un cappuccino al bar stamattina. (*Eva and Stefania had a cappuccino at the bar this morning.*)

16. hai fatto; Bruno, che cosa hai fatto sabato scorso? (*Bruno, what did you do last Saturday?*)

17. ho messo; Io non ho messo il miele nel tè oggi. (*I didn't put honey in my tea today.*)

18. abbiamo perduto/abbiamo perso; Liliana ed io abbiamo perduto/abbiamo perso il nostro libro due giorni fa! (*Liliana and I lost our book two days ago.*)

19. avete letto; Tu ed Elena avete letto Catcher in the Rye nella classe d'inglese sei mesi fa. (*You and Elena read* Catcher in the Rye *in English class six months ago.*)

20. hanno vinto; Massimo e Carlo hanno vinto la partita di calcio la settimana scorsa. (*Massimo and Carlo won the soccer game last week.*)

21. ha bevuto; Silvia ha bevuto molta acqua ieri. (*Silvia drank a lot of water yesterday.*)

22. hai visto/hai veduto; Amelia, hai visto/hai veduto tuo padre oggi? (*Amelia, have you seen your father today?*)

23. venuto/a/i/e

24. nato/a/i/e

25. salito/a/i/e

26. partito/a/i/e

27. tornato/a/i/e

28. stato/a/i/e

29. stato/a/i/e

30. morto/a/i/e

31. sceso/a/i/e

32. andato/a/i/e

33. uscito/a/i/e

34. diventato/a/i/e

35. sono andati; Antonio e Margherita sono andati in Porto Rico per le vacanze. (*Antonio and Margherita went to Puerto Rico during the vacation.*)

36. è partita; Chiara è partita per la festa alle 8:00 di sera. (*Chiara left for the party at eight in the evening.*)

37. sei venuto; Owen, a che ora sei venuto a scuola oggi? (*Owen, what time did you come to school today?*)

38. sono uscite; Olivia e Maria Caterina non sono uscite sabato sera. (*Olivia and Maria Caterina didn't go out on Saturday evening.*)

39. è morto; Mio nonno è morto 30 anni fa. (*My grandfather died thirty years ago.*)

40. siete nati; Ragazzi, quando siete nati? (*Folks, when were you born?*)

41. siamo rimasti; La settimana scorsa Sophia ed io siamo rimasti a casa tutta la sera. (*Last week, Sophia and I stayed home all evening.*)

42. è caduta; La gatta è caduta dalla finestra! (*The cat fell out of the window!*)

43. siete diventati; Tu e tua sorella siete diventati alti questo anno! (*You and your sister have gotten tall this year!*)

44. sono arrivati; 9 mesi fa, i nuovi studenti sono arrivati all'università. (*9 months ago, the new students arrived at the university.*)

45. Mi è piaciuta la pizza! (*I liked the pizza!*)

46. Ti è piaciuto il gelato? (*Did you like the icecream?*)

47. Le sono piaciuti gli spaghetti alla carbonara. (*She liked the spghetti alla carbonara.*)

48. Gli sono piaciute le melanzane alla parmigiana. (*We liked the eggplant alla parmigiana.*)

49. Ci è piaciuto vedere il film Cinema Paradiso. (*We liked seeing the film Cinema Paradiso.*)

50. Vi è piaciuto il film? (*Did you like the film?*)

(51) *Have you already done your homework?*

(52) *My daughter has never visited Lecce.*

(53) *Have you seen Susanna? I haven't seen her anymore.*

(54) *We haven't eaten the eel yet.*

(55) *My parents have always come for Christmas.*

Chapter **13**

Once Upon a Time: The Imperfect

The imperfect is a common past tense used to describe something that lasted for a while; to narrate things in the past, such as fairy tales; and to refer to physical or emotional states of being in the past.

Quando Mariapaola era giovane, andava ogni weekend a ballare. (*When Mariapaola was young, she went/used to go/would go dancing every weekend.*)

In English you can convey an imperfect action in the past with the formula *used to* + infinitive. (Please refer to Chapter 12 for the other common past tense, the **passato prossimo**.)

The imperfect is a simple tense. Although you encounter regular and irregular verbs, fortunately, the imperfect doesn't have many irregularities. I outline the major ones in this chapter. I also give you some guidelines on how to choose between the **passato prossimo** (present perfect tense) and the imperfect.

You can also find discussion of when to use the imperfect progressive (yes, Italian has that one, too), rather than the imperfect. And I mention the **trapassato prossimo** (past perfect tense), which you use when two things occurred in the past, but one is closer to you in time than the other.

Knowing When to Use the Imperfect

Because the imperfect allows you to talk about things that occurred over an indeterminate period of time in the past, you can use it to express ongoing states, such as feelings, emotions, physical attributes, states of affairs, and habits. Here are some situations that you can use as guidelines for choosing the imperfect over another past tense. You employ the imperfect tense to talk about

>> Conditions and states of being: **Quando ero bambino ero felice.** (*When I was a child, I was happy.*)

>> Physical descriptions: **Mia sorella era alta e aveva i capelli lunghi.** (*My sister was tall and had long hair.*)

>> Interrupted actions in the past: **Quando suo fratello ha telefonato, Ada scriveva una lettera.** (*When her brother called, Ada was writing a letter.*)

   The first verb, **ha telefonato** is in the **passato prossimo**: It interrupts an ongoing action (**scriveva**), which is in the imperfect.

>> Two ongoing contemporaneous actions in the past: **Ieri sera, Robert guardava la partita mentre Giancarla giocava con Nico.** (*Last night, Robert was watching the game while Giancarlo was playing with Nico.*)

>> Habitual activities: **Quando ero bambino, passavo sempre l'estate in montagna.** (*When I was a child, I used to spend/I would always spend the summer in the mountains.*)

>> Age in the past: **Mio padre aveva quindici anni quando è venuto negli Stati Uniti.** (*My dad was 15 years old when he came to the United States.*)

>> Desires/wishes in the past: Use the verbs **volere** (*to want*), **desiderare** (*to desire/to wish*), **sperare** (*to hope*, **amare** (*to love*), **piacere** (*to like*). **Da piccola volevo/desideravo diventare veterinaria.** (*When I was little I wanted to/I wished to become a veterinarian.*) **Anzi, amavo tutti gli animal**i. (*Actually, I loved all animals.*) **Mi piacevano tanto I cavalli.** (*I used to like horses a lot.*)

DISCOVER THE PAST THROUGH LYRIC, VERSE, AND TALE

If you like to experience the language holistically and in context, while also hearing and speaking it, treat yourself to the following.:

- Songs: **"La Gatta," Gino Paoli; "Come una pietra scalciata," Articolo 31**

- Poetry: **"La cavalla storna," Giovanni Pascoli**

- Fairy Tales: **"Cappuccetto Rosso," "Cenerentola," "L'omino di Pan di zenzero"**

Forming the Imperfect

Luckily for you, the imperfect is a very regular tense, even for verbs that are irregular in other tenses. And even with the few verbs that are irregular in the imperfect, what changes is the stem of the verb; the endings are always the same. In the following sections, I start by showing you the endings, and then I move on to the few irregularities you may encounter.

Adding endings to regular verbs

Italian has three conjugations, for which the endings are **–are**, **–ere**, and **–ire**. To form the imperfect, you add endings to the stem of the verb, which you get by dropping the infinitive ending. So the stem of **guardare** (*to look at/to watch*) is **guard–**, of **leggere** (*to read*) is **legg–**, and of **sentire** (*to hear*) is **sent–**. The endings that you apply for the imperfect vary depending on the verb's conjugation. I list the endings in Table 13-1 and then provide a sample conjugation.

Table 13-1   Endings of the Imperfect

Person	–are Verbs	–ere Verbs	–ire Verbs
io	–avo	–evo	–ivo
tu	–avi	–evi	–ivi
lui/lei/Lei	–ava	–eva	–iva
noi	–avamo	–evamo	–ivamo
voi	–avate	–evate	–ivate
loro/Loro	–avano	–evano	–ivano

TIP

Drill with the endings a few times, by either repeating them to yourself or writing them out, to help them sink in, even before you conjugate the verbs.

guardare (to watch/to look at)	
io guardavo	noi guardavamo
tu guardavi	voi guardavate
lui/lei/Lei guardava	loro/Loro guardavano

Loro guardavano un film. (*They were watching a movie.*)

REMEMBER

The auxiliary verb **avere** (*to have*) — as well as the modal auxiliaries **dovere** (*must/shall/to have to*), **potere** (*can/may*), **volere** (*will/want*), and **sapere** (*to know how to*), which usually are followed by a verb in the infinitive, form the imperfect regularly, but in other tenses, they're irregular. Their meaning alters slightly in the imperfect. The following list shows the meaning and usage of the modal auxiliaries in the imperfect tense. I provide them in the first-person singular, but you have to choose the appropriate person (first, second, or third-person singular or plural) when you use them.

>> **Dovevo** (*had to*): Conveys necessity, need, or obligation.

Dovevano parlare con Sandro prima di partire. (*They had to talk to Sandro before leaving.*)

>> **Potevo** (*could/was able to/was capable of*): Conveys capacity, power, or permission

Poteva lavorare solo due ore al giorno. (*She could work only two hours a day.*)

>> **Volevo** (*wanted to*): Conveys intention or desire

I bambini volevano giocare a calcio. (*The children wanted to play soccer.*)

>> **Sapevo** (*could*): Conveys skill and ability

Sapeva giocare a golf. (*She could play golf./She knew how to play golf.*)

PRACTICE

Conjugate the following verbs in the imperfect in the person suggested for each entry.

Q. noi _____ (**partire**)

A. **noi partivamo** (*we were leaving*)

1. tu _____ (**andare**)

2. lui _____ (**avere**)

3. noi _____ (**parlare**)

4. voi _____ (**mangiare**)

5. le ragazze _____ (**capire**)

6. mio padre _____ (**leggere**)

7. loro _____ (**guardare**)

8. io _____ (**prendere**)

9. il cane_____ (**dormire**)

10. io _____ (**amare**)

A few scoundrels: Irregular verbs

As I say throughout this book, in most cases, you can't really find any criteria for recognizing irregular verbs. I list them for you in the following sections (and throughout the book), and you just have to learn them by heart (or consult a dictionary). The following sections cover irregular verbs in the imperfect.

Essere (to be): Always irregular

The verb **essere** (*to be*) is irregular in all moods and tenses. In the imperfect, it takes a special stem, **er–**, and adds some imperfect **–are** endings (even though, in the infinitive, it's an

–**ere** verb). This table shows you its conjugation. (Quite honestly, it's easier to show you than to explain!)

essere (to be)	
io ero	noi eravamo
tu eri	voi eravate
lui/lei/Lei era	loro/Loro erano

Io ero stanca. (*I was tired.*)

Piacere (to like): Uses the third person

The verb **piacere** (*to like*) is special in every tense. Use only the third-person singular (**piaceva**) and plural (**piacevano**) in the imperfect in this book. Please check out Chapter 6 and Chapter 12 for a more close-up look at this verb's peculiarities in the present tense and **passato prossimo**, including the indirect object pronouns that frequently accompany it. Here's a brief summary of the usage of piacere in the imperfect tense, plus examples:

>> Use **piaceva** if what was liked (or wasn't liked) is singular or expressed by a verb in the infinitive.

   Non mi piaceva il formaggio quando ero piccolo. (*I didn't like cheese when I was little.*)

   Mi piaceva visitare la mia amica Suzanne. (*I used to like to visit my friend Suzanne*).

>> Use **piacevano** if what was liked is plural.

   Mi piacevano molto i ravioli. (*I used to like ravioli a lot.*)

Verbs that take an expanded stem

Because of space limitations, I can't list all the verbs that take an expanded stem in the imperfect, so I give you the most common ones in Table 13-2, along with their modified stems. These few verbs add the regular endings of the imperfect of –**ere** verbs to the expanded stem (–**evo**, –**evi**, –**eva**, –**evamo**, –**evate**, –**evano**).

tradurre (to translate)	
io traducevo	noi traducevamo
tu traducevi	voi traducevate
lui/lei/Lei traduceva	loro/Loro traducevano

Noi traducevamo Dante. (*We were translating/We used to translate Dante.*)

fare (to do/to make)	
io facevo	noi facevamo
tu facevi	voi facevate
lui/lei/Lei faceva	loro/Loro facevano

Noi facevamo alpinismo da giovani. (*We used to go climbing when we were young.*)

Table 13-2   Verbs with an Expanded Stem

Infinitive	Expanded Stem for the Imperfect
bere (*to drink*)	**bev–**
tradurre (*to translate*)	**traduc–**
dire (*to say/to tell*)	**dic–**
fare (to do/to make)	**fac–**

Conjugate the verbs in parentheses with the requested form of the imperfect.

PRACTICE

Q: A dieci anni, io _____ sempre nove grandi ravioli per cena. (mangiare)

A: A dieci anni, io mangiavo sempre nove grandi ravioli per cena. (*When I was 10, I would always eat nine large ravioli for dinner.*)

11 Quando Cristina _____ piccola, _____ con le sue amiche. (essere, giocare)

12 Che cosa _____ quando è cominciato a piovere? (fare, voi)

13 Mi _____ il formaggio una volta. (piacere)

14 Carlo _____ sempre il latte. (bere)

15 Noi _____ tutti insieme a casa. (parlare)

16 I miei nonni mi _____ sempre di essere brava. (dire)

17 _____ stare a scuola o a casa? (preferire, tu)

18 _____ in Italia ogni estate. (andare, io)

19 Io e mia cugina _____ un film ogni sabato quando _____ piccole. (vedere, essere)

20 Le mie sorelle _____ una passeggiata mentre i nostri genitori _____. (fare, dormire)

21 Mi dispiace, cosa _____? Non ho capito. (dire, tu)

22 Eleonora e i suoi studenti _____ la poesia. (tradurre)

23 _____ un bicchiere di acqua quando è arrivata la posta. (bere, io)

Crafting the Imperfect Progressive

In Chapter 5, I explain the present progressive.

> **Sto studiando.** (*I'm studying* — as in, this minute.)

I also walk you through how to conjugate the present progressive in the present, and how to form regular and irregular gerunds.

Like English, Italian has an imperfect progressive tense.

> **Io stavo leggendo.** (*I was reading.*)

You form the imperfect progressive by conjugating the verb **stare** (*to stay/to be*) in the imperfect and then adding the gerund of the main verb. The gerund is invariable (it has only one form), so you don't have to worry about making it agree with anything. You form the gerund by adding **–ando** to the stems of verbs ending in **–are**, and **–endo** to the stems of verbs ending in **–ere** or **–ire**.

In other words, the formula is as follows:

> Imperfect of **stare** + gerund

The following table gives you an example of a verb in the imperfect progressive.

guardare (to look at/to watch)	
io stavo guardando	noi stavamo guardando
tu stavi guardando	voi stavate guardando
lui/lei/Lei stava guardando	loro/Loro stavano guardando

Voi stavate guardando la partita di calcio. (*You were watching the soccer game* [at that precise moment].)

REMEMBER

In Italian, you use the imperfect progressive in the same way you use it in English: to emphasize what you were doing (or what was happening) at a given moment. If you ask the question, **"Che cosa stavano facendo?"** (*"What were they doing?"*), what you leave unsaid is that you want to know what they were doing at that moment or at the time that you're talking about.

In Italian, you use the progressive form to talk about emotional and mental states.

> **Stavo pensando di licenziarmi.** (*I was thinking of quitting my job.*)

But you don't use it to talk about conditions, which take the imperfect, as in **Indossava un vestito blu** (*She was wearing a blue dress*), or with the verb **essere** (*to be*), as in **Era carino con te** (*He was being nice to you*).

PRACTICE

In the following sentences, fill in the blanks with the appropriate person of the imperfect progressive.

Q. Quando ho visto quell'incidente, _____ dal negozio. (uscire)

A. Quando ho visto quell'incidente, stavo uscendo dal negozio. (*When I saw that accident, I was walking out of the store.*)

24 _____ e non ho sentito il campanello. (dormire, io)

25 Quando ho incontrato Sandro, lui _____ in palestra. (andare)

26 Roberto _____ un corso di vela quando ha conosciuto mia sorella. (fare)

27 Quando mi hai chiamato io _____ la pasta. (cucinare)

28 I bambini _____ i castelli di sabbia. (fare)

29 "Che cosa stavate facendo?" _____ a scacchi. (giocare, noi)

30 La moto è arrivata molto velcemente proprio mentre Ida _____ la strada. (attraversare)

When the Going Gets Tricky: The Imperfect and Passato Prossimo

In the following sections, I give you guidelines about

>> How to choose between the imperfect and the **passato prossimo** (present perfect)

>> What happens when you link sentences together, using the **passato prossimo** in one and the imperfect in the other. **Guardavo** [imperfect] **la TV quando è mancata** [present perfect] **la luce.** (*I was watching TV when the electricity went out.*)

>> Which keywords can trigger a lightbulb when you're trying to figure out which tense to use

>> What the special forms are for **sapere** (*to know*) and **conoscere** (*to know*)

Choosing one over the other: Imperfect or passato prossimo?

In Italian you use the **passato prossimo** to talk about situations that began and ended in the past (just like you do in English with the present perfect).

Il grande direttore d'orchestra è morto nella sua casa di famiglia. (*The great conductor died at his family's home.*)

REMEMBER

But in some situations, Italian uses the imperfect or the **passato prossimo**, and the English translation for both of the Italian tenses is the same.

Mia figlia era una bambina vivace. (*My daughter was a lively kid.*)

Mia figlia è stata in Spagna l'estate scorsa. (*My daughter was in Spain last summer.*)

In the first sentence, the verb *was* (**era**) needs to be in the imperfect in Italian because the sentence conveys a condition lasting over time. In the second sentence, the trip to Spain is an event that was concluded in the past, so you need the **passato prossimo** here to convey *was* (**è stata**). You have to get used to asking the following questions to decide whether to use the imperfect or the present perfect:

>> Am I talking about an event? If yes, use the **passato prossimo**.

>> Am I talking about a situation, a condition, or something lasting? If yes, use the imperfect.

Using different tenses in different sentences

Sometimes, you may find yourself in a situation where, when looking at a sentence in isolation, you can't figure out whether you're talking about a condition that lasted in the past or an event that happened and is over. You can't always clearly see whether to use the **passato prossimo** or the imperfect.

You need to appreciate the nuances in order to make the best decision. People can understand you if you use the wrong tense in situations, but if you want to communicate well, you need to develop sensitivity to those nuances.

Grasping key terms

If you're still in doubt about which past tense to use, for now, follow the lists in this section. I give you some trigger terms that can help you determine context and identify which tense to use.

Here are terms associated with the **passato prossimo**:

>> **all'improvviso** (*all of a sudden/suddenly*)

>> **immediatamente** (*immediately*)

>> **quando** (*when*)

>> **quella volta** (*that time*)

Di solito andavo alla riunione quella volta non sono andata. (*I usually went to the meeting, that time, I did not go.*)

This example shows the imperfect, and **passato prossimo** in the same sentence.

>> **ieri, ieri, invece** (*yesterday/yesterday/instead*)

>> **ad un tratto** (*suddenly*)

>> **due ore fa** (*two years ago*)

>> **il mese scorso** (*last month*)

>> **domenica** (*on Sunday;* or any other day of the week)

>> **una volta** (*once*)

   Una volta ho mangiato il cervo. (*I ate venison once.*)

>> **e quindi** (*and so*)

This list gives you some common terms associated with the imperfect:

>> **di solito** (*usually*)

>> **sempre** (*always*)

>> **spesso** (*often*)

>> **frequentemente** (*frequently*)

>> **d'estate** (*in the summer;* or any other season)

>> **ogni giorno** (*every day*)

>> **da piccolo/a** (*when I was little*) **quando ero piccolo/a** (*when I was little*): these two terms are pretty much interchangeable.

>> **da bambino/a** (*as a child*)

>> **da giovane** (*as a young person*)

>> **mentre** (*while*)

>> **la domenica, il lunedì** (*on Sundays, on Mondays,* and so on)

>> **c'era una volta** (*once upon a time*)

Looking at the forms of sapere and conoscere

TIP

The verbs **sapere** (*to know*) and **conoscere** (*to know*) have different meanings in the **passato prossimo** and in the imperfect.

Sapere in the present and in the imperfect means to know how to do something or to know any other piece of information, such as where, why, how, how many, who:

>> Present: **Non so nuotare.** (*I don't know how to swim.*)

>> Imperfect: **Non sapevo nuotare.** (*I didn't know how to swim.*)

   Sapevo pattinare una volta. (*I used to know how to skate once upon a time.*)

In the **passsato prossimo** however, **sapere** means to learn, to find out, or to hear.

   Ho saputo che George Clooney compra una casa a Como. (*I heard that George Clooney is buying a house in Como.*)

Conoscere in the present and imperfect means to know someone or something (like a city or restaurant).

>> Present: **Conosco Giulia.** (*I know Giulia.*)

>> Imperfect: **Conoscevo Giulia allora** (*I knew Giulia back then.*)

In the **passato prossimo**, however, **conoscere** means to meet someone for the first time.

Ho conosciuto Giulia quattro anni fa. (*I met Giulia 4 years ago.*)

PRACTICE

Decide whether you need the imperfect or the **passato prossimo** in the following sentences and conjugate the verbs accordingly. Look out for the trigger words (which I list in the preceding section), which should help you figure out the context.

Q. Mia madre _____ nel 1970. (**nascere**)

A. Mia madre è nata nel 1970. (*My mother was born in 1970.*)

31. Di solito i miei amici _____ a scuola in macchina; quel giorno, invece _____ in treno. (venire)

32. Sabato sera _____ (guidare, io) ma all'improvviso _____ un chighiale davanti a me. (vedere)

33. Mentre io _____ (fare) i compiti mio fratello mi _____ (dare) fastidio e quindi _____ via. (andare, io)

34. Quando _____ (avere) 6 anni, _____ (andare) in Italia per la prima volta. (io)

35. La mia famiglia _____ (andare) a Block Island ogni estate. Ci _____ molto (piacere). Un'estate _____ anche la famiglia di mio zio. (venire)

36. _____ (volere, io) uscire ieri sera, ma la mamma _____ di no! (dire)

37. Maria _____ ieri dalle 10:00 alle 11:30. (studiare)

38. (Io) _____ che George Clooney si sposa. (sapere = heard, found out, learned)

39. _____ suonare il piano una volta. (sapere) = (used to know how)

40. Non _____ mio marito 10 anni fa. (conoscere: I didn't know him).

41. _____ Giancarlo 11 anni fa. (conoscere:I met him)

42. Ieri sera Anna _____ triste ed è rimasta a casa. (essere)

43 (Consider this a narration, a story in the past, that begins with *It was terrible outside that evening...*)

_____ una brutta sera (essere). _____ (piovere) e _____ vento (tirare): tutto ad un tratto_____un grande rumore (a big noise). (sentire, io)

Conveying Two Past Actions in Sequence: The Past Perfect

In Italian, the past perfect is called **trapassato prossimo**. You need this tense when two actions occurred in the past and one occurred before the other. An example of this in English sounds like this: *The train had already left.* (**Il treno era già partito**).

You use the past perfect

>> When you're talking about an event that happened in the past before the situation you're describing. You convey the situation with the imperfect and the event with the past perfect.

Non sapevo [imperfect] **che tu gli avevi già telefonato** [past perfect]. (*I didn't know you'd already called him.*)

>> When you're describing a situation that lasted over time before an event you're talking about. You convey the event with the **passato prossimo** and the situation with the past perfect.

Quando siamo usciti [passato prossimo]**, aveva smesso di piovere** [past perfect]. (*By the time we went out, it had stopped raining.*)

You form the past perfect by conjugating the auxiliary verb **essere** or **avere** in the imperfect. Then you add the past participle of the main verb, such as **detto** (*said*) or **andato** (*gone*), to get **avevo detto** (*I had said*) or **ero andato** (*I had gone*). (Check out Chapter 12 to see which verbs take **essere** and which verbs take **avere** in a compound tense.)

TIP

Head to Chapter 12 for information about the following:

>> How to form the past participle: **amato** (*loved*), **fatto** (*done, made*), and so on

>> Where to place the adverb **già** (*already*), which you use frequently with the past perfect.

Il treno era già partito quando siamo arrivati. (*The train had already left when we arrived.*)

Quando ho visto i miei genitori avevano già cenato. (*When I saw my parents, they'd already had supper*).

>> How to choose between **essere**, and **avere** as the auxiliary

>> Which of the four endings of the past participle you need: **–o, –a, –i,** or **–e**

PRACTICE

Complete the following sentences by adding the past perfect in the person suggested in parentheses. Choose the appropriate auxiliary, and pay attention to the ending of the past participle.

Q. Ieri Anna ci ha portato il libro che _____. (chiedere, noi)

A. Ieri Anna ci ha portato il libro che avevamo chiesto. (*Yesterday, Anna brought us the book we asked for/had asked for.*)

44 Non sembrate sorpresi. _____ già _____ la notizia della sua promozione? (sapere, voi)

45 _____ sempre _____ un marito modello, ma un bel giorno è sparito. (essere, lui)

46 Mariella non sapeva che Anna e Luisa _____ in Olanda. (nascere, loro)

47 _____ già _____ le chiavi ad Emilia? Io non le trovo più. (dare, tu)

48 _____ a Pippo che andavamo in Grecia, ma non si ricordava. (dire, noi)

Answers to "Once Upon a Time: The Imperfect" Practice Questions

1. **tu andavi** (*you were going*)

2. **lui aveva** (*he had*)

3. **noi parlavamo** (*we used to speak/we were speaking*)

4. **voi mangiavate** (*you all were eating*)

5. **le ragazze capivano** (*the girls understood*)

6. **mio padre leggeva** (*my dad would/used to read*)

7. **loro guardavano** (*they were watching*)

8. **io prendevo** (*I used to get*)

9. **il cane dormiva** (*the dog was sleeping*)

10. **io amavo** (*I loved*)

11. **era, giocava; Quando Cristina era piccola, giocava con le sue amiche.** (*When Cristina was little she used to play with her friends.*)

12. **facevate; Che cosa facevate quando è cominciato a piovere?** (*What were you doing when it started to rain?*)

13. **piaceva; Mi piaceva il formaggio una volta.** (*I used to like cheese.*)

14. **beveva; Carlo beveva sempre il latte.** (*Carlo used to always drink milk.*)

15. **parlavamo; Noi parlavamo tutti insieme a casa.** (*We used to all talk together at home.*)

16. **dicevano; I miei nonni mi dicevano sempre di essere brava.** (*My grandparents always told me to be good.*)

17. **Preferivi; Preferivi stare a scuola o a casa?** (*Did you prefer to be at school or home?*)

18. **Andavo; Andavo in Italia ogni estate.** (*I used to go to Italy every summer.*)

19. **vedevamo, eravamo; Io e mia cugina vedevamo un film ogni sabato quando eravamo piccole.** (*My cousin and I used to see a film every Saturday when we were little.*)

20. **facevano, dormivano; Le mie sorelle facevano una passeggiata mentre i nostri genitori dormivano.** (*My sisters were taking a walk while our parents were sleeping.*)

21. **dicevi; Mi dispiace, cosa dicevi? Non ho capito.** (*I'm sorry, what were you saying? I didn't understand.*)

22. **traducevano; Eleonora e i suoi studenti traducevano la poesia.** (*Eleonora nd her students were translating the poem.*)

(23) **Bevevo; Bevevo un bicchiere di acqua quando è arrivata la posta.** (*I was drinking a glass of water when the mail arrived,*)

(24) **Dormivo; Dormivo e non ho sentito il campanello.** (*I was sleeping and didn't hear the doorbell.*)

(25) **stava andando; Quando ho incontrato Sandro, lui stava andando in palestra.** (*When I bumped into Sandro he was going to the gym.*)

(26) **stava facendo; Roberto stava facendo un corso di vela quando ha conosciuto mia sorella.** (*Roberto was taking a sailing class when he met my sister.*)

(27) **stavo cucinando; Quando mi hai chiamato io stavo cucinando la pasta.** (*When you called I was cooking the pasta.*)

(28) **stavano facendo; I bambini stavano facendo i castelli di sabbia.** (*The children were making sandcastles.*)

(29) **Stavamo giocando; "Che cosa stavate facendo?" Stavamo giocando a scacchi.** (*What were you doing? We were playing chess.*)

(30) **stava attraversando; La moto è arrivata molto velocemente proprio mentre Ida stava attraversando la strada.** (*The motorcycle arrived very fast right when Ida was crossing the street.*)

(31) **venivo; sono venuta/o; Di solito venivo a scuola in macchina; quel giorno, invece sono venuta/o in treno.** (*I used to come to school by car; that day, however, I came by train.*)

(32) **guidavo, ho visto; Sabato sera guidavo, ma all'improvviso ho visto un cinghiale davanti a me.** (*Saturday night I was driving, when all of a sudden I saw a wild boar in front of me.*)

(33) **Mentre io facevo i compiti mio fratello mi dava fastidio e quindi sono andato via.** (*While I was doing my homework my brother was bothering me and so I left.*)

(34) **avevo, sono andata; Quando avevo sei anni, sono andata in Italia per la prima volta.** (*When I was six years old, I went to Italy for the first time.*)

(35) **andava, piaceva, è venuta; La mia famiglia andava a Block Island ogni estate. Ci piaceva molto. Un'estate è venuta anche la famiglia di mio zio.** (*My family used to go to Block Island every summer. We really liked it. One summer my uncle's family came too.*)

(36) **Volevo, ha detto; Volevo uscire ieri sera, ma la mamma ha detto di no.** (*I wanted to go out last night but my mom said no.*)

(37) **ha studiato; Maria ha studiato ieri dalle 10:00 alle 11:30.** (*Maria studied from 10 until 11:30 last night.*)

(38) **ho saputo; (Io) ho saputo che George Clooney si sposa.** (*I heard that George Clooney is getting married*).

(39) **Sapevo; Sapevo suonare il piano una volta.** (*I used to know how to play the piano.*)

(40) **conoscevo; Non conoscevo mio marito 10 anni fa.** (*I didn't know my husband 10 years ago.*)

(41) **Ho conosciuto; Ho conosciuto Giancarlo 11 anni fa.** (*I met giancarlo eleven years ago.*)

(42) **era; Ieri sera Anna Maria era triste ed è rimasta a casa.** (*Last night, Anna Maria was sad and she stayed home.*)

43 **Era, Pioveva, tirava, ho sentito; Era una brutta sera. Pioveva e tirava vento: tutto ad un tratto ho sentito un grande rumore.** (*It was an ugly night. It was rainy and windy: all of a sudden I heard a big noise.*)

44 **Avevate, saputo; Non sembrate sorpresi. Avevate già saputo della sua promozione?** (*You don't seem surprised. Did you already know about her promotion?*)

45 **Era, stato; Era sempre stato un marito modello, ma un bel giorno è sparito.** (*He had always been a model husband, but one fine day he disappeared.*)

46 **erano nate; Mariella non sapeva che Anna e Luisa erano nate in Olanda.** (*Mariella didn't know that Anna and Luisa were born in Holland.*)

47 **Avevi, dato; Avevi già dato le chiavi ad Emilia? Io non le trovo più.** (*Had you already given the keys to Emilia? I can't find them.*)

48 **Avevamo detto; Avevamo detto a Pippo che andavamo in Grecia, ma non si ricordava.** (*We had told Pippo we were going to Greece, but he didn't remember.*)

Chapter **14**

Looking Ahead: The Future Tense

T he future tense is quite common and easy to form. The future is a tense you employ to talk about an event that hasn't yet taken place. Italian has a *simple future form* (**futuro semplice**).

> **Andrò.** (*I will go.*)

Italian also has a compound form called the **futuro anteriore** (*future perfect*).

> **Sarò andato** (*I will have gone*).

In this chapter, I cover details on when to use both future tenses and how to form the verbs.

Using the Two Future Forms

Here's when you use the simple future tense:

» To describe events happening in the future (usually a far or unspecified future)

Un giorno sarò ricco e famoso. (*One day I will be rich and famous.*)

» To express the intention to do something in the future

Penso che andrò in California il prossimo anno. (*I think I'll go to California next year.*)

» To express a possibility or probability

Hanno bussato alla porta, sarà l'UPS che consegna il pacco. (*Someone knocked on the door; it may be UPS delivering the package.*)

» When the first verb of a sentence (either a subordinate or main clause) is in the future

Quando finirai il liceo, andrai all'università. (*When you finish high school, you'll go to college.*)

Se mangerai da noi, ti preparerò le lasagne. (*If you eat at our house, I'll make lasagna for you.*)

You use the future perfect when a future event precedes another future event.

Quando tornerai a casa, Ugo sarà già partito. (*By the time you return home, Ugo will have already left.*)

Common Expressions Denoting the Future

Like in English, you frequently use Italian words and phrases that translate as, for example, *next* and *in x amount of time*. To start you off, Table 14-1 offers some common future tense expressions.

Table 14-1   Common Terms Denoting the Future

Term	Meaning
prossimo	*next*
l'anno prossimo	*next year*
il mese prossimo	*next month*
fra	*in*
fra 10 anni	*in 10 years*
fra 100 anni	*in 100 years*
domani	*tomorrow*
dopodomani	*day after tomorrow*
se	*if*
quando	*when*
nel futuro	*in the future*
nel 2050. . .	*in 2050 . . .*

Using the Present to Talk about the Future

All languages have rules, and even basic conjugations can be a challenge at first. Not only do Italian verb forms vary more than they do in English, but Italian also takes a few more liberties in using the present tense to describe the future.

In Italian you talk about the future by using the present tense in the following cases:

>> To mention an event that will happen soon

La vedo domenica. (*I'll see her on Sunday./I'm seeing her on Sunday.*)

>> To announce a decision that's more or less close in time

Quest'estate vado alle Maldive. (*This coming summer, I'm going to the Maldives.*)

>> To refer to an event that's part of a timetable

Il semestre autunnale inizia il 10 ottobre. (*The fall term begins on October 10.*)

>> To give instructions

Quando arrivi a Londra, va' direttamente alla stazione Vittoria. (*When you get to London, go straight to Victoria Station.*)

Forming the Simple Future Tense

REMEMBER

You form the future tense by adding the future endings to the infinitive stem of the verb (just like the condition, which you can read about in Chapter 16).

Regular verbs

The simple future tense in Italian is a thing of beauty: You conjugate all verbs — both regular and irregular, ending in **–are**, **–ere**, and **–ire** — in exactly the same way. So, you have to memorize only one set of endings.

In Table 14-2, I list the endings for all three conjugations, followed by a sample conjugation table. All verbs — regular and irregular — place the accent on the same vowels **ò** and **à**. Add stress to these syllables when speaking them (and also in your head when reading them).

Also remember that regular future infinitive stems take the infinitive and cut off the final **e**. And, in **–are** verbs, the **a** of the infinitive changes to **e**. For example:

>> **parlare** becomes **parler–**

>> **prendere** becomes **prender–**

>> **partire** becomes **partir–**

Table 14-2 — Endings for Regular and Irregular Verbs in the Future Tense

Person	Ending for –are/–ere/–ire Verbs
io	–ò
tu	–ai
lui/lei/Lei	–à
noi	–emo
voi	–ete
loro/Loro	–anno

The following table shows the future conjugation for an –are verb. Verbs ending in –ere and –ire conjugate in the same way.

guardare (to look at)	
io guarderò	noi guarderemo
tu guarderai	voi guarderete
lui/lei/Lei guarderà	loro/Loro guarderanno

Massimo non mi guarderà mai. (*Massimo will never look at me.*)

Stem-changing regular verbs

Verbs that end in –ciare and –giare, such as **cominciare** (*to begin*) and **mangiare** (*to eat*), drop the **i** to preserve the soft sound of the infinitive **c** (like in *cherry*) and **g** (like in *Jerry*). Remember to change the **a** to **e** in the stem, as well:

>> **cominciare** becomes **comincer–**

>> **mangiare** becomes **manger–**

Verbs that end in –care and –gare, such as **cercare** (*to look for*) and **pagare** (*to pay*), place **ch** and **gh** before the endings to preserve the hard sound of the infinitive **c** (as in *cat*) and **g** (as in *gondola*). You also need to change the **a** to **e** in the stem:

>> **pagare** becomes **pagher–**

>> **cercare** becomes **cercher–**

Select the correct verb in the following sentences, choosing among the options in parentheses.

PRACTICE

Q. (Pagheremo/Prenderanno/Servirete) noi il conto.

A. Pagheremo noi il conto. (*We will pay for the bill.*)

1. Gianni e Piero (balleranno/correranno/visiteranno) la Maratona di New York.

2. Io e i miei fratelli (prenderai/serviranno/daremo) una grande festa.

3. "Marco, (lascerò/partirai/saliremo) per Mosca fra un mese?"

4. "Signora, (cambierà/cancelleranno/ricorderete) il suo numero di telefono?"

5. "Tutti i presenti, (passerà/usciranno/entrerai) dalla porta numero 4."

6. Tu e i tuoi amici (finirete/annulleranno/daremo) la torta?

PRACTICE

Conjugate the following verbs. Keep in mind the spelling peculiarities you can find in the sections "Forming the Simple Future Tense" earlier in this chapter.

Q. Maria _____ Alberobello. (visitare)

A. Maria visiterà Alberobello. (*Maria will visit Alberobello*).

7. Il prossimo semestre, _____ il nuovo romanzo di Elena Ferrante. (leggere, noi)

8. Sofia e Giovanna _____ fra un mese. (partire)

9. Luca, dove _____ quest'estate? (lavorare)

10. Se _____, noi _____ a casa. (nevicare, mangiare)

11. Io _____ tutto alla fine del mese. (pagare)

12. Voi _____ la vostra vacanza fra 25 giorni. (cominciare)

Irregular verbs

You have to consider some irregular-verb issues when dealing with the simple future tense (just like any Italian tense). The irregular verbs conjugate starting from irregular future stems (which are the exact same in the conditional tense, so you only have to learn this set once). The endings of regular infinitive stems are exactly the same as the endings of regular verbs.

Working with essere and avere

The verb **essere** (*to be*) has an irregular stem.

sar– + the regular future ending

Avere (*to have*) is much less irregular.

avr– + the regular future ending

The following tables show their future-tense conjugations.

essere (to be)	
io sarò	noi saremo
tu sarai	voi sarete
lui/lei/Lei sarà	loro/Loro saranno

Dove sarai tra vent'anni? (*Where will you be in 20 years?*)

avere (to have)	
io avrò	noi avremo
tu avrai	voi avrete
lui/lei/Lei avrà	loro/Loro avranno

Guarda quei ragazzi: avranno vent'anni al massimo.
(*Look at those guys: They can't be older than 20.*)

Looking at dare, fare, and stare

What makes the verbs **dare**, **fare**, and **stare** irregular is that the **a** doesn't change to an **e**, unlike all the other regular **–are** verbs in the future tense.

>> **dare** (*to give*) becomes **dar–**

   Daremo una festa per Amalia. (*We're going to have a party for Amalia.*)

>> **fare** (*to do/to make*) becomes **far–**

   Cosa farai da grande? (*What are you going to be when you grow up?*)

>> **stare** (*to be/to stay*) becomes **star–**

   Annabella e Violetta staranno a casa stasera. (*Violetta and Annabella are staying home tonight.*)

Figuring out stem-changing irregular verbs

Just add the future endings (which you can find in the section "Forming the Simple Future Tense," earlier in this chapter) on to these irregular stems, and you're good to go.

Some of these future stems follow a pattern: Remove the final vowel and the second to last vowel to form the infinitive, whereas other verbs double up on the **r**. Noticing these patterns in the following list will help you to group them and remember them.

>> **andare** (*to go*): **andr–** + future ending

>> **cadere** (*to fall*): **cadr–** + future ending

>> **dovere** (*to have to/must*): **dovr–** + future ending

>> **potere** (*must/shall*): **potr–** + future ending

» **sapere** (*to know how to*): **sapr–** + future ending

» **vedere** (*to see*): **vedr–** + future ending

» **vivere** (*to live*): **vivr–** + future ending

» **venire** (*to come*): **verr–** + future ending

» **volere** (*to want*): **vorr–** + future ending

» **rimanere** (*to remain/to stay*): **rimarr–** + future ending

» **bere** (*to drink*): **berr–** + future ending

Here are just a few examples that use the irregular stems.

Dovrò ridare questo esame. (*I'll have to take this exam again.*)

Non so quando potrò vederti. (*I don't know when I'll be able to see you.*)

Non saprò mai sciare come te. (*I'll never be able to ski like you.*)

Vorranno conoscerti, prima o poi. (*They'd like to meet you, sooner or later.*)

Add the verb to the following sentences, choosing among the options in parentheses.

PRACTICE

Q. (Farai/Berrai/Avrà) una torta [tu]?

A. **Farai una torta?** (*Will you make a cake?*)

13　Io (uscirò/sarà/starò) a casa sabato sera.

14　Mamma e papà (staremo/faranno/avrete) un viaggio a dicembre.

15　Noi (potranno/dovremo/vorrete) vendere la barca, purtroppo.

16　"Signori, (vorremo/potrà/dovrete) lasciare la stanza."

17　"Signore, (andrà/sarai/lascerò) in Tunisia il mese prossimo?"

18　Stai tranquillo, domani (starai/farà/saremo) bello.

19　"Dove (farai/saremo/andrete) in Grecia tu e tua moglie?"

Conjugate the verb in the following sentences:

PRACTICE

Q. State attenti, _____benzina! (rimanere)

A. **State attenti, rimarrete senza benzina!** (*Be careful, you'll run out of gas!*)

20　Margherita _____ Liborio ad Amalfi. (vedere)

21　Al matrimonio io _____ alla salute degli sposi. (bere)

(22) Noi _____ in campagna per l'estate. (rimanere)

(23) "State attente voi due, _____ dalla scala!" (cadere)

(24) Voi _____ andare alla partita, immagino. (volere)

(25) I ragazzi _____ fare il bucato a mano. (dovere)

(26) _____ da noi a cena, Luciano? (venire)

(27) _____ in Africa per lavoro? (andare, voi)

(28) Giulia e Annika _____ sull'aereo a quest'ora. (essere)

(29) _____ una mano a mio padre. (dare, io)

(30) Come _____ il mondo tra 50 anni? (essere)

(31) Anche noi _____ andare al concerto! (potere, noi)

(32) _____ alla mia festa di compleanno? (venire, lei)

Forming the Future Perfect Tense

The future perfect is a compound tense that describes a future event happening before another future event. You form it by adding the simple future of the auxiliary verb **essere** (*to be*) or **avere** (*to have*) to the past participle of the verb.

In the section "Irregular verbs," earlier in this chapter, I explain how to form the future tense of **essere** and **avere**. Chapter 12 tells you which auxiliary to choose, how to form the past participle, and how to make the past participle with subjects.

The following tables give you the future perfect of **mangiare** (*to eat*), which uses **avere**; and **tornare** (*to return/to go back*), which uses **essere**.

mangiare (to eat)	
io avrò mangiato	noi avremo mangiato
tu avrai mangiato	voi avrete mangiato
lui/lei/Lei avrà mangiato	loro/Loro avranno mangiato

Il gatto avrà mangiato la bistecca. (*The cat probably ate the steak.*)

tornare (to return, to go back)	
io sarò tornato/tornata	noi saremo tornati/tornate
tu sarai tornato/tornata	voi sarete tornati/tornate
lui/lei/Lei sarà	loro/Loro saranno tornati/tornatetornato/tornata

Sarà tornato in ufficio. (*He must have gone back to work.*)

To understand how to use the future perfect, compare the verb tenses in the following example sentences:

>> Present: **Quando arriva in ufficio, gli telefono.** (*I call him when he gets to the office.*)

>> Future: **Quando arriverà in ufficio, gli telefonerò.** (*I will call him when he gets to the office.*)

>> Future perfect: **Quando sarà arrivato in ufficio, gli telefonerò.** (*I'll call him after he's arrived at the office.*)

PRACTICE

Conjugate the following verbs in the future perfect in this fictitious future.

Q. Guarda che pozzanghere! _____ tutta la notte. (piovere)

A. Guarda che pozzanghere! **Avrà/Sarà piovuto tutta la notte.** (*Look at these puddles! It must have rained all night.*)

33 Dove sono i ragazzi? Boh! _____ il treno. (perdere)

34 Pensate, fra 2 giorni _____ già _____ in Sicilia. (arrivare, noi)

35 "Chi era alla porta?" _____ il postino. (essere)

36 Il cane _____ il cibo del gatto. (mangiare)

Answers to "Looking Ahead: The Future Tense" Practice Questions

(1) **correranno; Gianni e Piero correranno la Maratona di New York.** (*Gianni and Piero will run the New York Marathon.*)

(2) **daremo; Io e i miei fratelli daremo una grande festa.** (*My siblings and I are going to throw a big party.*)

(3) **partirai; "Marco, partirai per Mosca fra un mese?"** (*"Marco, are you leaving for Moscow in a month?"*)

(4) **cambierà; "Signora, cambierà il suo numero di telefono?"** (*"Ma'am, will you be changing your phone number?"*)

(5) **usciranno; "Tutti i presenti usciranno dalla porta numero 4."** (*"All present will have to exit from gate number four."*)

(6) **finirete; Tu e i tuoi amici finirete la torta?** (*Will you and your friends finish the cake?*)

(7) **leggeremo; Il prossimo semestre, leggeremo il nuovo romanzo di Elena Ferrante.** (*Next semester we will read Elena Ferrante's new novel.*)

(8) **partiranno; Sofia e Giovanna partiranno fra un mese.** (*Sofia and Giovanni will be leaving in one month.*)

(9) **lavorerai; Luca, dove lavorerai quest'estate?** (*Luca, where will you work this summer?*)

(10) **nevicherà, mangeremo; Se nevicherà, noi mangeremo a casa.** (*If it snows, we'll eat at home.*)

(11) **pagherò; Io pagherò tutto alla fine del mese.** (*I'll pay everything the end of the month.*)

(12) **comincerete; Voi comincerete la vostra vacanza fra 25 giorni.** (*You're going to begin your vacation in twenty-five days.*)

(13) **starò; Io starò a casa sabato sera.** (*I'm going to stay home on Saturday evening.*)

(14) **faranno; Mamma e papà faranno un viaggio a dicembre.** (*Mom and Dad will take a trip in December.*)

(15) **dovremo; Noi dovremo vendere la barca, purtroppo.** (*We will have to sell the boat, unfortunately.*)

(16) **dovrete; "Signori, dovrete lasciare la stanza."** (*"Ladies and gentlemen, you will have to leave the room."*)

(17) **andrà; "Signore, andrà in Tunisia il mese prossimo?"** (*"Will you be going to Tunisia next month, sir?"*)

(18) **farà; Stai tranquillo, domani farà bello.** (*Don't worry, tomorrow it will be nice out.*)

(19) **andrete; "Dove andrete in Grecia tu e tua moglie?"** (*"Where will you and your wife go in Greece?"*)

(20) **vedrà; Margherita vedrà Liborio ad Amalfi.** (*Margherita will see Liborio in Amalfi.*)

(21) berró; Al matrimonio io berrò alla salute degli sposi. (*I'm going to drink to the health of the newlyweds at the wedding.*)

(22) rimarremo; Noi rimarremo in campagna per l'estate. (*We're going to stay in the countryside for the summer.*)

(23) cadrete; "State attente voi due, cadrete dalla scala!" (*"Be careful you two, you're going to fall off the ladder!"*)

(24) vorret; Voi vorrete andare alla partita, immagino. (*I suppose you want to go to the game.*)

(25) dovranno; I ragazzi dovranno fare il bucato a mano. (*The children will have to give a hand with the laundry.*)

(26) Verrai; Verrai da noi a cena, Luciano? (*Will you come to our place for dinner, Luciano?*)

(27) Andrete; Andrete in Africa per lavoro? (*Will you go to Africa for work?*)

(28) saranno; Giulia e Annika saranno sull'aereo a quest'ora. (*Giulia and Annika will probably be on the plane at this time.*)

(29) Darò; Darò una mano a mio padre. (*I will give my father a hand.*)

(30) sarà; Come sarà il mondo tra 50 anni? (*What will the world be like in 50 years?*)

(31) potremo; Anche noi potremo andare al concerto! (*We'll be able to go to the concert too!*)

(32) Verrà; Verrà alla mia festa di compleanno? (*Will she come to my birthday party?*)

(33) Avranno perso; Dove sono i ragazzi? Boh! Avranno perso il treno. (*Where are the kids? Beats me. They must have missed the train.*)

(34) saremo, arrivati; Pensate, fra due giorni saremo già arrivati in Sicilia. (*Just think, in two days we'll have already arrived in Sicily.*)

(35) Sarà stato; "Chi era alla porta?" Sarà stato il postino. (*"Who was at the door?" It must have been the letter-carrier.*)

(36) avrà mangiato; Il cane avrà mangiato il cibo del gatto. (*The dog probably ate the cat's food.*)

Chapter **15**

Commanding and the Imperative

The imperative is the mood of commands and exhortations, such as **Abbi fiducia!** (*Have faith!*) or the less-inspiring **Non dare fastidio a tuo fratello!** (*Don't bother your brother!*).

In this chapter, you can find out how to form the imperative, how to issue affirmative and negative commands, and what to do with pronouns, as in the command **"Svegliati!"** (*"Wake up!"*) and **"Maria e Lee, fateci vedere le vostre foto."** (*"Maria and Lee, let us see your photos."*)

Choosing the Imperative

The imperative in Italian always implies a direct command, and you mainly use it in conversation. Conversely, Italian uses the infinitive to give generic orders, or to give instruction in signs, advertisements, recipes, and directions. Here are a couple of examples:

» Imperative: **Andrea, mescola la farina!** (*Andrea, mix the flour!*)

» Infinitive: **La ricetta dice: "Mescolare la farina e aggiungere tre uova."** (*The recipe says: "Mix the flour and add three eggs."*)

A sentence such as **Andiamo! È tardi!** (*Let's go! It's late!*) lies between order and suggestion (more of an urging than a command). You use the imperative when addressing a person directly.

> **Passi prima Lei, Signora!** (*Please, you go first, Ma'am!*)

> **Prendete l'ascensore sulla destra!** (*Take the elevator on the right!*).

And the imperative is employed mostly (but not exclusively) in the second-person singular (**tu**) and plural (**voi**).

The Imperative Form of Regular Verbs

When you form an imperative in Italian, you have a sort of reverse rule for the **tu** and **Lei** forms — the **–are** conjugations are a flip of the **–ere** and **–ire** conjugations. For example, the imperative of the **–are** verb **cantare** (*to sing*) is **Canta!** (informal) and **Canti!** (formal). In contrast, the imperative forms of the **–ire** verb **dormire** (*to sleep*) are **Dormi!** (informal) and **Dorma!** (formal). Table 15-1 spells this out a little more clearly.

Informal usage

The imperative mood is used to give orders, advice, and suggestions. The informal imperative form addresses people with whom you are familiar, or when the degree of formality is low (with classmates, children, and coworkers, for example). The informal imperative forms of **tu**, **noi**, and **voi** are identical to the corresponding present tense forms with one exception: In the **tu** form of **–are** verbs, the **–i** becomes **–a**. Please note that the imperative form of **noi** corresponds to the English *Let's*.

> **Andiamo a Parigi!** (*Let's go to Paris!*).

TIP

Quickly review the present indicative tense, which you can find in Chapter 5, if you don't have it easily available in your memory bank.

Table 15-1 shows the different conjugations for informal usage of imperatives. Make a point of underlining or highlighting the imperative endings so that you can easily evoke them when needed.

Table 15-1 Informal Imperatives of Regular Verbs

Verb	Informal Singular	Informal Plural
guardare (*to look*)	**(tu) guarda!** (*[you] look!*)	**(noi) guardiamo!** (*let's look!*); **(voi) guardate!** (*[you] look!*)
prendere (*to take*)	**(tu) prendi!** (*[you] take!*)	**(noi) prendiamo!** (*let's take!*); **(voi) prendete!** (*[you] take!*)
dormire (*to sleep*)	**(tu) dormi!** (*[you] sleep!*)	**(noi) dormiamo!** (*let's sleep!*); **(voi) dormite!** (*[you] sleep!*)
finire (*to finish*)	**(tu) finisci!** (*[you] finish!*)	**(noi) finiamo!** (*let's finish!*); **(voi) finite!** (*[you] finish!*)

DIFFERENCES

Sometimes, the only difference between the imperative and the indicative is your tone of voice. Always include an exclamation point when writing or speaking in the imperative. For example, imagine how different these two sentences sound:

> **Guardate la partita.** (*You're watching the game.*)
>
> **Guardate la partita!** (*Watch the game!*)

Formal usage

The formal imperative (**Lei/Loro**) is used less frequently than the informal command form, but you must use it in certain situations. You go the formal route as a form of respect in situations where a certain degree of formality is required, such as when entering a store, interacting with wait-staff, addressing your own boss, talking to older people (such as your professors and your friends' parents), or talking to people whom you don't know or have just met.

REMEMBER

After you figure out how to conjugate **Lei** and **Loro** in the imperative, you can also conjugate verbs in the present subjunctive because the forms are identical. (Although I don't go into the present subjunctive because it is too advanced and beyond the scope of this book. If you want to continue in Italian after you complete this book, you'll have a leg up with this bit of knowledge.)

Although you may hear the formal imperative of **Loro** in some prescribed situations, everyday spoken Italian mostly uses the informal imperative form of **voi**.

> **Signore e signori, ascoltate con attenzione!** (*Ladies and gentlemen, listen carefully!*).

TIP

The best way to construct a formal imperative is to drop the **–are, –ere, –ire** from the verb and add the formal imperative endings. Table 15-2 shows some examples. Highlight or underline the endings to drive home the notion that **–are** verbs take **–i** endings, and that **–ere/–ire** take **–a** endings.

Table 15-2	Formal Imperatives of Regular Verbs	
Verb	Formal Singular	Formal Plural
guardare (*to look*)	**(Lei) guardi!** (*[you] look!*)	**(Loro) guardino!** (*[you] look!*)
prendere (*to take*)	**(Lei) prenda!** (*[you] take!*)	**(Loro) prendano!** (*[you] take!*)
dormire (*to sleep*)	**(Lei) dorma!** (*[you] sleep!*)	**(Loro) dormano!** (*[you] sleep!*)
finire (*to finish*)	**(Lei) finisca!** (*[you] finish!*)	**(Loro) finiscano!** (*[you] finish!*)

The Imperative Form of Irregular Verbs

Some Italian verbs have an irregular conjugation in the imperative. The following sections walk you through the conjugations of these verbs.

Verbs that are irregular in the informal imperative

The verbs **andare** (*to go*), **dare** (*to give*), **fare** (*to do, to make*), and **stare** (*to stay*) have both regular and irregular **tu** informal imperatives: **va'/vai, fa'/fai, da'/dai**, and **sta'/stai**. When speaking, you more commonly use the irregular imperatives than their regular forms.

> **Sta' zitto e fa' quel che dico!** (*Be quiet and do as I say!*).

The verb **dire** (*to say*) is irregular in the **tu, Lei and Loro** forms, as in **Di' la verità!** (*Tell the truth!*): The other persons are **dica!, dite!, diciamo!** and **dicano!**

REMEMBER

When you walk into a store, or when a server comes to take your order, you frequently hear, **"Dimmi!"** (if they're being informal with you) or **"Mi dica!"** or **"Dica pure!"** (if they're being formal). On these occasions, this usage means *"How can I help you?"* — not *"Say it!"/"Tell me!"*

Verbs that are irregular in the formal imperative

TIP

The best way to construct a formal Imperative of irregular verbs is to start from the **–io** form of the present tense.

These irregular verbs, whose stems change in the present tense form, are as follows.

- » **andare** (*to go/to leave*)

  Vado. (–**io**, present) (*I'm leaving.*)

  Vada! (**Lei**, imperative) (*Leave!*)

  Vadano! (**Loro**, imperative) (*Leave!*)

- » **bere** (*to drink*

  Bevo l'acqua. (io, present) (*I drink/am drinking water.*)

  Beva. . .! (Lei, imperative) (*Drink. . .!*)

  Bevano. . .! (Loro, imperative) (*Drink. . .!*)

- » **dire** (*to say*)

- » **fare** (*to do/to make*)

- » **rimanere** (*to remain*)

- » **salire** (*to climb*)

- » **sedere** (*to sit*)

- » **tenere** (*to hold/to take*)

- » **uscire** (*to go out*)

- » **venire** (*to come*)

First, conjugate them in the **–io** person in the present tense, and then add **–a** and **–ano** to form the formal imperative. (Check out these irregular present-tense stems in Chapters 5 and 6).

Follow these steps to form the formal imperative (Lei and Loro), with the verb **andare** (*to go/ to leave*) as an example:

1. **Conjugate the verb in the –io person in the present tense.**

   For **andare**, you conjugate it as **Io vado** because that's what it is in the present.

2. **Drop the –o from the present-tense version of the word.**

   This step leaves you with the present-tense verb stem.

   For example, when you drop the **–o** from **vado**, you're left with **vad–**.

3. **Add –a and –ano to the present-tense verb stem**

   In this **andare** example, you end up with **vada** and **vadano**.

The verbs **avere** (*to have*), **essere** (*to be*), **sapere** (*to know how to*), **dare** (*to give*), and **stare** (*to stay*) are irregular in the formal imperative. The modal auxiliaries **dovere** (*must/shall/should*) and **potere** (*can/may/able to*) don't have the imperative due to their meaning. But **volere** (*to want*) and **sapere** (*to know how to*) do have an imperative, even though you may not use them often. I break down the conjugations of some of the auxiliaries and modal auxiliaries in the following tables.

avere (to have)	
	noi abbiamo
tu abbi	voi abbiate
Lei abbia	Loro abbiano

Abbi pazienza con lei. (*Have patience with her.*)

essere (to be)	
	noi siamo
tu sii	voi siate
Lei sia	Loro siano

Sii gentile con lei. (*Be nice to her.*)

sapere (to know how to)	
	noi sappiamo
tu sappi	voi sappiate
Lei sappia	Loro sappiano

Sappi che io non vengo. (*Know that I won't come.*)

dare (to give)	
	noi diamo
tu da'/dai	voi date
Lei dia	Loro diano

Date una mano al babbo! (*Give Dad a hand!*)

stare (to be, to stay)	
	noi stiamo
tu sta'/stai	voi state
Lei stia	Loro stiano

State zitti! (*Be quiet!* [*you*, pl.])

You can tone down the imperious effect of the imperative by adding the word **pure** (*by all means/please*) after the command. You can also throw in **prego** (*please/by all means*).

> **"Venga pure!"/"Venite pure!"** (*"By all means, please come!"*)

> **"Prego, mi segua!"** (*"Please, follow me!"*)

TIP

Sometimes, you may hear someone say, **"Dai!" "Dai!"** doesn't necessarily mean *"Give!"*: **Dai!** can also mean *"Come on!"*

Dai! È tardi! (*Come on! It's late!*)

PRACTICE

Use the clues in parentheses to fill in the blanks with the appropriate verbs in the present imperative. I've mixed up all the persons, and thrown in regular and irregular verbs here, so *be careful!* (**stai attento!**)

Q. _____ a spasso il cane! (tu, portare)

A. Porta a spasso il cane! (*Walk the dog!*)

1 _____ il mio consiglio, Signora! (ascoltare)

2 _____ con tuo fratello, Mara! (giocare)

3 _____ il vostro nome e cognome in stampatello, Signori! (voi, scrivere)

4 _____ a me, è meglio rimandare la partenza! (Loro, credere)

5 _____ la passeggiata, anche se non siamo stanchi! (noi, finire)

6 _____ avanti, Signore e Signori! (Loro, venire)

7 _____ attenti quando andate in bici! (voi, stare)

8 _____ il compito prima di guardare la tivù, (tu, finire)

9 _____ pure! (finire, Lei)

10 Mocca, _____ qui! (venire) (Mocca is a dog, so use the **tu** with her!)

11 _____ pazienza, per favore! (avere, voi)

12 _____ all'inferno! (andare, tu)

13 _____! (mangiare, tu)

Negative Commands

All verbs that have an affirmative command also have a negative command. All of the negative imperative forms, except for the **tu** form, are the exact same in the negative as they are in the affirmative (which you can read about in the sections "The Imperative Form of Regular Verbs" and "The Imperative Form of Irregular Verbs," earlier in this chapter).

You form the negative imperative for **tu** by using the infinitive form of the verb preceded by **Non** (*Don't*).

> **Non spendere troppo!** (*Don't spend too much!*)

> **Non finire tutta la torta!** (*Don't finish the whole cake!*)

The informal forms of **noi** and **voi** imperatives are formed by using their affirmative imperative preceded by **Non**.

> **Non parlate così in fretta!** (*Don't speak so fast!*)

> **Non usciamo stasera!** (*Let's not go out tonight!*)

Similarly, you craft the negative form of the formal imperative (**Lei** and **Loro**) by adding **non** to the formal imperative.

> **Non usi quel telefono, non funziona!** (*Don't use that phone, it doesn't work!*)

REMEMBER

The negative informal imperatives of the irregular verbs follow the rules of the regular imperatives.

The only difference between a verb's conjugations in affirmative and negative commands is in the **tu** person. In negative **tu** commands, you use the infinitive preceded by **non**.

> **Non tornare tardi!** (*Don't come back late!*).

Following are some more examples:

» **essere** (*to be*)

  tu: Non essere cattivo! (*Don't be mean!*)

  lei: Non siamo cattivi!

  noi: Non siamo cattivi!

  voi: Non siate cattivi!

» **andare: Non andare!** (*Don't go!*)

>> **dire: Non lo dire!** (*Don't say it!*)

>> **fare: Non lo fare!** (*Don't do it!*)

>> **uscire: Non uscire!** (*Don't go out!*)

Table 15-3 compares the **tu** and **Lei** forms of the imperative in two sample verbs.

Table 15-3 — Comparing Affirmative and Negative Commands

Verb	Tu Affirmative	Tu Negative	Lei Affirmative	Lei Negative	Example
andare (*to go*)	**va'/vai**	**non andare**	**vada**	**non vada**	**Non andare troppo veloce!** (*Don't go too fast!*)
portare (*to bring*)	**porta**	**non portare**	**porti**	**non porti**	**Porti il conto, per favore!** (*Please bring the bill!*)

PRACTICE Each of the following questions contains a reproduced road sign. Use the clues to tell your driver first what they should do and then what they shouldn't do, based on what the sign says. Write short commands in the second-person singular affirmative, and then the second-person singular negative. But because perhaps you should be using the formal **Lei** form with the driver, also add the **Lei** affirmative and negative command.

Q. (rallentare)

A. **Rallenta!** (*Go slower!*), **Non rallentare!** (*Don't slow down!*)

Rallenti! (*Go slower!*), **Non rallenti!** (*Don't slow down!*)

(14) (dare la precedenza) _____

15. **(entrare)** _____

16. **(parcheggiare)** _____

17. **(sorpassare)** _____

18. **(girare a destra)** _____

 19 **(superare il limite di velocità)** _____

Adding Pronouns to Commands

Pronouns are important parts of speech in Italian. This book addresses the personal pronouns in Chapter 4, the indirect object pronouns (in the context of the verb **piacere**) in Chapter 6, and the reflexive pronouns in Chapter 17). But I also want to introduce the direct object pronouns because they frequently accompany commands.

> **Mangia la pasta! Mangiala!** (*Eat the pasta!, Eat it!*): **La pasta** is a feminine singular direct object: **la** replaces it.

> **Guardami, Principessa!** (*Look at me, Princess!*): **Mi** in this sentence is a direct object, even though it might not be in English.

REMEMBER

You might need to tell someone to leave you alone — or to just leave! Here are two different ways to get rid of them, using the **tu** imperative (with and without a direct object pronoun).

> **Lasciami in pace!** (*Leave me alone!*)

> **Vai via!** (*Go away!*)

When the pronoun follows the imperative

Sometimes a pronoun follows the imperative, like in the English commands "*Listen to me!*" and "*Kiss me!*" When the pronoun follows the imperative, the pronoun is actually attached to the informal imperative form of the verb, creating a new word.

Ascoltami! (*Listen to me!*)

Baciami! (*Kiss me!*)

Here's the formula for the informal imperative (in the affirmative):

> Imperative + pronoun attached to imperative

Here are the unstressed pronouns that you can attach to the imperative:

> » Direct object pronouns: **mi** (*me*), **ti** (*you*), **lo/la** (*him/her*), **ci** (*us*), **vi** (*you*), **li/le** (*them*)
>
> **Aiutala!** (*Help her!*) (**Aiuta** + **la**)

> » Indirect object pronouns: **mi** (*to/for me*), **ti** (*to/for you*), **gli/le** (*to/for him/her*), **ci** (*to/for us*), **vi** (*to/for you*), **gli** (*to/for him*); also **loro** (*to/for them*) placed after the verb. You use these pronouns with the verb **piacere**, as well (see Chapter 6).
>
> **Compriamogli un paio di guanti.** (*Let's buy him a pair of gloves.*) (**Compriamo-mo** + **gli**)
>
> **Credimi!** (*Believe me!*) (**Credi** + **a me**)

> » **Ci** (*here, there, about this/that*) and **ne** (*about him/her/them, of this/that*)
>
> **Andateci!** (*Go there!*)
>
> **Parlatene!** (*Talk about it!*)

> » Double pronouns: **me lo** (*that to me*), **te le** (*those to her*), **glielo** (*it/that to him/her*), **gliene** (*about that to him*), **ce ne** (*about that to us*).
>
> Don't worry about these double-object pronouns in this book: It's enough for you to know that they exist when you're getting your feet wet with Italian.
>
> **Diteglielo.** (*Tell [it to] him/her.*)
>
> **Parlamene.** (*Tell me everything about it.*)

Like the other pronouns, when using a reflexive verb with the affirmative informal commands, the pronoun follows and is attached to the imperative.

Alzati e lavati! (*Get up and get washed!*)

In negative **tu** commands, the pronoun may precede or follow the infinitive — it's up to you! When attached to the infinitive, the infinitive drops the final **–e** before the pronoun.

Non preoccuparti!/Non ti preoccupare! (*Don't worry!*).

Refer to Table 15-4 for the use of reflexive pronouns with the imperative mood. The negative informal imperatives of the irregular verbs listed in Table 15-4 follow the rules of the regular imperatives.

If you issue a negative command in the second-person singular, which uses the infinitive, you drop the final **–e** of the verb. You can attach the pronoun to the verb or insert the pronoun between **non** (*not*) and the verb. Here are examples of both options.

Non telefonargli! (*Don't phone him!*)

Non gli telefonare! (*Don't phone him!*)

Table 15-4   Reflexive Imperatives

Affirmative Commands	Translation	Negative Commands	Translation
Lavati!	*Wash yourself!*	**Non ti lavare!/Non lavarti!**	*Don't wash yourself!*
Si lavi!	*Wash yourself!* (f, sing.)	**Non si lavi!**	*Don't wash yourself!* (f, sing.)
Laviamoci!	*Let's wash ourselves!*	**Non laviamoci!/Non ci laviamo!**	*Let's not wash ourselves!*
Lavatevi!	*Wash yourselves!*	**Non lavatevi!/Non vi lavate!**	*Don't wash yourselves!*
Si lavino!	*Wash yourselves!* (f, pl.)	**Non si lavino!**	*Don't wash yourselves!* (f, pl.)

When the pronoun precedes the imperative

When using a formal imperative (**Lei/Loro**), the pronoun precedes the imperative and the verb.

> **Mi ascolti bene prima di parlare!** (*Listen to me carefully before speaking!*)

When you issue a negative command in the formal imperative, you always place the pronoun between **non** and the imperative.

> **Non si preoccupi, signora!** (*Don't worry, Ma'am!*)

TIP

Chapter 17 discusses reflexive verbs, such as **addormentarsi** (*to fall asleep*) and **lavarsi** (*to wash oneself*), which use reflexive pronouns placed before the verb in other tenses, as well. In the imperative form of these verbs, the same rules of the pronouns apply:

>> *Get up!*: **Si alzi!** (formal) versus **Alzati!** (informal)

>> **Accomodati!** (Come in/Follow me/Take a seat!) versus **Si accomodi!** (formal) (Come in/Follow me/Take a seat!)

REMEMBER

Pronouns are attached to the verb in **tu**, **noi**, **voi** imperative forms. Pronouns precede the verb in **Lei/Loro** imperatives.

PRACTICE

In the following practice questions, first, determine what person imperative you're dealing with and whether that person is formal or informal. That information tells you where to place the pronoun. Then, rewrite each sentence, replacing the underlined nouns with direct object pronouns (d.o.), indirect object pronouns (i.o.), and reflexive pronouns (r.). (*Hint:* For the last four questions, just add the reflexive pronouns and leave the verbs alone.)

Q. Mandiamo una cartolina <u>a Sandro</u>! (i.o.)

A. **Mandiamogli una cartolina!** (*Let's send him a postcard!*)

20 Compra <u>le patatine</u> per la festa! (d.o.)

21 Non mangiare <u>il gelato</u>! (d.o.)

22 Non comprate <u>la frutta</u>! (d.o.)

23 Di' la verità <u>a me</u>! (i.o.)

24. Saluti <u>Nicole</u> da parte mia, Signora! (d.o.)

25. Non parlino <u>al Presidente</u>! (i.o.)

26. Invitate <u>Mariapola e David</u> a cena! (d.o.)

27. Non fare <u>la torta</u> per me! (d.o.)

28. Non dare la macchina <u>a Olimpia</u>! (i.o.)

29. Offra un bicchiere di vino <u>a loro</u>! (i.o.)

30. Dica la verità <u>a me</u>! (i.o.)

31. Signora, non _____ preoccupi! (r.)

32. Ragazzi, lavate _____ le mani! (r.)

33. Prego, accomoda _____! (r.)

34. Grace, non innamorar _____ mai! (r.)

Here's a creative way to ask your neighbors to clean up after their dogs. The picture below contains three informal **tu** commands (two regular and one negative); two of them have pronouns attached. *Remember:* **Fare bella figura** means *make a good impression.* **Fare brutta figura** means *make a bad impression.*

35. What commands are given on this notice? _____

36. What pronouns are attached to commands? _____

37. Translate the commands. _____

RELAX WITH SOME COMMANDS

If you want some relaxing Italian practice, here are some recommendations. I suggest some songs that have many examples of the imperative. Challenge yourself to find as many examples as possible

- **"Lasciatemi cantare!"** by Toto Cotugno

- **"Ricominciamo!"** by Adriano Pappalardo

- **"Recitar!. . . Vesti la giubba"** written by Leoncavallo; look for Pavarotti's performance of it

Answers to "Commanding and the Imperative" Practice Questions

(1) **Ascolti il mio consiglio, Signora!** (*Listen to my advice, Madam!*)

(2) **Gioca con tuo fratello, Mara!** (*Play with your brother, Mara!*)

(3) **Scrivano/Scrivete il vostro nome e cognome in stampatello, Signori!** (*Print your name and surname, ladies and gentlemen!*)

(4) **Credano a me, è meglio rimandare la partenza!** (*Believe me, it's better to postpone your departure!*)

(5) **Finiamo la passeggiata, anche se siamo stanchi!** (*Let's finish the walk, even though we're tired!*)

(6) **Vengano avanti, Signore e Signori!** (*Come in, ladies and gentlemen!*)

(7) **State attenti quando andate in bici!** (*Be careful when you go by bike.*)

(8) **Finisci il compito prima di guardare la tivù.** (*Finish your homework before watching tv.*)

(9) **Finisca pure di parlare!** (*Please finish speaking!*)

(10) **Mocca, vieni qui!** (*Mocca, come here!*)

(11) **Abbiate pazienza, per favore!** (*Have patience, please! Be patient, please!*)

(12) **Va'/Vai all'inferno!** (*Go to the devil!/Go to hell!*)

(13) **Mangia!** (*Eat!*)

(14) **Da' la precedenza!** (*Yield!*), **Non dare la precedenza!** (*Don't yield!*)

Dia la precedenza! (*Yield!*), **Non dia la precedenza!** (*Don't yield!*)

(15) **Entra!** (*Enter!*), **Non entrare!** (*Don't enter!*)

Entri! (*Enter!*), **Non entri!** (*Don't enter!*)

(16) **Parcheggia!** (*Park!*), **Non parcheggiare!** (*Don't park!*)

Parcheggi! (*Park!*), **Non parcheggi!** (*Don't park!*)

(17) **Sorpassa!** (*Pass!*), **Non sorpassare!** (*Don't pass!*)

Sorpassi! (*Pass!*), **Non sorpassi!** (*Don't pass!*)

(18) **Gira a destra!** (*Turn right!*), **Non girare a destra!** (*Don't turn right!*)

Vai dritto! (*Go straight!*), **Non andare dritto!** (*Don't go straight!*)

Giri a destra! (*Turn right!*) **Non giri a destra!** (*Don't turn right!*)

Vada! (*Go!*) **Non vada!** (*Don't go!*)

19. **Supera il limite di velocità!** (*Go past the speed limit!*), **Non superare il limite di velocità!** (*Don't exceed the speed limit!*)

Superi il limite di velocità! (*Go past the speed limit!*), **Non superi il limite di velocità!** (*Don't exceed the speed limit!*)

20. **Comprale per la festa!** (*Buy them for the party!*)

21. **Non mangiarlo!** (*Don't eat it!*)

22. **Non compratela!** (*Don't buy it!*)

23. **Dimmi la verità!** (*Tell me the truth!*)

24. **La saluti da parte mia, Signora!** (*Greeting from me, madam!*)

25. **Non gli parlino!** (*Don't speak to him!*)

26. **Invitateli a cena!** (*Invite them to dinner!*)

27. **Non farla per me!** (*Don't do it for me!*)

28. **Non darle la macchina!** (*Don't give her the car!*)

29. **Gli offra un bicchiere di vino!** (*Offer him a glass of wine!*)

30. **Mi dica la verità!** (*Tell me the truth!*)

31. **si; Signora, non si preoccupi!** (*Ma'am, don't worry!*)

32. **lavatevi; Ragazzi, lavatevi le mani!** (*Children, wash your hands!*)

33. **accomodati; Prego, accomodati!** (*Come in/Follow me/Take a seat!*)

34. **innamorarti; Grace, non innamorarti mai!** (*Grace, don't ever fall in love!*)

35. **Non farmi fare, raccoglila, porta**

36. **mi, la**

37. *Don't make me make a bad impression! You pick it up! Bring a bottle of water with you to clean up the pee pee!*

Chapter **16**

Forming and Using Conditional Verbs

What would you do if you had a million dollars? How would you manage any number of situations? Where would you have gone on vacation? You might use the conditional mood to deal with such questions. This chapter tells you how to use the conditional, which is a mood that basically expresses conditions and contingencies, in Italian.

The conditional mood has a present and past tense:

» **Present conditional:** When you're talking about something that someone would like or is wishing right now.

La Signora Rossi ti vorrebbe parlare. (*Mrs. Rossi would like to talk to you.*)

» **Past conditional:** Conveys that something would have been desirable or appropriate, even though it's too late now to do anything about it.

Avrei visto volentieri quel film una seconda volta. (*I would have gladly seen that movie a second time.*)

In this chapter, I show you how to form and use the present and past conditional.

Shaping Verbs into the Present Conditional

The present conditional is a polite tense. You use it when you want to express events occurring under certain circumstances or conditions. It's also used to add politeness to offers, advice, and requests that would otherwise sound too blunt. The present conditional is a simple tense that you form by adding suffixes to the infinitive stem of the verb, depending on the verb's ending. In other words, the conditional shares the exact same stem as the future tense (see Chapter 14 for more about the future tense).

TIP

The conditional is frequently used with words such as **ma** (*but*).

Mangerei, ma non ho fame. (*I would eat, but I'm not hungry.*)

Regular verbs

The conjugations for regular verbs in the present conditional are awesomely simple: They have only one set of endings. These are attached to the future stem of the verb (see Chapter 14 for more on the future). Just follow this formula.

future (infinitive) stem + conditional ending

These regular infinitive stems of –**are**, –**ere**, –**ire** verbs are as follow:

>> **parlare** becomes **parler–** (the **a** in –**are** verbs turns into an **e**).

   Parlerei con tuo padre. (*I would talk to your dad.*)

>> **mettere** becomes **metter–**.

   Gix metterebbe il divano là (*Gix would put the couch there*).

>> **partire** becomes **partir–**.

   Partiremmo subito, ma Maria e Lee non sono ancora arrivati. (*We'd leave right away, but Maria and Lee haven't arrived yet.*)

SONGS TO SET THE (CONDITIONAL) MOOD

Do you want some songs to get you through the conditional and experience it in context?

Here are a few songs that provide several examples of the conditional mood. Download the lyrics and Google the song itself so that you can listen and sing along. If you want, you can highlight the conditional in the lyrics that you download.

- **"Il mondo che vorrei,"** by Laura Pausini

- **"Il mondo che vorrei,"** by Vasco Rossi

- **"Io vorrei,"** by Lucio Battisti

The present conditional endings are the same for the three conjugations (–**are**, –**ere**, and –**ire** verbs). See Table 16-1.

Table 16-1 Endings for Regular Verbs in the Present Conditional

Person	Conditional Endings
io	–ei
tu	–esti
lui/lei/Lei	–ebbe
noi	–emmo
voi	–este
loro/Loro	–ebbero

The following table shows you how to conjugate **guardare** (*to look at*).

guardare (to look at)	
io guarderei	noi guarderemmo
tu guarderesti	voi guardereste
lui/lei/Lei guarderebbe	loro/Loro guarderebbero

Non guarderemmo mai quel programma! (*We would never watch that show!*)

Verbs that end in –**ciare** and –**giare**, such as **cominciare** (*to begin*) and **mangiare** (*to eat*), drop the **i** before the endings to preserve the soft sounds (ch) (as in *chips*) and (gee) (as in *gee whiz!*). Verbs that end in –**care** and –**gare**, such as **cercare** (*to look for*) and **pagare** (*to pay*), add an **h** to the stem before adding the conditional endings to preserve the hard sound of the infinitive, as in the *c* as in *cat*, and *g* as in *get*.

DIFFERENCES

Here are those stems:

>> **cominciare: comincer–**

>> **mangiare: manger–**

>> **cercare: cercher–**

>> **pagare: pagher–**

Piacere (*to like*) is always unique across the tenses. In this book, you're concerned with **piacere** only in the third-person singular (if what you like is singular or an infinitive) or the third-person plural (if what you like is plural). See Chapter 6 for more on **piacere** (in the present tense, and also the indirect object pronouns you often need to use with it).

REMEMBER

Mi piacerebbe visitare le Isole Egadi un giorno. (*I'd like to visit the Egadi Islands one day.*)

Mi piacerebbe una pizza. (*I'd like a pizza.*)

Ti piacerebbero le zucchine o le melanzane alla griglia? (*Would you like zucchini or eggplant on the grill?*)

REMEMBER

Piacere in the conditional present is very similar to **volere** (*to want*) in the conditional — both mean *would like.*

Mi piacerebbe frequentare l'Università di Urbino/Vorrei frequentare l'Università di Urbino. (*I'd like to attend the University of Urbino.*)

Irregular verbs (Well, sort of)

All verbs that have an irregular future stem use the same stem for the conditional. So although it seems that the conditional has irregular verbs, the situation is sort of misleading; the future has the irregular conjugations, and the conditional is built on the future tense. Technically, the conditional does follow a regular pattern — you form it by adding the appropriate endings to the future stems of the verb (see Chapter 14).

You can use **essere** (*to be*) and **avere** (*to have*) by themselves or as auxiliaries in compound tenses (see Chapters 5 and 12 for details on these two lovely verbs). In the present conditional, the stems are the same as for the future tense:

>> **essere** becomes **sar-**

>> **avere** becomes **avr-** (you drop both **e**'s from the infinitive)

The following tables show the conjugations for both **essere** and **avere** in the future tense.

essere (to be)	
io sarei	noi saremmo
tu saresti	voi sareste
lui/lei/Lei sarebbe	loro/Loro sarebbero

Sarei felice di conoscerlo. (*I would be happy to meet him.*)

avere (to have)	
io avrei	noi avremmo
tu avresti	voi avreste
lui/lei/Lei avrebbe	loro/Loro avrebbero

Non avrebbe degli spicci? (*Would you happen to have change?*)

You definitely have to communicate with a moderated tone. People often use the conditional of the verbs **dovere** (*must/shall/ought/need to*), **potere** (*can/may/to be able to*), **volere** (*to want to*), and **sapere** (*to know how to*) to soften the impact of requests and demands.

dovere (must/shall)	
io dovrei	noi dovremmo
tu dovresti	voi dovreste
lui/lei/Lei dovrebbe	loro/Loro dovrebbero

Dovremmo pagare il conto. (*We should pay the bill.*)

potere (can/may)	
io potrei	noi potremmo
tu potresti	voi potreste
lui/lei/Leipotrebbe	loro/Loro potrebbero

Potresti richiamarmi? (*Could you [please] call me back?*)

sapere (to know how to)	
Io saprei	noi sapremmo
tu sapresti	voi sapreste
lui/lei/Lei saprebbe	loro/Loro saprebbero

Saprebbe dirmi dove posso trovare un buon ristorante? (*Would you be able to tell me where I can find a good restaurant?*)

volere (will/to want to)	
io vorrei	noi vorremmo
tu vorresti	voi vorreste
lui/lei/Lei vorrebbe	loro/Loro vorrebbero

Vorrei parlarti prima possibile. (*I would like to talk to you as soon as possible.*)

Conjugate the following verbs in the present conditional.

PRACTICE

Q. _____ un po' di silenzio, per favore. (volere)

A. **Vorremmo un po' di silenzio, per favore.** (*We'd like a little bit of silence, please.*)

1. _____ una pizza! (mangiare, noi)

2. _____ dormire! (volere, io)

3. Loro _____ contenti di andare in Italia. (essere)

4. _____ con lui in vacanza? (andare, tu)

5. Caterina ed io _____ ma dobbiamo fare I compiti. (venire)

6. Mia madre _____ sempre con le sue amiche! (uscire)

7   Io non _____ duecento dollari per quegli stivali: sono bruttissimi! (pagare)

8   I nostri amici _____ arrivare fra mezz'ora. (dovere)

9   Mi _____ conoscere Leonardo Di Caprio. (piacere)

10 _____ darmi una mano, per favore? (potere, tu)

11 Tu _____ la verità? (dire)

12 Scusi, _____ l'ora? (sapere, Lei)

PRACTICE

Practice answering these open-ended questions.

Q. **Dove ti picerebbe essere in questo momento?** (*Where would you like to be right now?*)

A. **Mi piacerebbe essere a Ravenna.** (*I'd like to be in Ravenna.*)

13 Cosa faresti con un milione di dollari?

14 Cosa potresti fare per migliorare il mondo?

15 Quale città italiana ti piacerebbe visitare e perché?

16 Che cosa mangeresti in questo momento?

17 Che cosa vorresti fare quest'estate?

Using the Conditional by Itself

If you want something, you can be very assertive and, say (as a child might), **"Voglio un gelato!"** (*"I want ice cream!"*). If you're talking to yourself, this sort of statement is okay, but if you're engaging in polite conversation, you may want to be a tad less aggressive.

The conditional enables you to

>> Tone down your demands

Sposteresti la macchina, per favore? (*Would you mind moving the car, please?*)

>> Express surprise and uncertainty

Ci crederesti? (*Can you believe that?*)

In such cases, you build independent sentences and put the verb in the conditional tense. The word *please* is often implied with the conditional in Italian.

REMEMBER

Italian also uses **sapere** (*to know how to*) as a modal auxiliary.

Sapresti aprire la cassaforte? (*Could/Would you be able to/would you know how to open the safe?*)

PRACTICE

Transform the verbs in the present tense in the following sentences into the conditional tense. Change only the verb. First, figure out the person. Then, remember what the infinitive of the verb is.

Q. Comprate del pane anche per me.

A. Comprereste del pane anche per me? (*Would you buy some bread for me, too?*)

18 Cristina e Mara, portate la valigia del nonno?

19 Signora, mi prepara il pacco per oggi pomeriggio?

20 Signori, giocano a bridge con noi?

21 Devi restituire i soldi a Barbara.

22 Vogliono passare per Madrid.

23 Possiamo comprare quella casa.

24 Lei vuole andarsene, mentre lui vuole rimanere.

It's Over Now! Forming the Past Conditional

Every time you say something like *You should have told me!* (**Avresti dovuto dirmi!**) or *I would have liked to come to the party!* (**Mi sarebbe piaciuto venire alla festa!**) you're using the past conditional tense. The past conditional expresses the idea that it's too late now and also describes an action that can't occur in the future, either. The present conditional describes an action that's still possible.

Potrei andare al cinema stasera. (*I could go to the movies tonight.*)

TIP

To provide more context, compare these two sentences, the first in the present conditional and the second in the past conditional.

Cosa faresti al mio posto? (*What would you do in my situation?*)

Cosa avresti fatto al mio posto? (*What would you have done in my situation?*)

The past conditional is a compound tense (made up of two parts) with the following formula:

Present conditional of **essere** (*to be*) or **avere** (*to have*) + past participle of the verb

The auxiliary you use depends on which main verb you're using. (Chapter 12 shows you how to decide which auxiliary verb to use, how to distinguish between transitive and intransitive verbs, as well as how to form the past participle and make it agree with subjects.)

For example, in the following sentence, you form the past conditional by using the auxiliary **essere** and the past participle of **venire** (*to go*), which is **venuto**.

> **Sarei venuto al cinema con te, ma ero troppo stanco.** (*I would've gone to the movies with you, but I was too tired.*)

These two tables show the past conditional of **leggere** (*to read*), which takes the **avere** (a transitive verb), and of **andare** (*to go*), which takes the **essere** (an intransitive verb).

leggere (to read)	
io avrei letto	noi avremmo letto
tu avresti letto	voi avreste letto
lui/lei/Lei avrebbe letto	loro/Loro avrebbero letto

Avrei letto il giornale, ma l'hai buttato via. (*I would've read the newspaper, but you tossed it.*)

andare (to go)	
io sarei andato/andata	noi saremmo andati/andate
tu saresti andato/andata	voi sareste andati/andate
lui/lei/Lei/esso sarebbe andato/andata	loro/Loro sarebbero andati/andate

I ragazzi non sarebbero mai andati alla festa senza di te. (*The boys and girls would've never gone to the party without you.*)

REMEMBER

Piacere (*to like*) always takes **essere** in a compound tense. And this book uses **piacere** only in the third-person singular and plural. See Chapter 12 for **piacere** in the **passato prossimo**, which also explains the agreement of the verb with whatever is being liked.

> **Mi sarebbe piaciuto conoscere il tuo ragazzo.** (*I would have liked to meet your boyfriend*)
>
> **Ti sarebbe piaciuta l'opera ieri sera!** (*You would have liked the opera last night!*)
>
> **Gli sarebbero piaciute queste spiagge.** (*He would have liked these beaches.*)

Conjugate the following verbs into the past conditional.

PRACTICE

Q. Domenico e Maria _____ in Italia, ma non stavano abbastanza bene. **(tornare)**

A. Domenico e Maria sarebbero tornati in Italia, ma non stavano abbastanza bene. (*Domenico and Maria would have returned to Italy, but they were not well enough*).

(25) _____ alla festa, ma ero stanca. (venire, io)

(26) I miei genitori _____ a casa. (rimanere)

(27) Che cosa _____ tu a posto mio? (fare)

(28) La nostra squadra _____ la partita, ma Olivia non ha giocato. (vincere)

(29) Noi _____ studiare di più ieri sera. (dovere)

(30) Laurie _____ medico. (diventare)

Answers to "Forming and Using Conditional Verbs" Practice Questions

(1) **Mangeremmo; Mangeremmo una pizza!** (*We could eat a piazza!*)

(2) **Vorrei; Vorrei dormire!** (*I'd like to sleep.*)

(3) **sarebbero; Loro sarebbero contenti di andare in Italia.** (*They'd be happy to go to Italy.*)

(4) **Andresti; Andresti con lui in vacanza?** (*Would you go on vacation with him?*)

(5) **verremmo; Caterina ed io verremmo ma dobbiamo fare i compiti.** (*Caterina and I would come, but we need to do our homework.*)

(6) **uscirebbe; Mia madre uscirebbe sempre con le sue amiche!** (*My mother would go out with her friends all the time!*)

(7) **pagherei; Io non pagherei duecento dollari per quegli stivali: sono bruttissimi!** (*I wouldn't pay $200 for those boots: they're awful!*)

(8) **dovrebbero; I nostri amici dovrebbero arrivare fra mezz'ora.** (*Our friends should be arriving in a half hour.*)

(9) **piacerebbe; Mi piacerebbe conoscere Leonardo Di Caprio.** (*I'd like to meet Leonardo Di Caprio.*)

(10) **Potresti; Potresti darmi una mano, per favore?** (*Would you please give me a hand?*)

(11) **diresti; Tu diresti la verità?** (*Would you tell the truth?*)

(12) **saprebbe; Scusi, saprebbe l'ora?** (*Excuse me, would you know the time?*)

(13) **Comprerei una villa ad Amalfi.** (*I'd buy a villa in Amalif.*)

(14) **Potrei riciclare, usare meno luce, fare volontariato.** (*I could recycle, use less electricity, volunteer.*)

(15) **Mi piacerebbe visitare Siracusa perché è una bella città con tanta storia.** (*I'd like to visit Siracusa because it's a beautiful city with much history.*)

(16) **Mangererei una pasta alla crema** (*I would eat a custard filled pastry*).

(17) **Vorrei visitare il Messico.** (*I'd like to visit Mexico.*)

(18) **portereste; Cristina e Mara, portereste la valigia del nonno?** (*Cristina and Mara, would you carry grandpa's suitcase?*)

(19) **preparerebbe; Signora, mi preparerebbe il pacco per oggi pomeriggio?** (*Ma'am, would you please prepare the package for me for this afternoon?*)

(20) **giocherebbero; Signori, giocherebbero a bridge con noi?** (*Would you play bridge with us?*)

(21) **Dovresti; Dovresti restituire i soldi a Barbara.** (*You should give the money back to Barbara.*)

(22) **Vorrebbero; Vorrebbero passare per Madrid.** (*They'd like to pass through Madrid.*)

(23) **Potremmo; Potremmo comprare quella casa.** (*We could buy that house.*)

24 **vorrebbe, vorrebbe; Lei vorrebbe andarsene, mentre lui vorrebbe rimanere.** (*She would like to leave, while he would like to stay.*)

25 **Sarei venuta; Sarei venuta alla festa, ma ero stanca.** (*I would have come to the party, but I was tired.*)

26 **sarebbero rimasti; I miei genitori sarebbero rimasti a casa.** (*My parents would have stayed home.*)

27 **avresti fatto; Che cosa avresti fatto tu al mio posto?** (*What would you have done in my situation?*)

28 **avrebbe vinto; La nostra squadra avrebbe vinto la partita, ma Olivia non ha giocato.** (*Our team would have won the game, but Olivia didn't play.*)

29 **avremmo dovuto; Noi avremmo dovuto studiare di più ieri sera.** (*We should have studied more last night.*)

30 **sarebbe diventata; Laurie sarebbe diventata medico.** (*Laurie would have become a doctor.*)

Chapter **17**

Everyday Communication with Reflexives

Come ti chiami? (*What's your name?*) **Mi chiamo Teresa.** (*My name is Teresa.*) This conversation uses the reflexive verb **chiamarsi**, which literally means *to call oneself*. In Chapter 1, I present this commonly used structure as a key to basic communication with introductions and greetings. You use reflexive verbs in everyday life, all the time, to talk about your daily routine and how you feel.

> **Non mi sento bene.** (*I don't feel well.*)

> **Mia figlia si veste in cinque minuti.** (*My daughter gets dressed in five minutes.*).

You use reflexive verbs when

» The subject is the object of its own action. This construct frequently suggests doing something to oneself.

Mi lavo il viso. (*I'm washing my face.*). Note that this sentence doesn't have a possessive adjective — *my*. You generally don't use possessive adjectives with reflexive verbs or body parts and items you wear.

>> Expressing a rich range of other actions or moments that don't necessarily imply an action reflected back to the self, such as with the verb **dimenticarsi** (*to forget*).

>> More than one person is involved (thus making it a reciprocal action), such as the verb **guardarsi** (*to look at each other*). For this reason, reciprocals are always in the three plural persons (**noi**, **voi**, **loro**):

- **ci guardiamo** (*we're looking at each other*)
- **vi guardate** (*you look at each other*)
- **si guardano** (*they're looking at each other*)

REMEMBER

All reflexive and reciprocal verbs take the auxiliary **essere** in a compound tense. The compound tenses that this book covers include the **passato prossimo** (Chapter 12), the past perfect (Chapter 13) and the past conditional (Chapter 16).

In this chapter, I show how an action is directed to a subject with reflexive verbs. I also present the reflexive pronouns. Then, I introduce reflexive verbs in the present tense and the **passato prossimo**. Finally, I walk you through how to express reciprocal actions.

Directing an Action to a Subject

In both Italian and English, a reflexive verb allows you to say that an action is directed at the subject who's performing it. Italian uses reflexive verbs more than English, employing them to convey that

>> The subject is performing an action on themselves.

Io mi lavo. (*I'm washing myself./I'm getting washed.*)

>> Something is happening to the subject themselves, even though it's not something the person is causing it to happen, as in **Mi annoio** (*I'm bored*).

Io mi sveglio. (*I'm waking up.*)

>> The action is directed at the subject and a part of themselves.

Io mi lavo le mani. (*I wash my hands./I'm washing my hands.*)

>> The action is directed at the subject and implies putting on or taking off articles of clothing or other objects.

Mi metto gli occhiali. (*I'm putting my sunglasses on.*)

>> Two or more people engage in a reciprocal action, which frequently translates as *to each other*.

Noi ci scriviamo. (*We write to each other.*)

Looking at when the subject is also the object: Reflexive pronouns

Reflexive pronouns convey that the subject is also frequently the recipient of the action.

Il mio gatto si lava sempre. (*My cat always washes himself.*)

You use reflexive pronouns with reflexive verbs. Table 17-1 presents the reflexive pronouns.

Table 17-1   Reflexive Pronouns

Singular	Plural
mi (*myself*)	**ci** (*ourselves*)
ti (*yourself*)	**vi** (*yourselves*, informal)
si (*himself/herself/itself*)	**si** (*themselves*)
Si (*yourself*, third-person sing., formal)	**Si** (*yourselves*, third-person pl., formal)

When conjugating a reflexive verb, conjugate it exactly as you would a verb that's not reflexive: The only difference is that you place the reflexive pronoun in front of the conjugated verb (usually). So, tackle the tenses in the preceding chapters in order to know how to conjugate the reflexive verbs. For example, review how to conjugate the present tense regular (Chapter 5) and irregular verbs (Chapter 6). In this example, **svegliarsi** (*to wake up*) and **alzarsi** (*to get up*) look just like –are verbs in the present tense.

Marco si sveglia ogni mattina alle 6:00 ma non si alza fino alle 6:30. Io mi sveglio alle 6:00 ma mi alzo subito. (*Marco wakes up every morning at 6:00, but he doesn't get out of bed until 6:30. I wake up every morning at 6:00, but I get up immediately.*)

TIP

You also get a dose of these reflexive pronouns and reflexive verbs when dealing with the imperative in Chapter 15. When dealing with imperatives, the position of the pronouns shifts, according to which grammatical person you're using.

PRACTICE

Fill in the blanks in the following letter with the correct forms of the reflexive pronouns.

Q. **I ragazzi si annoiano d'estate?** (*Do the children get bored in the summer?*)

A. **No, non si annoiano mai.** (*No, they never get bored.*)

Cara Loredana,

Ti scrivo per darti mie notizie. Io (1) _____ sento molto felice oggi perché Roberto mi ha chiesto di sposarlo e noi (2) _____ sposiamo/sposeremo a giugno. Sai che noi (3) _____ divertiamo sempre insieme ed è un po' che usciamo. E tu (4) _____ senti di essere la mia damigella? Volevo chiederti subito perché mia madre (5) _____ metterà subito ad organizzare tutto e mi è molto importante che tu ne faccia parte! Fammi sapere al più presto!

Un abbraccio,

Carla

Forming reflexive verbs

In order to tell a reflexive verb from a regular transitive or intransitive verb, first look for the ending **–si** attached to the stem of the infinitive without the final **–e**: **lavare** (*to wash*) becomes **lavarsi** (*to wash oneself*). Then conjugate the reflexive verb in the desired tense by following these steps:

1. **Conjugate the verb in whatever tense you need.**

   Maybe you need present tense, **passato prossimo**, imperfect, conditional, or something else.

2. **Add the auxiliary essere in compound tenses.**

   I bambini si sono addormentati. (*The children have fallen asleep./The children fell asleep.*)

   Turn to Chapter 12 for coverage of compound tenses.

3. **Make the past participle agree with the subject in compound tenses.**

   Le bambine si sono addormentate (*The little girls have fallen asleep*)

   You treat all reflexives like intransitive verbs (which take **essere**). Turn to Chapter 12 to find out about past participles and agreement.

4. **Place the appropriate reflexive pronoun before the verb.**

   Choose from **mi** (*myself*), **ti** (*yourself*), **si** (*himself/herself/itself/oneself*), **ci** (*ourselves*), **vi** (*yourselves*), **si** (*themselves*).

   I bambini si addormentano. (*The children are falling asleep.*)

Forming reflexive verbs in the present

Flip back to Chapters 4, 5, and 6 if you need to review the present tense. One of the tricks to handling the reflexive verbs in the present (or any other tense) is to remember the format.

> reflexive pronoun + conjugated verb (without the **–si** attached)

Consider the verb **lavarsi** in its infinitive form:

> » Take off the **–si** and drag it to the front as a place holder for whatever reflexive pronoun you need.
>
> Now you're left with **lavare**, or a regular -**are** verb (see Chapter 4).
>
> » X + lavare (now you can conjugate **lavare** like a regular –**are** verb)

The following tables show you four regular reflexive verbs conjugated in the present: an –**are**, –**ere**, –**ire**, and –**ire** (**isc**) verb. You can also find a table for an irregular reflexive verb, **farsi male** (*to get hurt/to injure oneself*).

REMEMBER

You don't need the personal pronouns (**io, tu, lui, lei, Lei, noi, voi, loro**) when conjugating the reflexive verbs; they're even redundant at times. I include the personal pronouns in the **lavarsi** table only to remind you what they are. You do need the reflexive pronouns in these conjugations, though.

lavarsi (to wash oneself)	
io mi lavo	noi ci laviamo
tu ti lavi	voi vi lavate
lui/lei/Lei si lava	loro/Loro si lavano

Ci laviamo le mani prima di mangiare. (*We wash our hands before eating.*)

mettersi (to put something on)	
mi metto	ci mettiamo
ti metti	vi mettete
si mette	si mettono

Mi metto le scarpe da ginnastica. (*I'm putting my sneakers on.*)

divertirsi (to have fun/to enjoy oneself/to have a good time)	
mi diverto	ci divertiamo
ti diverti	vi divertite
si diverte	si divertono

Ci divertiamo stasera! (*We're going to have fun this evening!*)

trasferirsi (to move [to a place])	
mi trasferisco	ci trasferiamo
ti trasferisci	vi trasferite
si trasferisce	si trasferiscono

Gigio si trasferisce a Ravenna quando va in pensione. (*Gigio's going to move to Ravenna when he retires.*)

farsi male (to get hurt/to injure oneself)	
mi faccio male	ci facciamo male
ti fai male	vi fate male
si fa male	si fanno male

Mi faccio male se gioco a calcio oggi. (*I'm going to get hurt if I play soccer today.*)

Table 17-2 lists some very common reflexive verbs. Pick out the ones that you find most useful.

Table 17-2   Common Reflexive Verbs

Reflexive Verb	Reflexive Verb
ricordarsi (*to remember*)	**scusarsi** (*to apologize*)
addormentarsi (*to fall asleep*)	**fidanzarsi** (*to get engaged*)
rilassarsi (*to relax*)	**sedersi** (*to sit*)
sentirsi (*to feel*)	**stancarsi** (*to get tired*)
arrabbiarsi (*to get angry*)	**lamentarsi** (*to complain*)
alzarsi (*to get up, to stand up*)	**innamorarsi** (*to fall in love*)
chiamarsi (*to be called*)	**spogliarsi** (*to get undressed*)
curarsi (*to take care of oneself*)	**sposarsi [con]** (*to get married*)
dimenticarsi (*to forget*)	**annoiarsi** (*to get bored*)
divertirsi (*to enjoy oneself*)	**svegliarsi** (*to wake up*)
farsi male (*to get hurt*)	**svestirsi** (*to undress*)
fermarsi (*to stop*)	**tagliarsi** (*to cut oneself*)
offendersi (*to get/be offended*)	**trasferirsi** (*to move one's residence*)
rendersi conto di (*to become aware of*)	**vestirsi** (*to get dressed*)

A note about **innamorarsi** (*to fall in love*): This verb can be both **reflexive** and **reciprocal.** **Innamorarsi** is reflective when you say **Mi innamoro facilmente** (*I fall in love easily*) and it's reciprocal when you say **Ci siamo innamorati** (*We fell in love with each other*), so you will also see this verb in the later section, "Engaging in Reciprocal Actions."

PRACTICE

Conjugate the following reflexive verbs into the present tense.

Q. _____ spesso. (**innamorarsi, io**)

A. **Mi innamoro spesso.** (*I fall in love frequently.*)

6 Giovanna ed io _____ dell'esame. (lamentarsi)

7 Mio padre _____ la barba la mattina. (farsi)

8 Cecilia e Maeve, a che ora _____ di solito? (svegliarsi)

9 Alessia ed Alessandro, _____ di più a Salerno o a Ferrara? (divertirsi)

10 Non _____ mai! (truccarsi, io)

11 Michele e Bruno _____ bene per il matrimonio di Beniamino. (vestirsi)

12 Guglielmo, _____ per l'esamino? (preoccuparsi)

13 Chiara non _____ spesso. (arrabbiarsi)

14 _____ sempre di prendere la posta! (dimenticarsi, io)

Reflexive verbs in the passato prossimo

Reflexive verbs take **essere** as the auxiliary verb in compound tenses. You form them in the same way that you form the intransitive **essere** verbs (as outlined in Chapter 12), then add the reflexive pronoun in front. This section covers how to use reflexive verbs in the **passato prossimo**.

Here's the formula for reflexive verbs in the **passato prossimo**:

Reflexive pronoun + **essere** + past participle (–**ato**, –**uto**, –**ito**, with four endings)

Table 17-3 shows the verb **alzarsi** in the **passato prossimo** for each conjugation. Follow this pattern for all reflexive verbs.

Table 17-3   Conjugation of Alzarsi (Get Up)

Verb	Example
mi sono alzato/a	**Mi sono alzata alle sei stamattina.** (*I got up at six this morning.*)
ti sei alzata/o	**Ti sei alzata/o alle sei stamattina.** (*You got up at six this morning.*)
lui si è alzato	**Rocco si è alzato alle sei stamattina.** (*Rocco got up at six this morning.*)
lei si è alzata	**Carla si è alzata alle sei stamattina.** (*She got up at six this morning.*)
Lei si è alzata/o	**Si è alzata/o alle sei stamattina.** (*You [formal] got up at six this morning.*)
ci siamo alzati/e	**Noi ci siamo alzate/i alle sei stamattina.** (*We got up at six this morning.*)
vi siete alzati/e	**Vi siete alzati/e alle sei stamattina.** (*You got up at six this morning.*)
si sono alzate/i	**I ragazzi si sono alzati alle sei stamattina.** (*The boys got up at six this morning.*)
	Le ragazze si sono alzate alle sei stamattina. (*The girls got up at six this morning.*)

PRACTICE

Conjugate the following reflexive verbs into the **passato prossimo**.

Q. Ieri sono caduta mentre giocavo a calcio e _____ la caviglia. (rompersi)

A. mi sono rotta; Ieri sono caduta mentre giocavo a calcio e mi sono rotta la caviglia.
(*Yesterday, I fell while playing soccer and broke my ankle.*)

15 Luca e io _____ al ballo sabato scorso. (divertirsi, noi)

16 Maria Caterina _____ i capelli questa mattina. (lavarsi)

17 I miei genitori _____ sessanta anni fa. (sposarsi)

18 Salvatore _____ a prima vista di Elena, ma poi la perde di vista per sempre.
(innamorarsi)

19 Antonio, a che ora _____ ieri sera? (addormentarsi)

20 Oggi non _____ le lenti a contatto perchè mi fanno male gli occhi.
(mettersi, io, f)

21 Caterina e Anna _____ a scuola ieri. (annoiarsi)

Transforming a transitive verb into a reflexive verb

In Italian, you can make most *transitive verbs* — verbs that require both a subject and an object — reflexive by adding the ending **–si** to the infinitive of the verb. You make a transitive verb reflexive when you need the speaker to perform the action of a regular transitive verb.

For more information on transitive verbs, turn to Chapter 12. You can turn most transitive verbs into reflexive verbs; as a rule of thumb, use discernment and context. Start by looking at the following statement.

> **Io mi guardo allo specchio.** (*I'm looking at myself in the mirror.*)

Now note the differences in these sentence types:

> » **guardare** is transitive (and takes **avere** in a compound tense): **Guardo un film.** (*I'm watching a film.*)/**Ho guardato un film.** (*I watched a film.*)

> » **guardarsi** is reflexive (and takes **essere**): **Mi guardo nello specchio.** (*I'm looking at myself in the mirror.*)/**Mi sono guardata nello specchio.** (*I looked at myself in the mirror.*)

> » **guardarsi** is in the reciprocal form (and takes **essere**): **Emilia ed io ci guardiamo negli occhi.** (*Emilia and I look each other in the eye.*)/**Emilia ed io ci siamo guardate negli occhi.** (*Emilia and I looked each other in the eyes.*)

TIP

Some reflexive verbs have a passive meaning, such as **rompersi** (*to break*). For example, in the sentence **Il bicchiere si è rotto** (*The glass was/got broken*), you're technically saying that the glass was damaged. But the verb used to express that idea is reflexive, even though the glass didn't really do anything to itself.

Acting on the body and clothing

When you talk about someone doing something to their body or putting on or taking off articles of clothing, you can build a reflexive meaning without using possessive adjectives.

REMEMBER

This construction adds emphasis and avoids confusion about the recipient of the action. If you say **Io lavo i capelli** (*I'm washing hair*), you aren't saying whether you're washing your own hair or someone else's. But if you add a reflexive pronoun and say **Io mi lavo i capelli** (*I'm washing my hair*), you can only be washing your own hair.

Following are some common verbs used in talking about yourself:

> » **lavarsi** (*to wash oneself*)

> » **mettersi** (*to put on*)

> » **pettinarsi** (*to comb one's hair*)

> » **prepararsi** (*to prepare*)

> » **pulirsi** (*to clean oneself*)

» **radersi/farsi la barba** (*to shave*)

» **rompersi** (*to break [a limb]*)

» **spazzolarsi** (*to brush one's hair*)

» **spogliarsi** (*to undress*)

» **tagliarsi** (*to cut oneself*)

» **tingersi** (*to dye [one's hair]*)

» **togliersi** (*to take off*)

» **truccarsi** (*to put on make-up*)

» **vestirsi** (*to get dressed*)

PRACTICE

Translate the following sentences from English into Italian. Use the present tense, and get out your Italian dictionary, if necessary. Remember that you don't use possessive adjectives with things you put on or with body parts.

Q. *A man is shaving.*

A. **Un uomo si rade.**

22 A woman combs her hair.

23 A boy brushes (washes) his teeth.

24 The actor is putting his make-up on.

25 I'm putting in my contact lenses.

26 A man is taking off his shirt.

27 The children get dressed.

Engaging in Reciprocal Actions

DIFFERENCES

People often engage in activities characterized by reciprocity: They speak to one another, write to one another, and so on. You convey this action in English with the verb in the active form accompanied by the phrases *each other/one another*, or by using the verb *to get* + a past participle. In Italian, you use a reflexive verb in the plural because the subject includes at least two people (the section "Forming reflexive verbs," earlier in this chapter, shows you how to form the plural reflexive verb).

Si conoscono da molti anni. (*They've known each other for many years.*)

Marina e Pietro si sono fidanzati. (*Marina and Pietro got engaged.*)

Of course, you can also use some verbs that convey reciprocity to instead convey an emotion or a state of mind, saying that the subject is feeling something about themselves.

Nadia si conosce bene. (*Nadia knows herself very well.*)

In a true reciprocal usage, you have two or more subjects.

Nadia e Maria si conoscono da due anni. (*Nadia and Maria have known each other for two years.*)

Here's a list of some verbs that you can use to convey reciprocity:

» **amarsi** (*to love each other*)

» **baciarsi** (*to kiss each other*)

» **chiamarsi**, **telefonarsi** (*to call each other/to telephone each other/to talk on the phone to each other*)

» **conoscersi** (*to know each other/to meet*)

» **fidanzarsi** (*to get engaged to each other*)

» **incontrarsi** (*to meet each other*)

» **innamorarsi** (*to fall in love with each other*)

» **odiarsi** (*to hate each other*)

» **parlarsi** (*to speak to each other/to talk to each other*)

» **presentarsi** (*to introduce oneself to each other*)

» **salutarsi** (*to greet each other*)

» **scriversi** (*to write each other*)

» **separarsi** (*to get separated from each other*)

» **sposarsi** (*to get married*)

» **stringersi la mano** (*to shake hands*)

» **vedersi** (*to see each other*)

» **volersi bene** (*to care for each other*)

REMEMBER

Remember these two important points when dealing with reciprocals. They're

» Always plural: **–ci**, **–vi**, **–si** (we/you all/they do something with each other,)

» Basically plural reflexive verbs (discussed in the section "Forming reflexive verbs in the present" earlier in this chapter)

Translate the following sentences from English into Italian using the reciprocal form.

PRACTICE

Q. *Giulio and Barbara are calling each other.*

A. **Giulio e Barbara si telefonano.**

28 A man and a woman meet (for the first time) each other.

29 Vincenzo and Daria are getting married to each other.

30 Rudi and Mor love each other.

31 A man and a woman say hello to each other.

32 Two men hate each other.

33 We love each other.

 Conjugate these verbs in the reciprocal form in the **passato prossimo.**

PRACTICE

Q. _____alla festa. (**presentarsi, noi**)

A. **Ci siamo presentati alla festa.** (*We introduced ourselves to each other at the party.*)

34 Prima Olivia e Margherita _____ un messaggino e poi hanno studiato. (scriversi)

35 Riccardo e Alana, dove _____? (conoscersi)

36 Natalia e io _____ ieri sera a cena. (vedersi)

37 Il cane e il gatto _____. (baciarsi)

Answers to "Everyday Communication with Reflexives" Practice Questions

1. **mi**

2. **ci**

3. **ci**

4. **ti**

5. **si**

6. **ci lamentiamo; Giovanna ed io ci lamentiamo dell'esame.** (*Giovanna and I are complaining about the exam.*)

7. **si fa; Mio padre si fa la barba la mattina.** (*Mi dad shaves in the morning.*)

8. **vi svegliate; Cecilia e Maeve, a che ora vi svegliate di solito?** (*Cecilia and Maeve, what time do you get up in the morning?*)

9. **vi divertite; Alessia ed Alessandro, vi divertite di più a Salerno o a Ferrara?** (*Alessia and Alessandro, do you have more fun in Salerno or Ferrara?*)

10. **mi trucco; Non mi trucco mai!** (*I never wear make-up.*)

11. **si vestono; Michele e Bruno si vestono bene per il matrimonio di Beniamino.** (*Michele and Bruno are dressing well for Beniamino's wedding.*)

12. **ti preoccupi; Guglielmo, ti preoccupi per l'esamino?** (*Guglielmo, are you worried about the quiz?*)

13. **si arrabbia; Chiara non si arrabbia spesso.** (*Chiara doesn't get angry frequently.*)

14. **Mi dimentico; Mi dimentico sempre di prendere la posta.** (*I always forget to get the mail.*)

15. **ci siamo divertiti; Luca ed io ci siamo divertiti al ballo sabato scorso.** (*Luca and I had fun at the dance last Saturday.*)

16. **si è lavata; Maria Caterina si è lavata i capelli questa mattina.** (*Maria Caterina washed her hair this morning.*)

17. **si sono sposati; I miei genitori si sono sposati 60 anni fa.** (*My parents were married 60 years ago.*)

18. **si è innamorato; Salvatore si è innamorato a prima vista di Elena, ma poi la perde di vista per sempre.** (*Salvatore fell in love at first sight with Elens, but then he loses track of her forever*).

19. **ti sei addormentato; Antonio, a che ora ti sei addormentato ieri sera?** (*Antonio, what time did you fall asleep last night?*)

20. **mi sono messa; Oggi non mi sono messa le lenti a contatto perchè mi fanno male gli occhi.** (*Today I didn't put on my contact lenses because my eyes hurt.*)

21. **si sono annoiate; Caterina e Anna si sono annoiate a scuola ieri.** (*Caterina and Anna were bored at school yesterday.*)

(22) **Una donna si pettina.**

(23) **Un bambino si lava i denti.**

(24) **L'attore si trucca.**

(25) **Mi metto le lenti a contatto.**

(26) **Un uomo si toglie la camcia.**

(27) **I bambini si vestono.**

(28) **Un uomo e una donna si conoscono/si incontrano.** (*A man and a woman meet each other.*)

(29) **Vincenzo e Daria si sposano.** (*Vincenzo and Daria are getting married.*)

(30) **Rudi e Mor si amano.** (*Rudi and Mor love each other.*)

(31) **Un uomo e una donna si salutano.** (*A man and a woman greet each other.*)

(32) **Due uomini si odiano.** (*Two men hate ech other.*)

(33) **Ci amiamo.** (*We love each other.*)

(34) **si sono scritte; Prima Olivia ed Margherita si sono scritte un messaggino e poi hanno studiato.** (*First Olivia and Margherita wrote a text to each other and then they studied.*)

(35) **vi siete conosciuti; Riccardo e Alana, dove vi siete conosciuti?** (*Riccardo and Alana, where did the two of you meet?*)

(36) **ci siamo visti/e; Natalia ed io ci siamo visti/e ieri sera a cena.** (*Natalia and I saw each other at dinner last night.*)

(37) **si sono baciati; Il cane e il gatto si sono baciati.** (*The dog and cat kissed each other.*)

5

The Part of Tens

Chapter **18**

Ten Practice Dialogues for When You're Out and About in Italy

When you go to Italy, you'll undoubtedly find yourself in a variety of situations in which you have to communicate, whether at the train station, the pharmacy, or a restaurant. This chapter gives you dialogues for ten sample situations, to get you familiar with phrasing that you can modify for actual dialogues in Italian.

Being out and about and navigating everyday life, whether you're a tourist visiting several cities or a scholar hunkering down to do research, you need to know the nuances of the language used in different situations. Because many of your conversations in Italian will probably relate to food and drink, I start with those, and then move on to other dialogues at places such as the shoe shop, beach, pharmacy, and train station.

Al Ristorante (at the Restaurant)

Michele and Lucy are out to dinner at a restaurant in the Positano. Here's a conversation between the **cameriere** (*waiter*) and the **clienti** (*customers*).

Michele: **Buona sera, siamo in due e non abbiamo prenotato.** (*Good evening, there are two of us, and we didn't make a reservation.*)

Cameriere: **Non c'è problema. Prego, accomodatevi. Ecco il menù.** (*That's not a problem. Please follow me. Here are the menus.*)

(*5 minutes later*)

Cameriere: Avete deciso? (*Have you decided?*)

Lucy: **Allora io comincerei con un'insalata verde, e poi le linguine alle vongole.** (*Well, I'm going to start with a green salad, and then linguine with clams.*)

Michele: **Anche per me le linguine alle vongole. E un'insalata mista, per favore.** (*I'll have the linguine with clams, as well. And a mixed salad, please.*)

Although salads are technically **un contorno** (*a side dish*) that accompanies a **secondo** (*meat or fish*), some people might start their meal with one, especially if all they are getting is a salad and a dish of pasta (**a primo**) or a pizza.

Lucy: **E due calici di prosecco più una bottiglia d'acqua. Grazie.** (*And two glasses of prosecco and a bottle of water. Thank you.*)

Cameriere: L'acqua la volete naturale o gasata? (*Would you like natural or carbonated water?*)

Michele and Lucy: **Gasata.** (*Carbonated.*)

Cameriere: Molto bene. (*Very well.*)

(*The server brings the steaming pasta dishes after Michele and Lucy finish their salads.*)

Buon appetito! (*Enjoy your meal!*)

(*Later*)

Michele: **Era tutto squisito, grazie.** (*Everything was delicious, thank you.*)

Cameriere: Gradite un secondo, un dolce? Abbiamo un'ottima delizia al limone, fatta in casa. (*Would you like a second course or a dessert? We have an excellent lemon cake that we make here.*)

Michele: **Devo provare la delizia al limone. Una, per favore**. (*I must try the delizia al limone. One please.*)

(*15 minutes later*)

Lucy: **Ci portii conto per favore.** (*No, the bill please.*)

Cameriere: Se preferite potete andare direttamente alla cassa, tavolo diciannove. Grazie, e buonasera! (*If you prefer, you can go directly to the cashier and pay, table nineteen. Thank you, and have a good night!*)

Michele and Lucy: **Va bene, buonasera e grazie.** (*Okay, good-bye and thank you.*)

Here's the order of a complete meal in Italy:

>> **antipasto** (*appetizer*)

>> **primo piatto** (*first course*; pasta, rice, or soup)

>> **secondo piatto** (*second course*; meat or fish)

» **contorno** (*side dish*)

» **dolce** (*sweet; dessert*).

These days, not many people go for the entire meal, but it's good to know the general order, just in case!

One more tip! You must ask for the bill in an Italian restaurant; otherwise they will not bring it.

Al Bar, Colazione e Aperitivo

Bars (*cafes*) in Italy are a popular place to have breakfast or to grab a drink and snacks before dinner.

Colazione (breakfast)

Emilia and Ross go into their local **bar** (*cafe*) in Urbino for breakfast. Because they know the barista, they don't have to pay and get their *receipt* (**lo scontrino**) first. Many times though, you do need to pay first and then take your receipt to the barista.

Barista: Buongiorno! Cosa prendete? (*Good morning! What will you have?*)

Emilia: **Buongiorno! Per me, un cappuccino e una brioche salata per favore.**
(*Good morning! A cappuccino and a savory pastry for me, please.*) (See Figure 18-1.)

Ross: **Un cappuccino e una pasta alla crema.** (*A cappuccino and a custard pastry.*)

Barista: Ecco le paste! Gradite un bicchiere d'acqua?/ (*Here are the pastries! Would you like some water?*)

FIGURE 18-1:
A *cappuccino,* an Italian coffee made by using equal parts double espresso and steamed milk, with milk foam on top.

Credit: Adobe Stock

Emilia: **Sì, grazie. Gasata.** (*Yes, thanks. Fizzy.*)

Ross: **Quanto le devo?** (*What do I owe you?*)

Barista: **Sono cinque euro. Ecco lo scontrino. Grazie e buona giornata!** (*That will be 5 euros. Here's your receipt. Thanks, and have a great day!*)

L'aperitivo

Now, Maria and Lee go to their **bar** for an **aperitivo** (*aperitif*), or before dinner or before lunch drink, which is a ritual in many parts of Italy.

Barista: **Ciao ragazzi! Cosa vi preparo?** (*Hi kids! What shall I make for you?*)

Maria: **Un Aperol Spritz, per favore.** (*I'll have an Aperol Spritz, please.*)

Lee: **Per me un Campari Spritz.** (*And I'll have a Campari Spritz.*)

Barista: **Ragazzi, accomodatevi fuori, ve li portiamo.** (*Go on outside, folks, and we'll bring them to you.*)

(*A few minutes later, the barista appears with the spritzes and a tray laden with snacks.*)

Barista: **Ecco gli spritz e qualche stuzzichino**. (*Here are the spritzes with some snacks.*)

Maria and Lee: **Grazie!** (*Thank you!*)

Aperitivi are generally served with snacks such as **noccioline** (*peanuts*), **patatine** (*potato chips*), **pizzette** (*canape-size pizzas*) and mini puff-pastry sandwiches filled with all sorts of things (see Figure 18-2). At some places, you can order (and pay for) more elaborate snacks. These places include the **cicchetti** (*snacks*) in Venice or other places that advertise **apericena** – a cross between **aperitivo** and **cena** (*dinner*).

FIGURE 18-2:
A table with drinks and snacks.

Credit: Adobe Stock

Alla Salumeria (at the Deli)

Salvatore is doing some marketing at the **salumeria** (*deli*) in Castellaneta. Here's a dialogue between Salvatore and the **commessa** (*salesperson*), Carolina. They are using the formal **Lei** with each other.

> Salvatore: **Buon giorno. 3 etti di prosciutto di Parma, per favore**. (*Good morning. 300 grams of prosciutto di Parma, please.*)

> **Commessa**/Carolina: **Ho questo San Daniele in offerta, è favoloso.** (*I have this prosciutto San Daniele on special; it's fabulous.*)

> Salvatore: **Va benissimo il S. Daniele, grazie. Sono fresche le burrate?** (*The San Daniele is great, thank you. Is the burrata fresh?*)

> **Commessa: Me le consegnano tutti i giorni da Gioia del Colle.** (*They deliver it to me every day from Gioia del Colle.*)

> Salvatore: **Bene, allora due burrate, e anche una treccia di mozzarella, e anche 2 etti di olive miste, per favore.** (*Good. Well then, I'll have two burrata and also a mozzarella braid. And 200 grams of mixed olives.*)

> **Commessa: Ecco qua, sono trentasette euro in tutto. Le do una sportina?** (*Here you go, that will be thirty-seven euros in total. Shall I give you a shopping bag?*)

> Salvatore: **No grazie, ce l'ho. Ecco cinquanta euro.** (*No thanks, I have one here. Here's 50 euros.*)

> **Commessa: Ed ecco il suo resto. Buona giornata a lei!** (*And here is your change. Have a good day!*)

Al Forno (to the Bakery)

Here's a dialogue between, Maria, a *customer* (**cliente**), and Domenico, a *baker* (**fornaio/panettiere**) at the *bakery* (**forno/panetteria**). Maria has been buying bread from Domenico for 63 years (so they use the informal **tu** with each other).

> Maria: **Buongiorno, Domenico.** (*Hello, Domenico.*)

> Domenico: **Ciao, Maria. Cosa ti do oggi?** (*Hi, Maria. What can I get for you today?*)

> Maria: **Oggi arrivano i miei figli e i miei sei nipoti. Quindi, prendo un *toscano* piccolo insipido, un *ferrarese*, e un chilo di pane di Matera. Che panini sono quelli là?** (*Today my children and six grandchildren are coming to visit. So, I'm going to have a small bland Tuscan loaf, a Ferrara bread, and a kilo of Matera bread. What kinds of rolls are those?*)

> Domenico: **Questi sono multicereali e questi sono integrali.** (*These are multigrain, and these are whole wheat.*)

Maria: **Va bene, dammi anche tre panini integrali, per favore. E aggiungi due focacce tonde al rosmarino, per cortesia.** (*Okay, please give me three whole wheat rolls, as well. And add two round rosemary focaccias, please.*)

Domenico: **Altro?** (*Anything else?*)

Maria: **Una crostata all'albicocca, e poi nient'altro.** (*An apricot crostata, and that's it.*)

Domenico: **Ecco tutto, sono trenta euro, Maria. Salutami la tua famiglia!** (*Here's everything, that will be 30 euros, Maria. Say hi to your family for me!*)

Maria: **Grazie, Domenico! Ciao!** (*Thank you, Domenico. Bye!*)

Note: The word **forno** also means *oven*, so it also appears in terms such as **pasta al forno** (*baked pasta*) and **forno a legna** (*wood-burning oven*).

Alla Spiaggia (at the Beach)

Rocco and Carla are at a beach club in Marina di Ravenna. They stop at the outdoor cash register/bar on the way in and speak with the **cassiere** (the person behind the register) who's also the barista.

Rocco: **Buongiorno! Comincerei con un caffè normale e un caffè macchiato, e mezzo litro d'acqua naturale. Poi, due lettini, e un ombrellone in prima fila.** (*Good morning! We're going to start with an espresso and a caffè macchiato, and a half liter of water. Then, two beach lounges and a beach umbrella in the first row.*)

Cassiere/Barista: **Ecco i caffè e l'acqua. Questo è lo scontrino per la spiaggia. Deve mostrarlo al bagnino giù in riva. In totale sono diciannove euro.** (*Here is the coffee. This is the receipt for the beach. You need to show it to the beach boy down at the water. That will be 19 euros.*)

Rocco: **Posso pagare con la carta?** (*May I pay with my card?*)

Cassiere/Barista: **Certamente, non c'è problema. Buona giornata.** (*Yes, of course, that's not a problem. Have a good day.*)

Rocco: **A lei!** (*You, as well!*)

Many establishments on the Adriatic (and elsewhere) offer services such as **bar/ristorante**, umbrellas and lounge chairs, and lockers and showers (see Figure 18-3). If you prefer things a little more natural, look for a **spiaggia libera** (a beach that doesn't offer those services, which you can access for free).

COFFEE TO GO?

You don't find different size **cappuccino** and **caffè macchiato** in Italy, and few places automatically give you a to-go cup, unless you are in a place that caters to tourists. You usually get one standard size for these drinks, served in a ceramic cup, that you consume either at the counter or at a table. A **latte** in Italy is precisely that, a glass of *milk*!

FIGURE 18-3:
Conversing
with a beach
service can
have you set
up and
enjoying
the sea.

Al Negozio di Scarpe (at the Shoe Store)

Colleen goes into a shoe shop because the summer sales have begun. The **commessa** (*salesperson*) comes over to help.

Colleen: **Buongiorno.** (*Hello.*)

Commessa: **Buongiorno. Mi dica, signora. Come la posso aiutare?** (*Good morning, ma'am. How can I help you?*)

Colleen: **Volevo provare i sandali verdi in vetrina, per favore.** (*I wanted to try on the green sandals in the window please.*)

Commessa: **Sono rimasti solo il trentasei e il trentotto. Ma questi calzano molto. Che misura porta?** (*I only have size 36 and size 38 left. But these [sandals] run large. What [shoe] size do you wear?*)

Colleen: **Di solito porto il trentasette, ma mi faccia provare il trentasei, per favore.** (*I usually wear a 37, but please let me try the 36.*)

Commessa: **Ecco il trentasei! È una pelle molto morbida, questi sandali sono fatti a mano qui vicino, a Bagnacavallo.** (*Here's the 36. It's very soft leather. These sandals are hand-made nearby, in Bagnacavallo.*)

Colleen: **Ooh, mi piacciono molto. Che prezzo hanno?/Quanto vengono?** (*Oh, I really like them. How much do they cost?*)

Commessa: Novanta euro, signora. Li ho messi in saldo proprio oggi. Prima costavano centottanta. (*Ninety euros, ma'am. I just put them on sale today. They used to cost 180 euros.*)

Colleen: **Li prendo, grazie. Ecco la mia carta di credito.** (*I'm going to take them, thank you. Here's my credit card.*)

Commessa: Prendiamo solo contanti o il bancomat per le cose scontate. (*We only take cash or debit card on sale items.*)

Colleen: **Va bene, ecco il mio bancomat./** (*Okay, here is my ATM card.*)

In general, when you go into a smaller shop, you can expect the **commessa** (*salesperson*) to come right over and stay with you the whole time. Shoe sizes are different than in the United States, so find a handy conversion chart if you plan on doing any shoe shopping.

Al Negozio di Abbigliamento (at the Clothing Store)

Qi and Angela run a popular **bancarella** (*stall*) at the weekly Saturday **mercato** (*market*) in Lecce. Purveyors of Italian fashion, they call their stall **La Moda** (*Fashion*). Here come Mariapaola and David, ready to stock up on linen and cotton.

Qi: **Buon giorno, prego!** (*Hello. How can I help you?*)

Mariapaola: **Buongiorno. Quanto costano questi pantaloncini di lino?** (*Hello. How much are these linen shorts?*)

Qi: **Dieci euro. Abbiamo tutti questi colori.** (*Ten euros. We have all of these colors.*)

Mariapaola: **E queste camicette?** (*And these blouses?*)

Qi: **Quindici euro. Se vuole, le può provare.** (*Fifteen euros. You can try them on if you want.*)

Mariapaola: **Che taglia avete?** (*What sizes do you have?*)

Qi: **È tutto taglia unica. Queste le stanno bene.** (*It's one size fits all. These will fit you well.*)

David: **Quanto vengono queste camicie da uomo qua?** (*How much are these men's shirts here?*)

Qi: **Quelle vengono ventitrè euro.** (*Those are 33 euros.*)

Mariapaola: **Allora provo questi pantaloncini bianchi e questa camicetta bianca.** (*Okay then, I'm going to try on these white shorts and this white blouse.*)

David: **Posso provare quella camicia blu, per favore? E anche un paio di pantaloni beige.** (*May I please try on this dark blue shirt? And also a pair of beige pants.*)

Angela: **Certo, accomodatevi dietro la tenda.** (*Of course, you can go try them on behind the curtain.*)

You use the word **taglia** for clothing size and **misura** for shoe size. Because size numbering differs greatly between countries, check a conversion chart before shopping.

Dal Medico (at the Doctor's)

Laurie and John are hiking in the Dolomites when Laurie trips and injures her ankle. They go to the **pronto soccorso** (*emergency room*). This dialogue uses the formal Lei.

> **Medico: Buon giorno. Mi dica cos'è successo.** (*Hello. Tell me what happened.*)
>
> Laurie: **Buongiorno, dottore. Stavo facendo trekking quando sono inciampata e sono caduta.** (*Hello, doctor. I was hiking when I tripped and fell.*)
>
> **Medico: Dove le fa male? Ha battuto la testa?** (*Where does it hurt? Did you hurt your head?*)
>
> Laurie: **La testa no, ma mi fa molto male la caviglia. Non riesco a camminare. Mi aiuti, per favore./** (*Not my head, but my ankle really hurts. I can't walk. Will you please help me?*)

OUCH! MY (BLANK) HURTS

When saying something hurts, use an indirect object pronoun + **fa male** (if what hurts is singular) or **fanno male** (if what hurts is plural). Here are some body parts to know in the singular that you use with **mi/ti/gli/le fa male** to express pain:

la testa (*head*)

l'occhio (*eye*)

la caviglia (*ankle*)

il piede (*foot*)

il dente (*tooth*)

il polso (*wrist*)

il cuore (*heart*)

l'orecchio (*ear*)

And here are some body parts that take the plural with the phrase **mi/ti/gli/le fanno male** to express pain:

gli occhi (*eyes*)

le gambe (*legs*)

le braccia (*arms*)

i piedi (*feet*)

Medico: Mmm. Mi faccia vedere. È molto gonfia. Sarà una storta oppure si sarà rotta la caviglia. Adesso le faccio fare le lastre, e poi vediamo. (*Hmm. Let me see. It is very swollen. It's probably a bad sprain, or you may have broken it. I'm going to have you take some x-rays, and then we'll see.*)

John: **Grazie, dottore. Si potrebbe dare un po' di ghiaccio a mia moglie mentre aspettiamo? Ha tanto dolore.** (*Thank you doctor. Is it possible for my wife to get some ice while we wait? She's in a lot of pain.*)

Medico: Dopo aver fatto le lastre, l'infermiere le darà il ghiaccio. (*As soon as she's had the x-rays, the nurse will give her some ice.*)

Although you don't need this word in the following dialogue, you may need it in the future: **Aiuto!** (*Help!*)

Alla Farmacia (to the Pharmacy)

Tracey goes into the pharmacy (see Figure 18-4) for some advice and medicine from the **farmacista** (*pharmacist*).

Tracey: **Salve. Credo si essere stata punta da un insetto. Mi dà molto prurito.** (*Hello. I think I was stung by an insect. It's very itchy.*)

Farmacista: Mi faccia vedere. Sono quei puntini lì? Mi sembrano punture di ragno o di pulci di mare. Le do questa pomata per uso esterno. Dovrebbe attenuare il prurito. Tre volte al giorno, sulla zona irritata. Ha delle allergie? (*Let me have a look. Those dots there? They seem to be spider bites or sea flea bites. I'm going to give you this topical cream to apply three times per day. That ought to help with the itchiness. Do you have any allergies?*)

FIGURE 18-4: Look for this symbol when trying to find a pharmacy.

Credit: Adobe Stock

Tracey: **No, non ho allergie.** (*No, I don't have any allergies.*)

Farmacista: **Bene. Le do anche queste pastiglie da prendere una volta ogni sei ore, solo se il prurito diventa insopportabile.** (*Well then, I am going to give you these pills to take once every six hours, only if the itch becomes unbearable.*)

Tracey: **Grazie, quanto le devo?** (*Thank you. How much?*)

Farmacista: **Sono dodici euro.** (*That will be 16 euros.*)

In Italy, you can ask the pharmacist to recommend something for minor ailments and injuries, and you generally can't just browse the aisles looking for what you think will do the trick.

TIP

You might need bandages if you're doing a lot of walking. Here's how you ask for them: **"Mi servono dei cerotti, per favore, ho le vesciche ai piedi."** (*I need some bandages please, I have blisters on my feet.*)

Alla Stazione dei Treni (at the Train Station)

Annamaria and Robert are at the train station buying tickets at the **biglietteria** (*ticket sales booth*) in Salerno. In Italy, train schedules follow a 24-hour clock.

Annamaria: **Buongiorno. Due biglietti di solo andata per Bologna. Con partenza domani, 22 maggio. Qual è il treno più veloce? E qual è il primo che parte?** (*Hello. Two one-way tickets to Bologna, departing tomorrow, May 22nd. What's the fastest train? And the earliest?*)

Bigliettaio (*ticket collector*): **C'è il Frecciarossa che parte da Salerno alle 5:38 e arriva a Bologna Centrale alle 9:53. La durata è quattro ore e quindici minuti: questo è il treno più veloce ed è anche il primo. C'è la prenotazione obbligatoria, e costa settantadue euro.** (*There's the Frecciarossa train that departs from Salerno at 5:38 a.m. and arrives at the Bologna Centrale station at 9:53 a.m.. It takes four hours and fifteen minutes. This is the fastest train as well as the earliest one. Reservations are required, and it costs seventy-two euros.*)

Annamaria: **D'accordo, grazie. Due biglietti per il Frecciarossa delle 5:38 per Bologna. Quanto è?** (*Okay, thank you. Two tickets for the 5:38 a.m. Frecciarossa for tomorrow morning for Bologna. How much?*)

Bigliettaio: **Sono 144 euro. Il treno partirà dal binario sessantatrè.** (*That will be 144 euros. It's going to depart from track number 63.*)

Annamaria: **Grazie mille. Buongiorno.** (*Thank you so much. Goodbye.*)

Chapter **19**

Ten Common Word Swaps to Avoid

T his chapter is a mix of Italian vocabulary tips intended to help you avoid some simple mistakes, as well as enrich your Italian communicative skills. I start with what are called in language-learning jargon *false friends* — words that look similar in Italian and English but have different meanings — and move on to other tricky things like words and expressions that defy a literal translation. In other words, this chapter is devoted to nuances of the language that should help you move toward greater fluency.

Assumere versus Presumere

The verb **assumere** means *to hire someone* or *to be hired*, whereas the word **presumere** means *to assume.*

» **assumere** (*to hire*): **Ti ho assunto perché eri il migliore.** (*I hired you because you were the best.*)

» **presumere** (*to assume*): **Non puoi presumere di essere la più brava.** (*You can't assume you are the best.*)

Batteria versus Batteria

Batteria means *drum*, but it also means *battery*, as in a car battery.

>> **batteria** (car *battery*): **L'auto non parte. Forse la batteria è scarica.** (*The car isn't starting. Maybe the battery is dead.*)

>> **batteria** (*drums*): **Marco alla batteria, Giorgio al basso e Mina alla chitarra.** (*Marco on the drums, Giorgio on the base, and Mina on the guitar.*)

Fare Domanda versus Essere Esigente

Fare domanda means *to apply* (as in, to a university or for a job) and **essere esigente** means *to be demanding*.

>> **Faccio domanda per quel lavoro.** (*I'm applying for that job.*)

>> **Come sei esigente!** (*You're so demanding!*)

REMEMBER

The noun **la domanda** (*question*) comes from the verb **domandare** (*to ask*).

Dottore versus Medico

Whereas **dottore** means *someone with a degree*, **medico** means a *physician*.

>> **dottore** (*college graduate*): **Quando ti laurei in Italia diventi dottore.** (*When you graduate from college in Italy, you become a doctor.*)

>> **medico** (*physician*): **"I miei genitori sono medici."** (*"My parents are doctors."*)

Educato versus Colto

Educato means *polite*; **colto** means *educated*.

>> **educato** (*well-mannered*): **Grace è sempre molto educata quando viene a visitarci.** (*Grace is always so polite when she comes to visit us.*)

>> **colto** (*educated/cultured*): **Laura è una persona molto colta: risponde alle domande con descrizioni, interpretazioni e analisi dettagliate.** (*Laura is a very knowledgeable person: she answers questions with detailed descriptions, interpretations and analyses.*)

Fabbrica versus Stoffa and Fattoria

So even though the word **fabbrica** looks like the word *fabric* it means *factory*, and the word **fattoria** looks like *factory* but it means *farm*.

>> **fabbrica** (*factory*): **La FIAT è una fabbrica italiana di automobili.** (*FIAT is an Italian car factory.*)

>> **stoffa** (*fabric*): **La stoffa di questo abito è morbido e naturale.** (*This suit's fabric is soft and natural.*)

>> **fattoria** (*farm*): **"Nella vecchia fattoria ia-ia-o."** (*"Old Macdonald had a farm, ee-i-ee-i-o."*)

Affettare versus Influenzare

Affettare means *to slice* (and not to affect) and **influenzare** means *to influence* or *affect someone or something.*

>> **Il macellaio affetta il prosciutto.** (*The butcher is slicing the prosciutto.*)

>> **I giovani sono spesso influenzati dagli amici.** (*Young people are frequently influenced by their friends.*)

Partita versus Festa

If you want to have a party you use the word **festa**, and if you're going to a game you use the word **partita**.

>> **partita** (*sports game*): **I ragazzi hanno una partita di basket dopo scuola oggi.** (*The children have a basketball game after school.*)

>> **festa** (*party*): **Mia cugina Kathy dà una festa per Jane e Matthew.** (*My cousin Kathy is having a party for Jane and Matthew.*)

Incidente versus Accidenti!

Accidenti! means *Wow!*, and **incidente** means accident.

>> **Incidente** (*accident*): **Danny ha avuto un terribile incidente con la bicicletta.** (*Danny had a terrible accident with his bike.*)

>> **Accidenti!** (*Wow!*): **Accidenti! che panorama!** (*Wow! What a view!*)

Straniero versus Estraneo

The word **straniero** means *foreigner* and the word **estraneo** means *outsider* or *stranger*.

» **straniero** (*foreigner*): **Ci sono molti stranieri in visita a Firenze.** (*There are many foreigners in Florence.*)

» **estraneo** (*stranger/outsider*): **Riunione insegnanti: Vietato l'ingresso agli estranei.** (*Teacher meeting: Outsiders not allowed.*)

6

Appendixes

IN THIS PART . . .

Go from English to Italian with the dictionary in Appendix A.

Get Italian words translated into English in Appendix B's dictionary.

Appendix A

English-Italian Dictionary

Here are some of the Italian words used throughout this book, arranged alphabetically in English, to help you when writing or speaking Italian.

a, an: **un, uno** (m)/**una** (f)
about, of: **di**
above: **sopra, di sopra**
after: **dopo**
again: **di nuovo**
against: **contro**
all: **tutto, tutti**
already: **già**
also, too: **anche,**
although: **sebbene**
always: **sempre**
among, in: **tra, fra**
and: **e**
ankle: **caviglia**
to answer: **rispondere**
anyone: **chiunque**
anything: **qualcosa, qualsiasicosa**
any: **alcuni, alcune**

around: **intorno**
to arrive: **arrivare**
as much, as many: **quanto, quanta, quanti, quante; tanto, tanta, tanti, tante**
as soon as: **appena**
at: **a, in**
bad: **cattivo**
badly: **male**
to be: **essere**
to be used to: **essere abituato**
beach: **spiaggia**
beautiful: **bello**
because: **perché**
before: **prima**
to begin: **incominciare**
behind: **dietro**
to believe: **credere**
below: **sotto, di sotto**

best, great: **ottimo, migliore**
better: **meglio, migliore**
between: **tra, fra**
big: **grosso**
bill: **conto**
bitter: **amaro**
to bore: **annoiare**
to borrow, to loan: **prendere, in prestito**
boy: **ragazzo**
to be born: **nascere, essere nato**
both . . . and: **sia . . . sia**
bread: **pane**
to bring: **portare**
brother: **fratello**
to build: **costruire**
but: **ma**
to buy: **comprare**
by: **da, in** (+ means of transportation)
to call: **chiamare, telefonare**
to call back, to recall: **richiamare**
can, to be able to, may: **potere**
to cancel: **annullare, cancellare, disdire**
car: **macchina, automobile**
to change: **cambiare**
cheap: **a buon mercato, economico**
to choose: **scegliere**
to clean: **pulire**
close: **vicino**
to close: **chiudere**
to come: **venire**
to correct: **correggere**
currently, now: **attualmente, ora, adesso**
day: **giorno**
dear: **caro**
to defend: **difendere**
to die: **morire**
difficult: **difficile**
to divorce: **divorziare**
to do: **fare**
down: **giù**
to drink: **bere**
to drive: **guidare**
early: **presto**
easy: **facile**
to eat: **mangiare**
either . . . or: **o . . . o**
to end, to finish: **finire**
enough: **abbastanza**
to enter: **entrare**
ever: **mai**

everyone: **ciascuno, tutti**
everything: **tutto**
everywhere: **dappertutto**
eye: **occhio**
to exit: **uscire**
exit: **uscita**
expensive: **caro, costoso**
to fall: **cadere**
to fall in love: **innamorarsi**
far: **lontano**
fast: **veloce, velocemente, in fretta**
fat: **grasso**
ferry: **traghetto**
a few: **alcuni**
few: **pochi**
finally: **finalmente**
to find: **trovare**
to finish: **finire**
to fly: **volare**
for: **per**
to forget: **dimenticare, dimenticarsi**
to forgive: **perdonare**
fresh: **fresco**
to frighten: **spaventare**
from: **da, di** (origin)
to get: **prendere, ricevere**
to get married: **sposarsi**
to give: **dare, donare**
to give back, to return: **restituire**
gladly: **volentieri**
to go: **andare**
to go out: **uscire**
good: **buono**
grapes: **uva**
great: **grande**
to grow: **crescere**
hand: **mano**
happy: **felice**
to hate: **odiare**
to have: **avere**
he: **lui**
head: **testa**
to hear: **sentire**
her, hers: **lei, (il) suo, (la) sua, (i) suoi, (le) sue**
here: **qui, qua**
him, his: **lui, (il) suo, (la) sua, (i) suoi, (le) sue**
to hold: **tenere**
to hope: **sperare**
hour: **ora**
how: **come**

how much, how many: **quanto, quanta, quanti, quante**

hunger: **fame**

I: **io**

if: **se**

in: **in, a**

in front of, before: **di fronte (a)**

inside: **dentro**

intelligent: **intelligente**

interesting: **interessante**

its: **(il) suo, (la) sua, (i) suoi, (le) sue**

to keep, to hold: **tenere**

key: **chiave**

kind: **gentile**

to know: **sapere, conoscere**

large: **grande**

late: **tardi**

least: **minimo**

to leave: **lasciare, partire**

left: **sinistra**

leg: **gamba**

to lend: **imprestare**

less, less than: **meno, meno di/che**

to let: **lasciare, permettere**

to like: **piacere**

to listen to: **ascoltare**

a little, a little of: **un po', un po' di**

little: **piccolo**

to live: **vivere, abitare**

to look at: **guardare**

to look for: **cercare**

to lose: **perdere**

a lot: **molto, molta, molti, molte**

to love: **amare**

to make: **fare**

man: **uomo**

to marry: **sposare**

me: **me**

to meet: **incontrare**

meeting: **riunione**

milk: **latte**

mine: **(il) mio, (la) mia, (i) miei, (le)] mie**

more, more than: **più, più di/che**

most: **Massimo, più**

to move: **muovere, muoversi**

must: **dovere**

my: **(il) mio, (la) mia, (i) miei, (le) mie**

near: **vicino**

need: **avere bisogno di**

neither ... nor: **né ... né**

never: **non ... mai**

new: **nuovo**

night: **notte**

no: **no**

no, no one, none: **nessuno**

not: **non**

not yet: **non ancora**

nothing: **niente, nulla**

now: **ora, adesso**

of: **di**

to offer: **offrire**

often: **spesso**

old: **vecchio, anziano**

on: **su, sopra**

one: **uno, una, si**

only: **solo, soltanto**

to open: **aprire**

or: **o**

our, ours: **(il) nostro, (la) nostra, (i) nostri, (le) nostre**

outside: **fuori**

over: **sopra**

to own: **possedere**

pants: **pantaloni**

parents: **genitori**

to pass: **passare**

to pay: **pagare**

people: **gente**

to play: **giocare, suonare (uno strumento)**

please: **per favore, per piacere**

to prefer: **preferire**

pretty: **carino**

to put: **mettere**

quickly: **rapidamente, in fretta, subito**

to receive: **ricevere**

relatives: **parenti**

to remember: **ricordare, ricordarsi**

to rent: **affittare (un appartamento), noleggiare (un'automobile)**

to repeat: **ripetere**

to reserve: **prenotare**

to return: **ritornare, restituire**

right: **destra**

right away: **subito**

sad: **triste**

same: **stesso**

sandwich: **panino**

to say, to tell: **dire**

to see: **vedere**

to sell: **vendere**

to send: **mandare**

serious: **serio**

shall: **dovere**

she: **lei**

to ship, to send: **spedire**

shirt: **camicia**

short: **piccolo, basso**

to shut: **chiudere**

sister: **sorella**

since: **da quando**

size: **taglia** (clothing), **numero/misura** (shoes)

to sleep: **dormire**

slowly: **lentamente, piano**

small: **piccolo**

so: **così**

some: **un po' di, del, alcuni, alcune**

something: **qualcosa**

soon: **presto**

to speak: **parlare**

to spend: **spendere**

to stay: **stare**

still: **ancora**

to stop: **fermare, fermarsi**

straight: **dritto**

stupid: **stupido**

to succeed, to be able to: **riuscire**

sweet: **dolce**

to take: **prendere, portare**

to talk: **parlare**

tall: **alto**

to tell: **dire, raccontare**

thank you: **grazie**

that: **che**

the: **il, la, lo, l', i, gli, le**

their, theirs: **(il) loro, (la) loro, (i) loro, (le) loro**

them: **loro**

then: **allora, poi**

there: **là, lì**

they: **loro**

thin: **magro**

to think: **pensare**

thirst: **sete**

this: **questo**

tired: **stanco, stanca, stanchi, stanche**

to travel: **viaggiare**

to try: **cercare, provare**

to: **a, in, da**

too much, too many: **troppo, troppa, troppi, troppe**

toward: **verso**

through: **attraverso, per**

ugly: **brutto**

until: **finché, fino a**

up: **su**

us: **noi**

to use: **usare**

very: **molto**

to wait: **aspettare**

to walk: **camminare**

to want, will: **volere**

a want, a craving: **voglia**

to watch: **guardare**

water: **acqua**

we: **noi**

to wear: **indossare, portare**

well: **bene**

well, so, then: **allora**

what: **che, che cosa**

when: **quando**

where: **dove**

whereas: **mentre**

whether: **se**

which: **che, quale**

while: **mentre**

who, whom: **che, chi**

why: **perché**

to wish: **desiderare, gradire**

with: **con**

without: **senza**

woman: **donna**

to work: **lavorare**

worse: **peggio, peggiore**

worst: **pessimo, peggiore**

yes: **sì**

yet: **ancora**

you: **tu, voi, lei, loro**

young: **giovane**

your, yours: **(il) tuo/vostro, (la) tua/vostra, (i) tuoi/vostri, (le) tue/vostre, (il) suo, (la) sua, (i) suoi, (le) sue**

Appendix B

Italian-English Dictionary

Here are some of the Italian words used throughout this book, arranged alphabetically in Italian, to help you when writing or speaking Italian.

a: *at, in, to*

abbastanza: *enough*

abitare: *to live*

adesso, ora: *now*

affittare (un appartamento): *to rent (an apartment)*

aiuto: *help*

alcuno, alcuni: *a few, any, some*

allora: *then, well, so*

alto: *tall*

amare: *to love*

amaro: *bitter*

anche: *also, too*

ancora: *still, yet, more*

andare: *to go*

annoiare: *to bore*

annullare: *to cancel*

aprire: *to open*

arrivare: *to arrive*

ascoltare: *to listen to*

aspettare: *to wait*

attraverso: *through*

attualmente: *currently, now*

avere: *to have*

avere bisogno di: *to need*

basso: *short, low*

bello: *beautiful*

bene: *well*

bere: *to drink*

biglietto: *ticket*

brutto: *ugly*

a buon mercato: *cheap*

buono: *good*

cadere: *to fall*

cambiare: *to change*

camicia: *shirt*

camminare: *to walk*
cancellare: *to cancel*
carino: *pretty, cute*
caro: *dear, expensive*
cattivo: *bad*
caviglia: *ankle*
cercare: *to look for, to try*
che: *that* (conj. and relative pron.), *who, whom, which*
che, che cosa: *what*
chi: *who, those who*
chiamare: *to call*
chiamarsi: *for one's name to be*
chiave: *key*
chiudere: *to close, to shut*
chiunque: *anyone, whoever*
ci: *here, there, us*
come: *how, what*
comprare: *to buy*
con: *with*
conoscere: *to be acquainted with, to know*
contro: *against*
correggere: *to correct*
così: *so*
costoso, caro: *expensive*
costruire: *to build*
credere: *to believe*
crescere: *to grow*
da: *by, from, through*
dappertutto: *everywhere*
dare, donare: *to give*
dei: *some, any*
del: *a little, some, of the*
dentro: *inside*
desiderare: *to wish*
destra: *right*
di: *about, of, from*
dietro a: *behind*
difendere: *to defend*
difficile: *difficult*
dimenticare, dimenticarsi: *to forget*
dire: *to say, to tell*
divorziare: *to divorce*
dolce: *sweet*
donna: *woman*
dopo: *after*
dormire: *to sleep*
dove: *where*
dovere: *must, shall, to have to, to be obliged to*
dritto: *straight*

e: *and*
entrare: *to enter*
essere: *to be*
essere abituato a: *to be used to*
facile: *easy*
fare: *to do, to make*
fare spese: *to go shopping*
fare spesa: *to go grocery shopping*
felice: *happy*
fermare, fermarsi: *to stop*
finché, fino a quando: *until*
finire: *to end, to finish*
formaggio: *cheese*
forte: *strong, fast*
fra: *among, between*
fratello: *brother;* fra: *bro*
fresco: *fresh, cool*
in fretta: *fast, quickly, rush*
di fronte [a]: *in front of, before*
fuori: *out, outside*
gente: *people*
gentile: *kind*
già: *already*
giocare: *to play*
giorno: *day*
giovane: *young*
giù: *down*
grande: *great*
grasso: *fat*
grosso: *big*
guardare: *to watch, to look at*
guidare: *to drive*
il, i, gli, le: *the*
in, in (+ means of transportation): *in, at, to, by*
incominciare: *to begin*
incontrare: *to meet*
indossare, portare: *to wear*
innamorarsi: *to fall in love*
intelligente: *intelligent*
interessante: *interesting*
intorno: *around*
io: *I*
la: *the*
là: *there*
lasciare: *to leave, to let*
latte: *milk*
lavorare: *to work*
lei: *she, her*
lentamente: *slowly*
lì: *there*

lontano: *far*
loro: *they, them*
loro, il loro: *their, theirs*
lui: *he, him*
ma: *but*
magro: *thin*
mai: *ever*
male: *badly*
mandare: *to send*
mangiare: *to eat*
massimo: *most*
me: *me*
meglio: *better*
meno, meno di/che: *less, less than*
meno: *less, minus*
mentre: *while, whereas*
mettere: *to put*
migliore: *better*
minimo: *least*
mio, il mio: *my, mine*
in modo da/che: *so as*
molto, molti: *very, much, many, a lot*
morire: *to die*
muovere, muoversi: *to move*
nascere, essere nato: *to be born*
ne: *of this, of that, of him, of them*
né . . . né: *neither . . . nor*
da nessuna parte: *nowhere*
nessuno: *no, no one, nobody*
niente: *nothing*
no: *no*
noi: *we, us*
noioso: *boring*
noleggiare (un'automobile):
    to rent (a car)
non: *not*
non ancora: *not yet*
non appena: *as soon as*
non . . . mai: *never*
nostro, il nostro: *our, ours*
notte: *night*
nulla: *nothing*
nuovo: *new*
di nuovo: *again*
o: *or*
o . . . o: *either . . . or*
occhio: *eye*
odiare: *to hate*
offrire: *to offer*
ora: *hour, now*

ottenere: *to get*
ottimo: *best, great*
pagare: *to pay*
pane: *bread*
panino: *sandwich, roll*
pantaloncini: *shorts*
pantaloni: *pants*
parecchio: *a lot, several*
parenti: *relatives*
parlare: *to talk, to speak*
partire: *to leave*
passare: *to pass*
peggio: *worse*
peggiore: *worse*
pensare: *to think*
per: *for, through*
perché: *because, why*
perdere: *to lose*
perdonare: *to forgive*
pessimo: *worst*
piacere: *to like*
piano: *slowly*
piccolo: *small, short*
più, più di/che: *more, more than*
di più: *more*
pochi: *few*
poco: *too little, small*
poi: *then*
portare: *to bring, to take*
possedere: *to own*
potere: *can, may*
preferire: *to prefer*
prego: *you're welcome, please, by all means, after you*
prendere: *to take, to have (in a restaurant/**caffè**)*
prenotare: *to reserve*
prestare: *to lend*
presto: *early, soon*
prima: *before*
primo: *first*
prossimo: *next*
provare: *to try*
pulire: *to clean*
qua, qui: *here*
da qualche parte: *somewhere*
qualcosa: *anything, something*
qualcuno: *someone, somebody*
quale: *which, what*
qualsiasi cosa: *anything*
quando: *when*
da quando: *ever since*

quanto, quanta, quanti, quante: *how much,*
   how many, as much, as many
quello: *that, the one*
questi/queste: *these*
questo/questa: *this*
racontare: *to tell*
ragazzo: *boy*
rapidamente: *quickly, fast*
restituire: *to give back, to return*
ricevere: *to receive, to get*
richiamare: *to call back, recall*
ricordare qualcosa a qualcuno: *to remind someone*
   of something
ricordare, ricordarsi: *to remember*
ripetere: *to repeat*
rispondere: *to answer*
ritornare: *to return*
riunione: *meeting*
riuscire: *to succeed*
sapere: *to know*
scegliere: *to choose*
se: *if, whether*
sempre: *always*
sentire: *to hear*
sete: *thirst*
senza: *without*
serio: *serious*
si: *one, we, they*
sì: *yes*
sia . . . sia: *both . . . and*
sinistra: *left*
solo, soltanto: *only*
sopra: *over*
sopra, di sopra: *above*
sotto, di sotto: *below*
spaventare: *to frighten*
spedire: *to send, to ship*
spendere: *to spend*
sperare: *to hope*
spesso: *often*
sposare: *to marry*
sposarsi: *to get married*
stanco: *tired*

stare: *to stay*
stesso: *same*
stupido: *stupid*
su: *on, up, over*
suo, il suo: *his, her, hers, its*
suonare: *to play, to ring*
tanto, tanti: *as much, so much, as many, so many*
tardi: *late*
te: *you*
telefonare: *to call, to telephone*
tenere: *to hold, to keep*
testa: *head*
tra: *among, between*
triste: *sad*
troppo, troppi: *too much, too many*
trovare: *to find*
tu: *you*
tuo, il tuo: *your, yours*
tutti: *everyone, all*
tutto: *everything, all*
ultimo: *last, latest*
un po', un po' di: *a little, a little of*
un/uno, una: *a, an, one*
uomo: *man*
uovo, uova: *egg, eggs*
usare: *to use*
uscire: *to exit, to go out*
vecchio: *old*
vedere: *to see*
veloce: *fast, quick*
velocemente: *fast, quickly*
vendere: *to sell*
venire: *to come*
verso: *toward*
viaggiare: *to travel*
vicino: *near, close*
vivere: *to live*
voi: *you*
volare: *to fly*
volentieri: *gladly*
volere: *to want, will*
vostro, il vostro: *your, yours*

Index

Y

About the Author

Teresa Picarazzi, PhD, has been teaching Italian for over 35 years. A former college professor (Dartmouth College, The University of Arizona, Wesleyan University), Teresa is currently in her 18th year at the Hopkins School (New Haven). She was the 2021 recipient of the AATI Distinguished Service Award, K-12 (American Association of Teachers of Italian). Teresa has lived, studied and worked in Cortona, Ferrara, Urbino, Siena, Florence, and Ravenna. Teresa loves to spend the summer in Ravenna with her husband Giancarlo and daughter Emilia.

Author's Acknowledgments

I have to thank many people for helping me complete this book. First, the team at Wiley: Acquisitions Editor Lindsay Lefevere for bringing me on to work on another project for For Dummies; Project Editor Linda Brandon, for walking me through the book step by step and for her incisive editing; Copy Editor Laura K. Miller and Technical Editor, friend Di Pietro, for their attentive reading and crucial comments. (Any errors you find in this book are entirely my responsibility.) I would also like to thank my brilliant friends in Ravenna, who spent hours with me talking about gender, culture, and current language usage this past summer: Nadia Pagani, Laura Gambi, Barbara Domenichini, and Serena Simoni. Thank you as well to my parents, Mary and Domenico, for instilling in me an incomparable work ethic, and for actively cheering me on throughout each phase of this project. Finally, I need to thank Giancarlo and Emilia for putting up with me, and encouraging me to spend a good chunk of our time in Italy at the Biblioteca Classense in Ravenna, so I might meet the deadlines for this book.

Dedication

This book would not exist, and I would not know how to teach, without my students, and so I dedicate it with love to all of my students, present and past.

Publisher's Acknowledgments

Acquisitions Editor: Lindsay Lefevere

Project Editor: Linda Brandon

Copy Editor: Laura K. Miller

Technical Editor: Antonietta Di Pietro

Production Editor: Tamilmani Varadharaj

Cover Image: © Alliance/Adobe Stock Photos

Leverage the power

Dummies is the global leader in the reference category and one of the most trusted and highly regarded brands in the world. No longer just focused on books, customers now have access to the dummies content they need in the format they want. Together we'll craft a solution that engages your customers, stands out from the competition, and helps you meet your goals.

Advertising & Sponsorships

Connect with an engaged audience on a powerful multimedia site, and position your message alongside expert how-to content. Dummies.com is a one-stop shop for free, online information and know-how curated by a team of experts.

- Targeted ads
- Video
- Email Marketing
- Microsites
- Sweepstakes sponsorship

20 MILLION PAGE VIEWS EVERY SINGLE MONTH

15 MILLION UNIQUE VISITORS PER MONTH

43% OF ALL VISITORS ACCESS THE SITE VIA THEIR MOBILE DEVICES

700,000 NEWSLETTER SUBSCRIPTIONS TO THE INBOXES OF

300,000 UNIQUE INDIVIDUALS EVERY WEEK

PERSONAL ENRICHMENT

Staying Sharp	**Facebook**	**Guitar**	**Investing**	**Beekeeping**	**Digital Photography**
9781119187790	9781119179030	9781119293354	9781119293347	9781119310068	9781119235606
USA $26.00	USA $21.99	USA $24.99	USA $22.99	USA $22.99	USA $24.99
CAN $31.99	CAN $25.99	CAN $29.99	CAN $27.99	CAN $27.99	CAN $29.99
UK £19.99	UK £16.99	UK £17.99	UK £16.99	UK £16.99	UK £17.99

Meditation	**Pregnancy**	**Samsung Galaxy S7**	**iPhone**	**Crocheting**	**Nutrition**
9781119251163	9781119235491	9781119279952	9781119283133	9781119287117	9781119130246
USA $24.99	USA $26.99	USA $24.99	USA $24.99	USA $24.99	USA $22.99
CAN $29.99	CAN $31.99	CAN $29.99	CAN $29.99	CAN $29.99	CAN $27.99
UK £17.99	UK £19.99	UK £17.99	UK £17.99	UK £16.99	UK £16.99

PROFESSIONAL DEVELOPMENT

 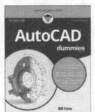     

Windows 10	**AutoCAD**	**Excel 2016**	**QuickBooks 2017**	**macOS Sierra**	**LinkedIn**	**Windows 10 All-in-One**
9781119311041	9781119255796	9781119293439	9781119281467	9781119280651	9781119251132	9781119310563
USA $24.99	USA $39.99	USA $26.99	USA $26.99	USA $29.99	USA $24.99	USA $34.00
CAN $29.99	CAN $47.99	CAN $31.99	CAN $31.99	CAN $35.99	CAN $29.99	CAN $41.99
UK £17.99	UK £27.99	UK £19.99	UK £19.99	UK £21.99	UK £17.99	UK £24.99

SharePoint 2016	**Fundamental Analysis**	**Networking**	**Office 2016**	**Office 365**	**Salesforce.com**	**Coding**
9781119181705	9781119263593	9781119257769	9781119293477	9781119265313	9781119239314	9781119293323
USA $29.99	USA $26.99	USA $29.99	USA $26.99	USA $24.99	USA $29.99	USA $29.99
CAN $35.99	CAN $31.99	CAN $35.99	CAN $31.99	CAN $29.99	CAN $35.99	CAN $35.99
UK £21.99	UK £19.99	UK £21.99	UK £19.99	UK £17.99	UK £21.99	UK £21.99

dummies
A Wiley Brand

Learning Made Easy

ACADEMIC

9781119293576
USA $19.99
CAN $23.99
UK £15.99

9781119293637
USA $19.99
CAN $23.99
UK £15.99

9781119293491
USA $19.99
CAN $23.99
UK £15.99

9781119293460
USA $19.99
CAN $23.99
UK £15.99

9781119293590
USA $19.99
CAN $23.99
UK £15.99

9781119215844
USA $26.99
CAN $31.99
UK £19.99

9781119293378
USA $22.99
CAN $27.99
UK £16.99

9781119293521
USA $19.99
CAN $23.99
UK £15.99

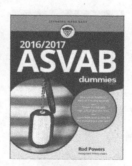

9781119239178
USA $18.99
CAN $22.99
UK £14.99

9781119263883
USA $26.99
CAN $31.99
UK £19.99

Available Everywhere Books Are Sold

dummies.com

dummies®
A Wiley Brand

Small books for big imaginations

GETTING STARTED WITH Coding
Get Creative with Code!
Camille McCue, PhD

9781119177173
USA $9.99
CAN $9.99
UK £8.99

MODDING Minecraft
Build Your Own Minecraft Mods!
Sarah Guthals, PhD
Stephen Foster, PhD
Lindsey Handley, PhD

9781119177272
USA $9.99
CAN $9.99
UK £8.99

MAKING YouTube VIDEOS
Star in Your Own Video!
Nick Willoughby

9781119177241
USA $9.99
CAN $9.99
UK £8.99

DESIGNING Digital Games
Create Games with Scratch!
Derek Breen

9781119177210
USA $9.99
CAN $9.99
UK £8.99

GETTING STARTED WITH Raspberry Pi
Program Your Raspberry Pi!
Richard Wentk

9781119262657
USA $9.99
CAN $9.99
UK £6.99

EXPERIMENTING WITH Science
Think, Test, and Learn!
Chris J. Mullins, PhD

9781119291336
USA $9.99
CAN $9.99
UK £6.99

CREATING Digital Animations
Animate Stories with Scratch!
Derek Breen

9781119233527
USA $9.99
CAN $9.99
UK £6.99

GETTING STARTED WITH Engineering
Think Like an Engineer!
Camille McCue, PhD

9781119291220
USA $9.99
CAN $9.99
UK £6.99

WRITING Computer Code
Learn the Language of Computers!
Chris Minnick and Eva Holland

9781119177302
USA $9.99
CAN $9.99
UK £8.99

Unleash Their Creativity

dummies.com